To
Martin Moore,
who has shown
genuine promis
a student at St. D
High School,
all the best,
Irving H. King
May 16, 1995

The COAST GUARD under SAIL

The COAST GUARD under SAIL

The U.S. Revenue Cutter Service 1789-1865

Irving H. King

Naval Institute Press • Annapolis, Maryland

Library of Congress Cataloging-in-Publication Data
King, Irving H.
The Coast Guard under sail : the U.S. Revenue Cutter Service, 1789–1865 / Irving H. King.
p. cm.
Sequel to: George Washington's Coast Guard.
Bibliography: p.
Includes index.
ISBN 0-87021-234-6
1. United States. Revenue-Cutter Service—History. I. Title.
HJ6645.K49 1989
359.9'7'0973—dc19 89-12445
CIP

Printed in the United States of America

9 8 7 6 5 4 3 2

First printing

To my children

Michael B. King
Gregory D. King
Elizabeth A. King
Patrick C. King

Contents

Preface

This book is the second part of a series that, upon completion, will cover the history of the U.S. Coast Guard. The first, *George Washington's Coast Guard*, forms the basis for chapters one and two of this volume, which thus stands alone as a complete account of the Coast Guard from its inception as the U.S. Revenue Cutter Service in 1790 to the end of the Civil War. This period was the age of sail. Of course, steam cutters operated before 1865, and some sailing cutters continued in service after that date; but basically, the service depended on wind and sail until the end of the war, and on steam power after that.

This volume, like its predecessor, emphasizes the dual character of the Revenue Cutter Service as an adjunct to the naval establishment and as a servant that met U.S. maritime needs. In the former capacity, it helped to build the U.S. Navy and then fought alongside it in the Quasi-War with France, the War of 1812, the war against piracy in the Caribbean, the Seminole War, the Mexican War, and the Civil War. In the latter role, it collected revenue for the nation. At this task it succeeded quickly, establishing a measure of respect for the new constitutional government and its laws, something that had proven beyond the means of both the British Colonial Customs Service and the Confederation. This was the result of a policy that combined a spirit of enterprise with a proper acknowledgment of the freedoms of American citizens. And because of the success of the Revenue Cutter Service, the national government also turned to it for such delicate tasks as enforcing Jefferson's embargo, upholding national sovereignty in the Nullification Controversy, and returning fugitive slaves to their masters under the Compromise of 1850.

The Revenue Cutter Service cooperated from the beginning with other agencies that ultimately joined it to form the U.S. Coast Guard: the Lighthouse Service, the Life-Saving Service, and the Steamboat Inspection Service. For a brief time before the Mexican War, the first military commandant of the Revenue Cutter Service, Captain Alexander Fraser, took action to combine three of these organizations, but the sectionalism of the 1850s terminated the trend toward unity and saw the ouster of the service's military leadership.

The Revenue Cutter Service continued throughout the period to aid mariners in distress. It added winter cruising for that purpose in 1831–32, and following the Mexican War extended its services into the Pacific Ocean.

Like the first work of this series, the present volume is founded extensively on primary source materials, in particular the correspondence between customs collectors and secretaries of the treasury. Many have helped me to search the records, and I want to express my gratitude to them. The staff at Waesche Hall, the U.S. Coast Guard Academy Library, especially Paul Johnson, the head librarian, gave much-needed and continual assistance. Dorothy Brewington of the G. W. Blunt White Library at Mystic Seaport generously provided me with a folder of notes that her late husband Marion Brewington gathered in the 1930s on early revenue cutters. Thanks go also to the staffs of the Federal Archives and Records Center at Waltham, Massachusetts, the National Archives, the John Carter Brown Library, the Smithsonian Institution, the Naval Historical Center, the New York Public Library, the New York Historical Society, the Connecticut Historical Society, the Louisiana State Museum, the Smith College Library, the Boston Public Library, the Colonial Williamsburg Foundation, the Mariners' Museum, the Yale University Art Gallery, the Connecticut College Library, the U.S. Customs Service, the Metropolitan Museum of Art, the Independence National Historical Park, and Robert L. Scheina, historian at U.S. Coast Guard headquarters.

Finally, I am most grateful to my wife, Ann E. King, for her encouragement during the writing of this volume, and for her many helpful suggestions when she read the final draft.

The COAST GUARD under SAIL

CHAPTER ONE

Launching the Revenue Cutter Service

In New York City on the morning of 30 April 1789, George Washington stepped forward and took the oath of office as the first president of the United States. Earlier, after leading the colonies to victory over the mighty British empire, Washington had taken leave of his officers at Fraunces's Tavern in New York and retired to his beloved Mount Vernon, hoping to lead a quiet life. But America's independence was troubled by internal social, economic, political, and cultural divisions and soon the Confederation government crumbled.[1] A constitution was drafted that established a federal system, and to ensure its success the electors unanimously chose George Washington as the nation's first chief executive. Alas, he was compelled out of retirement by duty.

In his first inaugural address on that April day, the president spoke of his fear upon learning of his election. "[T]he magnitude and difficulty of the trust to which the voice of my Country called me," he wrote, "being sufficient to awaken in the wisest and most experienced of her citizens, a distrustful scrutiny into his qualifications, could not but overwhelm" one who had inherited "inferior endowments from nature" and was "unpracticed in the duties of civil administration. . . ."[2] Though underestimating his qualifications, he did have legitimate concerns. Before everything else he had to make an experimental government work while protecting the nation's liberties, a task that required new administrative branches. Britain and Spain still occupied American territory. Secession threatened in the West. The army was small, the navy now nonexistent, the treasury empty. The United States owed debts to its citizens and to foreign countries. There was no revenue flowing into the treasury, and although Congress quickly passed an import tariff to raise some, no organization existed to collect it; until such an organization was established, none of the new president's problems could be solved.

Washington gave the job of creating a revenue-raising organization to Alexander Hamilton. Hamilton became the first secretary of the treasury. The department he established in 1789 was initially the biggest in the government. By 1801 over half the country's federal civil servants worked there, performing an enormous variety of important jobs. As the department's duties grew, Hamilton delegated an increasing amount of authority to collectors of customs. It says something of the significance attached to these customs posts that Washington often filled them with trusted veterans of the Revolutionary army.[3]

Some collectors were men of national reputation who had attained high rank during the Revolution. Benjamin Lincoln, a major general who had served as secretary of war and accepted Cornwallis's surrender at Yorktown, was the first federal collector at Boston. Brigadier General John Lamb, the first collector at the port of New York, had accompanied Benedict Arnold on his daring military march to Quebec and had played an important role in the defeat of General Burgoyne's forces at Saratoga. And Otho H. Williams, who had served as General Nathaniel Greene's adjutant general throughout the southern campaigns of the Revolution, was the first collector at Baltimore.[4]

Few other collectors rivaled Lincoln, Lamb, and Williams in reputation, but they were all men of prominence in their regions and they all played important roles in establishing the early Revenue Cutter Service.

Many of the collector's duties were directly related to commerce and trade. The collector had to make sure that duties were paid on imported goods. He registered, licensed, and inspected vessels and cleared ships engaged in foreign trade.[5] Collecting tariffs and tonnage duties was his most important task, for the nation desperately needed the revenue, and his most difficult. It was this that led to the creation of the Revenue Cutter Service.

By 1789 smuggling was not only a well-established custom; it had also gained recognition as a meritorious national enterprise. More than a century of hated British restrictions on colonial trade, decades of resistance to British customs officials during the Revolution, and after independence, years of smuggling to continue trade with the empire had schooled Americans in the art of avoiding tariffs. Goods shipped from around the world were offloaded onto coastal islands or into small boats to be taken past collectors' eyes under the cover of darkness. Manifests carried false statements about the type, quantity, and quality of cargo. Local customs officials and merchants were in collusion to defraud the government. When all else failed, Americans sometimes resorted to force, as when the crew of John Hancock's *Liberty* threw British customs officials into Boston Harbor rather than obey the law.

Nature had shaped an Atlantic coast of harbors, inlets, rivers, and offshore islands that further complicated efforts to collect revenue. Smugglers had access to many harbors of safe refuge, and the West Indies, for centuries a smugglers' haven, lay not far off the U. S. coast.

During Confederation states had tried to prevent smuggling. They had their own customs laws, collectors, and naval officers. Some states even employed revenue boats and barges in their harbors. The Virginia assembly authorized two inspection boats, the *Patriot* and the *Liberty*, to cut down on smuggling and to enforce a sophisticated set of mercantile regulations, but in 1786 Charles Lee explained to the Council of the State of Virginia that his experience as the naval officer for the state's south Potomac district led him to believe that smuggling could not be stopped.[6]

In April and May 1789, during congressional discussions about the establishment of customs duties for the new constitutional government, state representatives expressed views similar to Lee's. Congressman Ames of Massachusetts told his colleagues that it would be impossible to guard the entire coast of Massachusetts. Thomas T. Tucker argued that lower tariffs were desirable to avoid an unfair advantage for smugglers, and Elias Boudinot, the president of the Continental Congress, added that such a task would require the efforts of extraordinary men:

> When I recollect, that numerous volumes of laws made to secure and regulate this point, the inefficiency of them all, though accompanied with the most terrible denunciations and penalties, and the careful observing eye of long experienced officers—I say, when I recollect all this, and consider it may be necessary for the United States to adopt a similar plan, I own that I almost shrink from the task as an extraordinary work, requiring the most superior abilities.[7]

Alexander Hamilton. (*Courtesy* U.S. *Naval* Institute.)

Fully aware of the difficulties he faced, Hamilton sent out two Treasury Department circulars, dated 2 October 1789 and 23 September 1790, asking collectors whether there was smuggling in their districts and if they needed boats to secure revenue.[8] In reply, the collectors variously explained that smuggling, which had been rampant under state control, continued unabated under federal regulations.[9] Sharp Delany, the collector at Philadelphia, then the busiest port in the nation, was forceful in advocating the employment of boats in inspections and deserves much of the credit for convincing Hamilton of the need for them.[10]

Armed with the collectors' correspondence, Hamilton presented Congress with a bill on 22 April 1790 calling for the establishment of the U. S. Revenue Cutter Service. He proposed the employment of ten boats to collect the revenue: "two, for the coasts of Massachusetts and New Hampshire; one for Long Island Sound; one for New York; one for the Bay of Delaware; two for the Chesapeake (these of course to ply along the neighboring coasts); one for North Carolina; one for South Carolina; and one for Georgia."[11] He thought that "boats of from thirty-six to forty feet keel" would "answer the purpose, each having one Captain, one Lieutenant, and six marines, and armed with swivels." He expected to build each boat, fully equipped, for $1,000 and estimated that it would cost $18,560 a year to operate the ten boats—$13,560 for salaries, $3,000 for provisions, and $2,000 for wear and tear.[12]

On 4 August 1790 Congress passed Hamilton's bill empowering the president to build and equip ten boats to collect revenue. The bill authorized the employment of forty officers, one master, and a first, second, and third mate for each cutter and made them "officers of the customs."[13] A product of the dire needs of the nation, the Treasury Department, and the collectors, this bill was the birth certificate of the U. S. Revenue Cutter Service, the eighteenth century ancestor of today's U. S. Coast Guard.

Realizing that the newly created service would be only as good as the men who commanded its vessels, Hamilton told Congress, "The utility of an establishment of this nature must depend on the exertion, vigilance, and fidelity of those to whom the charge of the boats shall be confined. If they are not respectable characters, they will rather serve to screen, than detect fraud."[14] Sharing Hamilton's concern, President Washington joined him in seeking information about candidates from many sources but kept close personal control over the final selection process.[15] In fact, Washington retained for himself the exclusive right to appoint the masters of cutters.

Hamilton started his search by writing to collectors north of New York. Ultimately he extended his inquiry as far south as Savannah, Georgia. On

10 September 1790, he explained his actions and intentions to the president:

> There not being sufficient light with regard to characters for officering the Cutters destined for the eastern coasts, particularly Massachusetts, I have written private letters to the Collectors of Boston and Portsmouth on the subject: when their answers arrive, the persons who appear to have most in their favor from New York inclusively eastward shall be noted for your determination.[16]

In response to his inquiry, collectors from Passamaquoddy Bay, Maine, to Savannah flooded the secretary with information, and he passed the contents of their correspondence on to Washington.[17]

America's merchants and businessmen supported candidates for cutter assignments. Thaddeus Burr, a Connecticut merchant, endorsed Jonathan Maltbie's successful bid to command the revenue cutter *Argus* at New London, Connecticut.[18] Comfort Sands, director of the Bank of New York, Benjamin Walker, director of the Society for Establishing Useful Manufactures in America, and eighteen prominent New York City businessmen put forward John Tanner as a mate on the revenue cutter *Vigilant* at New York. Several prominent citizens of Pennsylvania supported the candidacy of James Montgomery as master and Isaac Roach as first mate of the revenue cutter *General Greene* at Philadelphia.[19]

Political patronage played a role in the selection of first officers as politicians sought jobs for friends and allies. U. S. Senator James Gunn of Georgia recommended John Howell to command the revenue cutter *Eagle* at Savannah, declaring him "a man of unblemished integrity" with "a perfect knowledge of our Coast." Gunn also stressed that Howell's bid was supported by the governor of Georgia and all the state's principal officials.[20] Howell got the job, as did others who were endorsed by political patrons.[21]

In at least one instance, the political influence that helped a candidate to secure an initial appointment may have cost him a subsequent, better assignment. Both John Foster Williams and Nathaniel B. Lyde wanted to command the revenue cutter *Massachusetts*, and both had impressive support. Williams, the victor, was endorsed by the collector of the port of Boston, Benjamin Lincoln, and by Governor John Hancock, while Lyde, the vanquished, was the choice of Vice President John Adams.[22] Williams skippered the first two Massachusetts cutters, and when in 1798 a third "Boston cutter," the 187-ton brig *Pickering*, was launched for service in the Quasi-War with France, he sought command of the newer and bigger warship. But John Adams was president by 1798, and he was advised against appointing Williams to the new command. The nephew of Secretary of State Timothy Pickering explained to his uncle that it would be a mistake to give command of the ship to Williams because he was "old, without enterprise, & has been not a little *tainted* in his politics." The nephew had heard of no one better qualified than Captain Jonathan Chapman of Boston.[23] About a month later, President Adams, evidently receptive to the above advice, gave command of the *Pickering* to Chapman and left Williams in command of the older *Massachusetts*.[24]

At least one officer successfully sought command for himself. Hopley Yeaton met President Washington at Portsmouth, New Hampshire, on 2 November 1789, and had the honor of taking the president fishing in the harbor there. The following evening Washington danced with the attractive Mrs. Yeaton at a ball given in his honor. About one month later Yeaton sought from the president "such offices" in the state of New Hampshire "or any other in the Union" that the president thought him equal to. We may be sure that this request reached Washington, for Tobias Lear of Portsmouth was the president's private secretary, and Yeaton had sailed with Lear aboard the latter's privateer *Polly* during the American Revolution. Together the two men had suffered the indignity of capture by the British and the subsequent relief of rescue. It was Lear who drew up successive lists of leading candidates for cutter command, and Yeaton appeared first on every one.[25]

Washington played an active role in the selection of commanding officers for cutters sailing out of Southern ports. He told Hamilton to extend his "enquiries respecting proper characters to command these vessels . . . to the States south of Virginia." For the Virginia post Washington had already decided to appoint Richard Taylor. For the additional posts, he took a trip through the South and selected masters after meeting the candidates. William Jackson, who toured with Washington, informed Hamilton from Wilmington, Delaware, on 25 April 1791 that the president thought Captain William Cooke should be made captain of the revenue cutter there. Tobias Lear was duly ordered to fill out Cooke's commission. Prior to his tour, the president had intended to appoint William Hall master of the South Carolina cutter to please William Loughton Smith, a Federalist member of the House of Representatives. But on 8 May 1791, a day after attending a gala celebration in Charleston in his honor, he commissioned Robert Cochrane master of the South Carolina cutter.[26]

During the tour Washington was confirmed in his intention to appoint John Howell as commander of the revenue cutter *Eagle* at Savannah, Georgia. Senator James Gunn had strongly recommended Howell for the job, and Washington told Hamilton to inform the captain that his appointment was assured, provided the secretary knew of no reason to counteract the recommendation. Hamilton asked if they might not await additional recommendations for the purpose of comparison. The president agreed. Later, on 20 May 1791, he wrote Hamilton from Augusta, Georgia, that he had appointed John Howell commander, Hendricks Fisher first mate, and John Wood second mate, of the Georgia revenue cutter.[27]

The president did not have enough information to make a good decision on a commander for the Baltimore cutter. Having planned to appoint to that post Joshua Barney, a close personal friend and naval hero of the Revolution, he had not bothered to meet other candidates on his Southern tour. When Barney subsequently turned down the offer, Washington had no leads except the names of Simon Gross and David Porter, provided by Barney without any statement of preference. Gross was listed first, and so Washington appointed him master of the *Active*.[28] This turned out to be a mistake. Gross appointed his own junior officers without consulting Washington, and continued to do so even after Hamilton told him in no uncertain terms to submit candidates' names through his office, which would then submit them to the president.[29] Washington decided to take personal charge of the matter. On a trip through Baltimore in the summer of 1792, he discussed Gross's misconduct with customs officials and then removed him from command, replacing him with David Porter, his first mate.[30] There was to be absolutely no question in anyone's mind who had the final authority to select officers for the Revenue Cutter Service.

To backtrack, by the fall of 1790 Hamilton had gathered an enormous amount of information about candidates from sources throughout the nation. In a letter to Washington dated 29 September 1790 he listed the leading candidates and the cities and states from which they hailed. Washington returned the list on 6 October with orders to notify the men of his intention to appoint them to command.[31] On 21 March 1791, then, the president signed the commissions of the first masters of the Revenue Cutter Service. Hopley Yeaton headed the list and thus became the first seagoing officer commissioned by the new government of the United States. Others commissioned that day were John Foster Williams of Massachusetts, Jonathan Maltbie of Connecticut, Patrick Dennis of New York, James Montgomery of Pennsylvania, Simon Gross of Maryland, and Richard Taylor of Virginia. Washington subsequently took his trip to the South and completed the list by commissioning William Cooke of North Carolina on 25 April 1791, Robert Cochrane of South Carolina on 8 May 1791, and John Howell of Georgia on 20 May 1791.

The integrity and good character of the first ten officers had been attested to by prominent collectors of customs, Revolutionary War officers, businessmen, and politicians. What were their experiences before becoming masters in America's first seagoing service?

They had diverse backgrounds, but all were seamen with command experience—every one had served at sea during the Revolution as a naval, marine, or privateering officer—and some had held jobs as state or federal customs officials. Yeaton, Maltbie, Dennis, Porter, and Howell had sailed as merchant captains before the Revolution. Taylor had served as an officer in the Virginia customs service before taking command of the federal cutter that bore that state's name, and Montgomery and Porter had accepted minor jobs in the federal customs service prior to joining the Revenue Cutter Service as masters of the Pennsylvania and Maryland cutters respectively.[32]

Thus Washington had commissioned competent, mature officers of sound judgment to command the U.S. cutters. They faced a formidable task, one that had defied solution under British rule and Confederation alike, but they were equal to the challenge.

They began by supervising the construction of their own cutters, a task undertaken at the suggestion of Washington. The president realized that the government would benefit from having cutters built under the watchful eyes of the men who would ultimately command them. Some skippers started this job even before they were commissioned, and Hamilton speeded up the command selection process in order to advance the date of construction. The first masters contracted with lumberjacks, shipyards, carpenters, and sailmakers and oversaw the building of their craft from the laying of the keel to the launching.[33] Subsequent presidents have continued this practice, both in the Coast Guard and in the navy, of having commanders supervise new construction.

Hamilton laid the groundwork for construction by gathering information about shipbuilding in the United States and abroad. Ten months before the founding of the Revenue Cutter Service, he asked the collectors at Alexandria (Virginia), Portsmouth, Boston, and Philadelphia about methods of construction, the cost of a fully rigged and equipped vessel, and the type and duration of materials used. The collectors informed him that construction costs in the United States were about two-thirds those in France and England, and that the best materials for shipbuilding were live oak and cedar, both grown in the South. Vessels built of these materials in New York and Philadelphia lasted as long as the best-built vessels of Europe. In New England, vessels were constructed of native timber and planks; hemp, cordage, and sailcloth from Europe; iron from Philadelphia; and turpentine and tar from the Carolinas. New England builders used oak for timbers and outside planks, white pine for decks and masts, and spruce for smaller spars, yards, and topmasts. Ships built in Massachusetts were touted as comparable to those coming from Britain and France and were credited in addition with a good turn of speed.[34]

Armed with this information, Hamilton ordered the collectors at Newburyport (Massachusetts), Portsmouth, New London, New York, Philadelphia, Baltimore, Hampton (Virginia), Washington (North Carolina), Charleston, and Savannah to make arrangements for the construction of their cutters. Realizing that some would oppose the activities of the Revenue Cutter Service, and hoping to win support for it instead, Hamilton proposed that the cutters be built in various locations around the nation, an idea that Washington approved of. To further minimize opposition to the service, Hamilton insisted that each vessel be built for no more than $1,000.[35]

Design and construction was carried out in ten states by independent builders. Even so, the vessels turned out quite similar, their designs being the product both of function and of Hamilton's demand for economy. Cutters would have to spend a lot of time at sea, and therefore seaworthiness was an important consideration. For law enforcement, they would have to have speed, a shallow draft, and the ability to sail to windward, and they would have to carry guns.[36]

Howard I. Chapelle wrote in *The History of American Sailing Ships* that the schooner was "the national rig, quite satisfactory as to speed and weatherliness, and a type that both officers and seamen would be well acquainted with. . . ."[37] As a result, the service rigged at least eight and probably all ten of the cutters as schooners.

It is important to stress that the service chose to build the first ten cutters. It could just as easily have purchased vessels already afloat, as some within the organization had suggested. Sharp Delany wanted to purchase a vessel that was about to be condemned for illegal activity, and he appealed to Hamilton's desire for economy by noting that it could be purchased for less than half the cost of building a new cutter. The skipper of the revenue cutter *Virginia*, Richard Taylor, expressed doubts about his ability to build an adequate cutter for $1,000. Concerned about having a fast vessel, he recommended that the service buy a pilot boat with proven speed. But Hamilton decided against this course of action.[38]

How does one explain the secretary's actions? He was anxious to keep down costs to minimize political opposition to the service, and yet refused to purchase perfectly good vessels at reasonable prices. To understand his actions, one must remember that both he and Washington wanted to develop a naval establishment. Like others who had lived through the Revolution, they well understood one of the basic lessons taught by the naval phase of that conflict. As General Washington had explained to Lafayette, within a month after the battle of Yorktown,

> no land force can act decisively, unless it is accompanied by a maritime superiority; nor can more than negative advantages be expected without it. For proof of this, we have only to recur to the instances of the ease and facility with which the British shifted their ground, as advantages were to be obtained at either extremity of the continent, and to their late heavy loss the moment they failed in their naval superiority.[39]

In addition to national defense Hamilton had economic and political motives for fostering a naval establishment. He wanted in particular to promote the growth of American commerce and trade. In the *Federalist Papers* he wrote that the

> institution of a navy would have an internally unifying and stimulating effect on [the] . . . national economy. Each section would benefit not only from the display and exercise of naval power, but also from the process of naval development. Each possessed some peculiar advantage for this establishment. The Southern States, for example, produced especially fine ship timber and naval stores; the Middle States yielded "a greater plenty of iron, and of better quality"; while seamen would be drawn chiefly from the North. And the force thus created by the joint efforts of the whole country would provide the people of America with a tangible symbol of their national unity and power.[40]

Thus Hamilton hoped by building vessels not only to acquire revenue cutters but also to reap the military, economic, and political benefits that would flow from the cutter establishment.

Delany, who did not understand Hamilton's larger concept, was understandably frustrated by orders to purchase a new cutter for $1,000. The sum seemed much too small. Though he did everything humanly possible to satisfy the secretary's wishes, the cost of the *General Greene* exceeded $1,500. Apparently it was the citizens of Philadelphia who paid for the cost overrun.[41]

Several other cutters exceeded Hamilton's limit. Recognizing that a cutter that could operate off the Massachusetts coast in winter would have to be bigger than average, Hamilton himself authorized the expenditure of $1,440 for the revenue cutter *Massachusetts*. Even that sum proved inadequate: the *Massachusetts* cost $2,050. Thus one of the first vessels ever built by the U.S. government exceeded the amount authorized by over forty percent.[42]

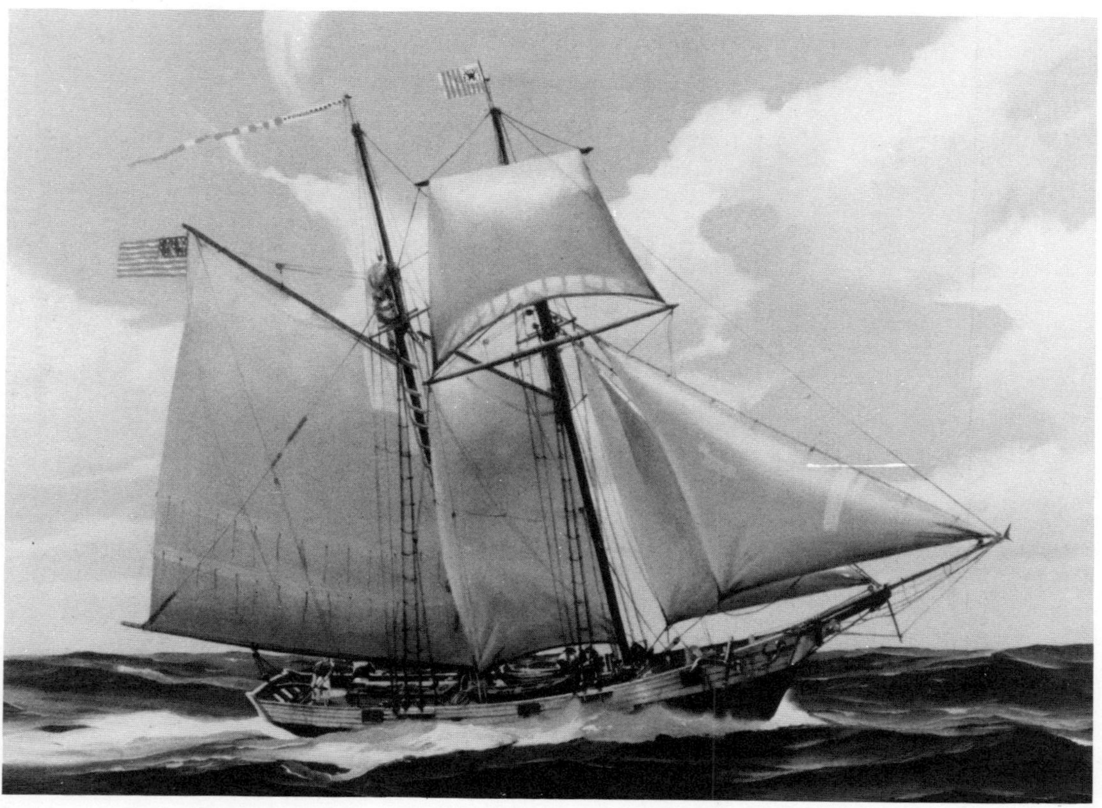

The USRC Massachusetts. (*Courtesy* USCG *Public Affairs Staff.*)

Searle and Tyler built the *Massachusetts* at Newburyport, where she was launched on 23 July 1791. Hamilton had wanted cutters of from 36′ to 40′ in length on the keel. The *Massachusetts*, the biggest, had the following measurements: 60′ upper deck, 17′ 8″ beam, 7′ 8″ depth of hold, and over 70 tons burden. She was a two-masted schooner with a handsome Indian figurehead, quarter badges, and considerable carved work about her square stern, and she had a long quarterdeck and deep bulwarks. Unfortunately, this biggest and most expensive of the cutters was a terrible disappointment to her master, a very dull sailer. As a result she was replaced by a second *Massachusetts*, a small sloop built by Adna Bates at Cohasset for $1,600 in June 1793.[43]

The other cutters were closer in size and cost to Hamilton's wishes, as can be seen in the following table:

HAMILTON'S REVENUE CUTTERS

Name	Built at	Launched	Length	Beam	Draft	Burden (tons)	Rig	Cost	Sold
Massachusetts	Newburyport	23 July 1791	60′	17′8″	7′8″	70 43/95	Schooner	$2,050	9 Oct. 1792
Scammel	Portsmouth area	24 Aug. 1791	57 6/10′	15 8/10′	6′6″	51 88/95	Schooner	$1,255	16 Aug. 1798 for $565
*Argus**	New London	1791	47′9″	16′3″	6′2″	35	Schooner	@ $1,000	1804
						48 8/95	Sloop		
Vigilant†	New York	1791	48′ keel	15′	4′6″	35	Schooner	@ $1,000	1798 for £348
							Sloop		
General Greene	Philadelphia	5 Aug. 1791							
Active	Baltimore	12 Apr. 1791							
Virginia	Hampton	1791	40′ keel	17′					
Diligence	Washington, N.C.	Commissioned June/July 1792							
South Carolina	Charleston	1792/1793							
Eagle	Savannah	Early 1793							

*The *Argus* was launched as a 35-ton schooner. In 1804 she was sold as a 48-9/95-ton sloop. Her rig was changed and her size increased after her launching.

†The *Vigilant* was launched as a schooner and had her rig changed to a sloop before she was sold in 1798.

HAMILTON'S REVENUE CUTTERS (*continued*)

Draft	Burden (tons)	Rig	Cost	Sold
		Schooner	Over $1,500	Dec. 1797
	50	Schooner	@ $1,000	26 Feb. 1800 for $733.50
6′6″	47	Schooner	@ $1,000	1797
	40	Schooner		5 Nov. 1798 for $310
	35	Schooner	@$1,000	1798
	50	Schooner	@$1,000	1799

The typical cutter was about 40 tons burden, measured from 40′ to 50′ in length, and was rigged as a schooner or a sloop.

Searle and Tyler promised to deliver the *Massachusetts* with two boats and seven sails, including a mainsail, foresail, jib, flying jib, fore-topsail, maintopsail, and square sail. On 14 December 1792 Hamilton ordered Sharp Delany to purchase nine bolts of no. 1 and three bolts of no. 8 Boston sailcloth for the *Eagle* at Savannah. That was the same amount of sailcloth that Searle and Tyler were supposed to have delivered to the *Massachusetts*, indicating that the *Eagle*, and perhaps the other cutters, had the same sail plan as she.[44] We definitely know that all of the first ten cutters sailed with Boston sailcloth.[45]

The *Massachusetts* went to sea armed with either four or six swivel guns. The other cutters mounted three or four swivels, and all the cutters carried ten muskets, ten bayonets, and twenty pistols.[46]

Most of the cutters were named for a Revolutionary War hero or for the state from which they sailed. The rest bore a name that symbolized the optimism and drive of the revolutionary generation.

When in 1794 actions were taken leading to the eventual launching of the first U.S. naval vessel, in 1797, and the establishment of the U.S. Navy, in 1798, the government sought help from and followed the precedents set by the Revenue Cutter Service.

In his first annual address to Congress, George Washington explained that "to be prepared for War is one of the most effectual means of preserving peace. A free people ought not only to be armed but disciplined, . . . their safety and interest require, that they should promote such manufactories, as tend to render them independent on [*sic*] others for essential, particularly for military supplies." In response to Washington's address, the House of Representatives directed Alexander Hamilton to prepare "a proper plan . . . for the encouragement and promotion of such manufactories as . . . [would] tend to render the United States independent of other nations for essential, particularly for military supplies." To carry out this mandate Hamilton asked Benjamin Lincoln, the customs collector at Boston, to help him to acquire precise information about the state of manufacturing in Massachusetts. As directed by Congress, he inquired particularly about the production of military supplies.[47]

Although Lincoln's response has not been found, we know from subsequent correspondence he and Hamilton agreed that the United States should foster the manufacture of domestic, specifically Boston, sailcloth for national security purposes, and that the sailcloth should be tried out on the first revenue cutters. As mentioned, the first cutters, though built in the districts they would serve, all carried sails made of sailcloth manufactured in Boston.[48]

In 1793, events unfolded that gave added significance to the testing of sailcloth by the Revenue Cutter Service. That fall Barbary corsairs intensified their attacks on American ships. Algerines seized eleven merchant ships and enslaved more than one hundred officers and seamen. Many of the Founding Fathers had previously advocated the establishment of a navy, but it was the corsairs' insults to the flag that stimulated Congress to pass a naval act which the president signed into law on 27 March 1794. The act called for the construction of six frigates and provided for the cessation of construction should the pirates accept a treaty of peace.[49]

Such a treaty was signed early in 1796, and the navy did stop building three of the frigates.[50] But France and Britain had gone to war in 1793 and the United States, an active neutral carrier, was soon embroiled in difficulties with both belligerents. This crisis, which resulted in the Quasi-War with France, prompted Congress to pass a bill signed by President Washington on 20 April 1796 authorizing him to continue work on the three unfinished naval vessels. Under the pro-navy Federalist president John Adams, the additional frigates were rushed to completion and a separate department was set up for the navy.

When work was started on the naval frigates, Hamilton returned again to Benjamin Lincoln for advice about proper sails. The secretary's letter of 28 June 1794 is worth quoting because it expresses his desire to stimulate domestic manufacturing and his reliance on the Revenue Cutter Service for the testing of domestic sailcloth:

> What Sail Cloth shall we use for the Frigate, that of Domestic or that of Foreign Manufacture? National pride and interest plead for the former, if the quality be really good, but is it really good? Objections are made; that which is principally insisted upon is that it shrinks exceedingly.
>
> Let me know with certainty what experience has decided. I ask your

The Frigate Constitution. (*Courtesy* U.S. *Naval Historical Center.*)

> opinion because I rely on your impartiality as well as judgement. It would be terrible to mistake the Public & I, personally, who must provide, am materially interested that there be none. Let me hear from you as soon as may be.[51]

A week later Lincoln wrote assuring Hamilton that Boston sailcloth was superior to that produced abroad. Though such a claim could not have been made honestly two years before, experience had proven that the Boston cloth was strong and less liable to mildew than the European.[52] Lincoln made his case by citing the experience of cutters and mentioning the positive endorsement of Captain James Magee of Boston, who had sailed his ship *Margaret* to Canton and back using two new suits of sails, one of Boston manufacture and one of foreign. When Magee returned home, Lincoln had asked him specifically about the Boston duck and was told that nothing could be better.[53]

In September 1794 the government signed a contract with the "Boston company, for sail cloth, sufficient for one entire suit of sail cloth for each frigate."[54] Miscellaneous smaller orders were placed with other manufacturers. The *Old Ironsides* carried some Rhode Island sailcloth, as well as sails of flax made in Boston's Old Granary Building in 1797–98.[55]

Everyone familiar with the history of America's sailing navy is aware that the first frigates gained an international reputation for speed. We now know that this was in part the result of good Boston sailcloth. We also know that the domestic sailcloth industry was consciously developed for defense purposes by President Washington, Alexander Hamilton, Benjamin Lincoln, and the Revenue Cutter Service.

The service provided additional experience that proved invaluable to the nation during the infancy of the U.S. Navy. When Secretary of War Knox was deciding what capabilities American warships should have to meet the challenge of corsairs, he consulted a number of advisers. They cannot all be identified with certainty, but John Foster Williams, the master of the *Massachusetts*, was one, and his advice was said to have been influential.[56] Knox ultimately decided to build six forty-four-gun frigates that would be powerful enough to fight any frigates in the world and fast enough to outrun any ships-of-the-line.

On 27 December 1794, Knox submitted a report to the House of Representatives on the construction of the first six frigates. In it he included basic principles that were clearly in keeping with the precedents set by the Revenue Cutter Service. The six frigates were built at Portsmouth, Boston, New York, Philadelphia, Baltimore, and Norfolk, "in order, as well to distribute the advantages arising from the operation, as to ascertain at what places they can be executed to the greatest advantage." All six of the states these ports were located in and four of the ports themselves were used as sites for cutter construction to win support for the Revenue Cutter Service. In Baltimore David Stodder, the shipbuilder who had constructed the cutter *Active*, was hired to build the first navy frigate to put to sea, the *Constellation*.[57]

Knox established a policy in the navy, which derived from Washington and Hamilton's policy in the revenue service, of having frigate captains superintend the construction and equipment of their own vessels.[58]

Realizing that he could not simply contract for a completed ship at a given yard, Knox opened accounts in each yard for the principal materials and items used in construction, such as timber, iron, masts, spars, hemp, and anchors. This policy was based on a lesson learned by Alexander Hamilton and Joseph Whipple when they built the revenue cutter *Scammel* at Portsmouth.[59]

While the government rented shipyards and organized the business end of construction, the Treasury Department made arrangements to collect construction materials. The department naturally turned for help to the officials who, from their work with the Revenue Cutter Service, had experience in shipbuilding and contracting. The job of procuring shipwrights, axmen, carpenters, timber, lumber, and armaments fell most heavily on the shoulders of Commissioner of Revenue Tench Coxe. Coxe was put in charge of the procurement of military and naval supplies, and he turned for help to Collectors of the Customs Isaac Holmes of Charleston, John Habersham of Savannah, and Jedediah Huntington of New London. All had worked with the Revenue Cutter Service.[60]

The frigates were built of live oak, red cedar, and pitch pine from Georgia, North Carolina, and South Carolina, all procured by the Treasury Department. The department hired John T. Morgan, a master shipwright from Boston, "to search for the timber, to superintend the cutting and forming it . . . , and to procure it to be shipped for the six several ports at which the frigates were to be built." Collectors Holmes and Habersham were appointed to draw up the contracts for the timber in North and South Carolina and in Georgia. Most of the lumberjacks and carpenters who cut the timber were found in Connecticut, Massachusetts, and Rhode Island by Collector Huntington. The rest of the woodcutters were hired by Habersham. The Treasury Department dispatched the New Englanders to Savannah, whence they were transported to St. Simons aboard the revenue cutter *Eagle*.[61]

When in December 1794 it was decided that twenty anchors should be imported from Europe to use on the frigates, Hamilton ordered Thomas Pinckney, who was then minister plenipotentiary to the Court of St.

James, to procure and ship them. In keeping with Hamilton's economic nationalism, the minister was ordered to give "a preference . . . to American Bottoms" when he shipped the anchors.[62]

The influence of the Treasury Department on the navy did not end with the construction of the first six frigates. During the Quasi-War with France the department, under Secretary Oliver Wolcott, Hamilton's protégé and successor, arranged contracts and purchased cannon, cannon carriages, and masts for the navy. Customs collectors, moreover, assisted the Treasury Department in securing naval agents.[63] Benjamin Stoddert, the first secretary of the navy, was a successful merchant and a staunch Federalist from Georgetown, Maryland, who proved to be a hard-working and competent administrator. But he did not know as much about ships as the secretary of the treasury, and he admitted as much in a letter to Wolcott.[64]

Subsequently, Stoddert expressed his desire for a single navy yard on the Potomac River. But once again he acknowledged the valuable experience of the Revenue Cutter Service by asking Wolcott to consider the subject seriously and to give his "candid opinion, without the least respect to . . . [Stoddert's] prejudices or follies." Later he submitted to Congress a comprehensive report on naval matters that reflected Wolcott's input. It called for an immediate building program using domestic materials and for a judicious distribution of shipyards, storehouses, and dry docks in the big cities along the Atlantic seaboard. Among other things, the idea was to "distribute more equally amongst the States, the advantage which may arise, from supplying the Materials and the Labour."[65]

In the last days of the John Adams administration, Stoddert and the president rushed to build navy yards and dry docks. They pushed through Congress legislation for the construction of six ships-of-the-line and for the purchase of ship's timber and timberlands. Stoddert acquired land for navy yards at Portsmouth, Boston, New York, Philadelphia, Washington, and Norfolk. All of this was done to assure that the nation had a permanent shore organization and an adequate naval establishment prior to the inauguration of the anti-navy Jefferson.[66]

In conclusion, the Revenue Cutter Service established precedents that were of consequence to the nation in the 1790s, and remain so to this day. Hamilton's small fleet of revenue cutters tested the sailcloth that powered the first six frigates of the U.S. Navy. Treasury Department officials, who learned about shipbuilding by constructing cutters, made important contributions to the construction of frigates. And the political and economic advantage of using locally manufactured products in the construction of public vessels, as well as of distributing shore facilities over a wide area, was first learned by Hamilton in the Revenue Cutter Service and subsequently recognized by the Navy Department.

CHAPTER TWO

Getting Under Way

The first revenue cutters were generally too small, slow, and lightly armed for combat. Thus the coming of the Quasi-War with France led to the construction of a whole new class of bigger, faster, and more heavily armed cutters, including the 187-ton brigs *Pickering* and *Eagle*, the 187-ton schooners *Scammel*, *Governor Jay*, *Virginia*, *Diligence*, and *South Carolina*, and the 98-ton sloop *General Greene*.[1]

America's troubles began when revolutionary France declared war on Great Britain and Spain on 1 February 1793. Recognizing the potential danger in this clash of titans, President Washington made a proclamation of U.S. neutrality, but France ignored it and sent Citizen Edmond Genet to the United States to wage a maritime war against France's enemies. From Charleston and Philadelphia, Genet fitted out privateers that seized British and Spanish prizes, some within the three-mile limit of the U.S. coast. The Revenue Cutter Service tried with little success to stop this illicit activity. In the spring of 1793, Captain William Cooke of the revenue cutter *Diligence* did charge Commander F. H. Hervieux of the privateer

Vainqueur de la Bastille with breaking the nation's revenue laws, and confiscated $40,000 in gold that belonged to the Spanish government, but this case was an exception. In February 1794, when John Foster Williams of the revenue cutter *Massachusetts* was prevented from boarding a small British ship anchored in Nantasket Roads for purposes of identification, all he could do was to report the incident to the Boston customs office. On 2 January 1795, the revenue cutter *General Greene* failed in an attempt to stop the French privateer *Jumeaux* from sailing from Philadelphia down the Delaware River.[2]

In general, the enforcement agencies were in a quandary. They received little or no local support. According to Melvin H. Jackson's *Privateering in Charleston, 1793–1796*, Judge Thomas Bee handed down a decision that "the President's wishes did not have the force of law and hence were not binding." Wholesale violations followed this decision in both Charleston and Philadelphia. Even the pro-British Hamilton was reluctant to declare unequivocally that customs officials should seize French vessels and their prizes, for France had claimed rights under the 1778 Franco-American Treaty of Alliance, and Hamilton wanted to avoid a confrontation over conflicting interpretations of treaty rights.[3] The small revenue cutters were, after all, the only armed vessels that the nation possessed at the time.

Thus French privateers continued to enter U.S. ports until 30 June 1796, when the secretary of the treasury finally ordered customs collectors to deny admission to privateers of all nations. His action followed the signing of Jay's Treaty by the United States and Great Britain. Brought on by a desire to avoid war with Great Britain, the greatest naval power of the day, Jay's Treaty improved Anglo-American relations at the expense of Franco-American friendship. Article 24 of the treaty stipulated that the signatories would stop arming enemy privateers and prevent the sale of their prizes. Enforcement of this article ended French privateering in American waters.[4]

It also convinced France that the United States had become a British satellite and started a series of events that led to an undeclared war. France stepped up her interference with American shipping. Her prize courts "exceeded even the worst of Britain's colonial courts in the arbitrariness, corruption, and cynicism with which they treated American vessels brought in on a bewildering array of charges. . . ." Brutality marked French treatment of American seamen. In the hopes of electing the Francophile Thomas Jefferson, the French minister to the United States, Pierre Adet, who had succeeded Citizen Genet, intervened in the 1796 presidential election. Adet's indiscretion hurt Jefferson's candidacy and angered

John Adams, who subsequently lashed out against France in his inaugural address. When President Adams later tried to settle Franco-American problems peacefully by sending John Marshall, Charles Cotesworth Pinckney, and Elbridge Gerry to France as envoys, France insulted the United States by demanding a bribe of $250,000, a loan of $10 million, and an apology from Adams. The Federalists refused to make such concessions, and adopted instead a policy of undeclared war.[5]

Congress did not declare war because it was divided on the issue. Some legislators believed that American ships would be more vulnerable in a declared war, and many hoped that peace would be more easily restored if war were not declared.[6]

The Quasi-War differed from others in that unarmed ships were not seized. French merchant ships that entered American ports were released and sent out of U.S. waters, and trade with France continued even during the conflict.[7]

The original revenue cutters were the only armed vessels that the United States had at sea when troubles started with France. Thus, on 14 June 1797, Congress ordered them to stop American citizens from privateering against the ships of friendly nations. On 1 July Congress added to this order the obligation to defend the nation's coast and to repel any attack on American commerce that occurred within U.S. waters. These demands revealed the inadequacy of the original cutters and gave birth to a new fleet.[8]

The only cutters capable of carrying out their new roles were the new *Virginia* and the *General Greene*. The former was armed with six 6-pounders on her main deck and four 4-pound howitzers in her cabin, and the latter had the capacity to carry eight 4-pounders. According to Secretary of the Treasury Oliver Wolcott, "none of the other cutters" could have been "armed with any prospect of advantage." Some were worn out. Others needed extensive repairs, and all had been built with limited resources for peacetime functions.[9]

A new building program added at least eight cutters before the end of the Quasi-War. The above-mentioned *Virginia* and *General Greene* had been built in 1797 at Norfolk and Baltimore, respectively. Before the year was out the *Diligence* was added at Philadelphia. Six cutters were launched in 1798: the *Governor Jay* at New York on 27 June, the *Unanimity* at Charleston and the *Pickering* at Newburyport in July, the *Eagle* at Philadelphia on 4 August, the *Scammel* at Portsmouth on 11 August, the *South Carolina* at Charleston on 27 November, and the *Governor Gilman* at Portsmouth. William Pritchard started the construction of the 195-ton brig *Pinckney* in his

Charleston shipyard, but the navy took her over from the Revenue Cutter Service before she was launched, on 13 October 1798.[10]

The service was proud of these new cutters. Some of the most famous naval architects in America participated in their construction. Josiah Fox designed the *Pickering, Eagle, Diligence, Governor Gilman*, and *Scammel*. Nathan and Orlando Merrill, the inventor of the lift model, built the *Pickering*, William and Abra Brown, the *Eagle*, Joshua Humphreys, the *Diligence*, and James Hackett, the *Governor Gilman* and the *Scammel*. A contemporary observer described this last cutter as being of fine workmanship, neat in finish, and beautiful in appearance. A reporter who witnessed the *Pickering*'s passage from Newburyport to Boston wrote in the *Philadelphia Daily Advertiser* that the cutter had sailed against the tide under a light breeze and was "a fine sail boat."[11]

With the exception of the 98-ton sloop *General Greene*, all the new cutters were rigged as "double topsail schooners or 'jackass brigs,' with fore and main square topsails." The *Diligence, Governor Jay, Scammel, Virginia*, and *South Carolina* were the schooners, and the *Eagle, Pickering, Unanimity*, and *Pinckney* the brigs. Howard Chapelle saw a set of plans in the Washington Navy Yard that was probably "a preliminary design or a rather hasty copy of a working drawing" of one of the schooners. Her measurements were as follows: 77′ 0″ between perpendiculars, 58′ 0″ straight rabbet, 20′0″ molded beam, 9′0″ depth of hold, and 187 tons burden. She had a square tuck stern with tumblehome topsides. All the new schooners and brigs except the *Pinckney* and the *Virginia* were probably about the same length as the cutter described by Chapelle. The *Pinckney* was a 195-ton brig with a 62′ keel, 23′ beam, and 10½′ depth of hold, and the schooner *Virginia* had a 50′ 0″ straight rabbet, 18′ 10″ molded beam, and 8′ 6″ depth of hold.[12]

Other cutters were either purchased or seized by the Revenue Cutter Service during the conflict. It bought the *Maria* and the *North Carolina*, and the revenue cutter *Eagle* seized the French schooner *Bon Père*, which sailed as a cutter under the name *Bee*.[13]

The new cutters mounted between ten and sixteen guns throughout the war. The most heavily armed, the *Eagle*, carried sixteen 9-pounders. In addition they carried a variety of small arms, including ten or twelve muskets, ten cutlasses, and twenty boarding pikes.[14]

Their crews were much bigger than those of the original cutters. On 1 July 1797, Congress authorized up to thirty seamen and marines for each cutter. A year later that number was increased to seventy. On 10 October 1798 the *Pickering, Governor Jay, General Greene, Eagle, Diligence, Vir-*

ginia, and *Scammel* received orders to cruise under the direction of Secretary of the Navy Benjamin Stoddert. That same day the *Pickering* (Captain Jonathan Chapman), *Governor Jay* (Captain John W. Leonard), and *Eagle* (Captain Hugh G. Campbell) were ordered to take aboard seventy men and boys, at least thirty-five of whom had to be able seamen. Captains Francis Bright of the *Virginia*, John Brown of the *Diligence*, George Price of the *General Greene*, and John Adams of the *Scammel* were each ordered to recruit thirty men and boys, of which number not more than fifteen were to be able seamen.[15]

On 25 February 1799 Congress authorized President John Adams to place all revenue cutters in the naval establishment, which he did, thereby redefining the maritime character of the Revenue Cutter Service and giving it the dual character of a military establishment and a maritime service.[16]

The war also led to a definition of the service that had been wanting before 1799. In 1790 Alexander Hamilton had asked Congress to commission revenue cutter officers as officers of the navy, saying, "This will not only induce fit men the more readily to engage, but will attach them to their duty by a nicer sense of honor."[17] But the colonial experience had left many congressmen opposed to any standing military establishment, so they designated the officers masters and mates and made them "officers of the customs" rather than reestablishing the American navy, which had sold off its last vessel in 1785.[18] Although maritime ranks were appropriate for officers of the new service, many of these men had served in the navy during the American Revolution and preferred naval titles. They sought a legal change in their status throughout the 1790s, and during the Quasi-War with France, on 2 March 1799, Congress granted their wish and made them captains and lieutenants.[19]

That same year, President Adams authorized cutters to fly an ensign that would distinguish them from other vessels. On 1 August Oliver Wolcott ordered collectors of customs to provide the cutters on their stations with an ensign "consisting of sixteen perpendicular stripes, alternate red and white, the Union of the Ensign to be the Arms of the United States, in dark Blue, on a white Field." A description of the flag was provided to the masters of all merchant ships.[20]

The Revenue Cutter Service did more than play a significant role in the building of the nation's naval establishment; it joined the navy in fighting the Quasi-War with France. A total of forty-five U.S. vessels served in combat between 1798 and 1801. Of these, eight were the new revenue cutters *Pickering*, *Eagle*, *Scammel*, *Diligence*, *Governor Jay*, *Virginia*, *South Carolina*, and *General Greene*. The Treasury Department built and manned these cut-

USRC *Ensign.* (*Courtesy USCG Public Affairs Staff.*)

ters and paid all their expenses until they actually cruised with the navy. Thereafter the navy picked up the bills and assigned officers and crews, in some cases retaining revenue cutter officers in command, in others giving command to naval officers.[21]

Secretary of the Navy Stoddert decided early in the war that smaller vessels should sail in company with at least one bigger ship. Thus, when the first cutters went to sea to protect the coast and American commerce along it, they sailed in squadrons with bigger naval vessels.[22]

In the summer of 1798, the *Pickering* joined the ship *Herald* on a cruise between Georges Bank and the western end of Long Island. The *General Greene* and the *Governor Jay* sailed between Long Island and Cape Henry in company with the frigates *Constellation* and *United States*, the ships *Delaware* and *Herald*, and the Indiaman *Ganges*. The coast between Cape Henry and the southern limits of the United States was patrolled by the *Virginia* and the *Constitution*. The *Diligence* sailed between Capes Fear and Hatteras, and the *Eagle* joined the *Montezuma* between the capes of Delaware and Virginia until the fall, when the cutter moved to the waters between Savannah and St. Marys.[23]

On 22 October 1798 the *Scammel* left Portsmouth, New Hampshire, carrying orders to sail as far east as Machias and as far south as Cape Cod and Nantucket. The orders for her captain, John Adams, are interesting because they reveal that he was expected to show both initiative and

The USRC Eagle, 1799–1801. (*Drawing by John A. Tilley, courtesy* USCG *Public Affairs Staff.*)

energy. Timothy Pickering wrote, "You are not confined to any distance from the coast, but are allowed to indulge a spirit of Enterprize; And if you should hear of Enemy Vessels further North or South than your Limits, you will consider that you are not confined to Limits."[24]

Because it seemed unlikely that French ships would cruise off the Atlantic coast during the winter of 1798–99, the navy moved four squadrons against enemy ships in the West Indies. Revenue cutters cruised with each of the squadrons.

Four cutters, the *Pickering*, *Eagle*, *Scammel*, and *Diligence*, sailed with the most powerful squadron, under the command of Commodore John Barry. It rendezvoused at Prince Rupert Bay on the island of Dominica and cruised to the windward of St. Christopher. The second squadron, under the command of Commodore Thomas Truxton, included the *Virginia*; it rendezvoused at St. Kitts and cruised between that island and Puerto Rico. The third squadron, under Commodore Thomas Tingey, cruised between Cuba and Haiti. The brig *Pinckney* and the revenue cutter *South Carolina* sailed with Tingey's squadron. The *General Greene* and *Governor Jay* cruised with the fourth squadron, under Commodore Stephen Decatur, in the vicinity of Havana and guarded the windward passage between Cuba and Santo Domingo.[25]

The cutters that sailed with the four squadrons in the West Indies had a positive effect on American commerce. They convoyed American merchantmen, patrolled the more "dangerous bottlenecks where the shipping was most vulnerable," and attacked French armed vessels. Robert G. Albion wrote that "most of the trouble in those waters came not from French cruisers, but from the privateers, which were able to bully defenseless merchantmen but could not and would not stand up against a well-armed warship." The squadrons offered plenty of protection for American commerce, and Secretary Stoddert was able to boast with justice that the navy more than paid for itself in reduced insurance rates.[26]

Secretary of the Treasury Wolcott, concerned about the prolonged absence from revenue work of revenue cutters serving with the navy, asked Benjamin Stoddert in May 1799 if he intended to keep cutters in the naval establishment. At just about the same time Stoddert, after consulting Commodore Truxtun, decided to return all cutters except the *Eagle*, *Scammel*, and *Pickering* to the Revenue Cutter Service. The *Eagle* and the *Scammel* served with the navy until the end of the war, when they were sold. The *Pickering* sank in a gale with all hands while bound from New Castle, Delaware, to Guadeloupe in September 1800. The *Diligence*, *General Greene*, *Governor Jay*, *Virginia*, and *South Carolina* were all returned to the Revenue Cutter Service in the summer of 1799.[27]

The USRC Eagle *Capturing the* Mehitable *during the* Quasi-War *with* France. (*Claire White-Peterson photo, courtesy* USCGA *Library.*)

The cutters had seized their fair share of enemy vessels while on duty with the navy. In his *Naval Documents of the Quasi-War with France*, Dudley Knox listed ninety-nine armed French vessels that were captured by U.S. warships between July 1798 and January 1801, claiming that cutters captured thirteen (actually fifteen) of those vessels without assistance and aided in the capture of four (actually five) more. Cutters also freed twenty American vessels that had been taken by French ships.[28]

When the war ended on 3 February 1801 the United States had a growing, dynamic naval establishment. And fifteen vessels that had served as revenue cutters were still in service.

Protecting the nation's revenue continued to be the primary obligation of the Revenue Cutter Service throughout the Quasi-War with France. When Congress authorized the use of cutters to protect American commerce, it had stressed that the president show due regard for their primary duty of protecting the revenue. Oliver Wolcott made the same point when he ordered Benjamin Lincoln to build a new, more heavily armed cutter for the Massachusetts station. And, although Secretary of the Navy Stoddert did not always show an adequate appreciation of the cutters' principal obligation, he was conscious of the nation's need for revenue and of the service's role in meeting that need.[29]

At first, the United States depended completely on revenue from merchant shipping to survive. No other federal taxes were collected during the nation's first five years under the Constitution. Even after excise taxes were levied, taxes on imports and tonnage continued to account for all but a small fraction of the revenue. Between 1 January and 30 September 1795, receipts from imports and tonnage duties amounted to $4,234,046. A tax on distilled spirits, which produced the second greatest amount of revenue during the same nine months, produced a mere $210,016. In December 1799 Oliver Wolcott wrote Fisher Ames that revenue had fallen one million dollars short the previous year, adding, "that is, the duties on imports decreased from seven million and a half, to six and a half million. . . ."[30]

The Revenue Cutter Service played an important role in the nation's successful collection of tariffs and tonnage duties. The first two secretaries of the treasury, Hamilton and Wolcott, were convinced that this was the case, as were the collectors of customs. In the summer of 1791 Joseph Whipple, the collector at Portsmouth, wrote that revenue cutter officers faced tremendous problems in trying "to reconcile a people accustom'd almost to no laws but their will, to strict observance of Revenue Laws. . . ." Six years later, Whipple asked Wolcott to replace the *Scammel* and was confident of success because he was sure that cutter had prevented or detected a great number of frauds on her station. After the revenue cutter *Massachusetts* went to sea, Benjamin Lincoln reported that duties were paid cheerfully and on time, and that no suits had been filed on any bond for more than a year.[31]

Such success was not a foregone conclusion, and contrasted sharply with the experience of Great Britain in North America. From the beginning of their service in America, British customs officers were unpopular. By the 1760s they were viewed as "wretches" of infamous character whom no merchant could trust. They were not even able to justify their presence by collecting revenue. At the end of the French and Indian War in 1763, an investigation "revealed that in most colonies the customs service was at best inefficient and at worst corrupt, and that the officers did not even collect enough money to cover the expenses." As every American school child knows, Britain strengthened the authority of the collectors after 1763 and employed her military might to collect taxes. The result was the American Revolution and the loss of an empire.[32]

The success of the Revenue Cutter Service cannot be explained by recounting its authority and methods of operation, although these are important. Congress authorized customs officers to board, search, and check the manifest of every ship bound for the United States that approached within four leagues of the coast. They could secure the hatches and openings to the holds of a ship and even have officers stay aboard until arrival in the United States. Acts of Congress obliged ships bound for the United States to carry manifests detailing their name, home port, tonnage, and master. The nature, quantity, port of origin, and destination of all cargo had to be listed. Laws required masters to enter an American port within twenty-four hours of arriving from abroad, and to report the cargo and deliver their manifests to a customs collector within forty-eight hours. Failure to comply with the laws of Congress was punishable by fine and even forfeiture of one's vessel.[33]

Alexander Hamilton ordered the Revenue Cutter Service to enforce congressional laws by stationing cutters at strategic ports along the coast: Boston, Portsmouth, New London, New York, Philadelphia, Norfolk, Baltimore, Wilmington (North Carolina), Charleston, and Savannah. He wisely encouraged skippers to ply the entire length of coast within their stations and to keep on the move as much as possible.[34]

But more important was Secretary Hamilton's instruction to masters about the proper attitude of an officer in his dealings with the free citizens of the nation:

> While I recommend in the strongest terms to the respective Officers, activity, vigilance & firmness, I feel no less solicitude that their deportment

> may be marked with prudence, moderation & good temper. Upon these last qualities not less than upon the former must depend the success, usefulness & consequently *continuance* of the establishment in which they are included. They cannot be insensible that there are some prepossessions against it, that the charge with which they are entrusted is a delicate one, & that it is easy by mismanagement to produce serious & extensive clamour, disgust & odium.
>
> They will always keep in mind that their Countrymen are Freemen & as such are impatient of every thing that bears the least mark of a domineering Spirit. They will therefore refrain with the most guarded circumspection from whatever has the semblance of haughtiness, rudeness or insult. If obstacles occur they will remember they are under the particular protection of the Laws, & that they can meet with nothing disagreeable in the execution of their duty which these will not severely reprehend. This reflection & a regard to the good of the service will prevent at all times a spirit of irritation or resentment. They will endeavor to overcome difficulties, if any are experienced, by a cool and temperate perseverance in their duty, by address & moderation rather than by vehemence or violence.[35]

Hamilton's advice was sound in 1791, as it is today. And it was the good fortune of the nation to have an administrator of Hamilton's genius who recognized the need for tact and courtesy on the part of revenue cutter officers, and who had the energy and force of will to guarantee compliance with his wishes.[36]

The men of the Revenue Cutter Service boarded most ships without incident, proving that reaction to the service by American merchants was favorable.[37] This was in part the result of Hamilton's insistence upon manly but tactful behavior. It was also a product of the service that cutters rendered to distressed mariners. The crew of the *Massachusetts* often pulled ships off beaches or rocks. Revenue cutters bailed out sinking boats, refloated those that had sunk, and towed damaged boats to shore. In the winter of 1800 the *Argus* piloted ships out of New London through the ice. And, of course, Northern merchants generally supported the Federalist government of Washington and Adams.[38]

By the end of the Quasi-War with France, the role of the service had expanded in noncombat areas from preventing smuggling to charting rivers and harbors, tending aids to navigation, establishing lighthouses, writing shipping directions, protecting public health, suppressing the slave trade, and carrying out ceremonial functions. Hamilton had always expected this expansion beyond the scope of the authority originally granted by Congress. From the beginning he assumed that the Revenue Cutter Service would chart the nation's coastal waters and assist the Treasury Department with the placement and maintenance of aids to navigation.[39] But a national tradition of using revenue cutters to respond to new needs on the high seas also accounted for the pre-1801 growth.

Although the service was not explicitly associated by law with the establishment and maintenance of aids to navigation, customs collectors who controlled cutters under the direction of the secretary of the treasury also controlled the U.S. Lighthouse Service, and they used cutters for a number of applicable purposes. Cutters located proper sites for lighthouses and transported supplies to their keepers. They tended buoys, sounded harbors, and wrote sailing instructions for Massachusetts Bay.[40]

The job of protecting public health evolved from an ability to meet an emerging need. In the fall of 1793, the *Eagle* took up a position at Cockspur on the Savannah River "to prevent vessels or passengers from coming up from places infested with malignant diseases, . . . without a permit from the Health Officer." When Baltimore authorities feared "that yellow fever might be imported into the city from the West Indies" in the summer of 1794, they established a quarantine and employed the revenue cutter *Active* to enforce it. Although concerned about the diversion of the cutter from revenue work, Hamilton consented to its use in this capacity after the governor of Maryland appealed personally for help. Two years later, Congress ordered the nation's customs collectors to help states to enforce quarantine laws. The Revenue Cutter Service continued to assist health officers throughout the Federalist era.[41]

The service utilized the skills of Isaac Roach, first mate of the *General Greene* at Philadelphia, to solve a very different maritime problem. In May 1792 Delaware Bay pilots struck for higher wages and stopped almost all shipping into Philadelphia. Fearing the strike would hurt the nation's economy and that the pilots might damage beacons and buoys in Delaware Bay, Hamilton called upon Roach for assistance. Roach, who had been a bay pilot before his commissioning as a revenue cutter officer, restored commercial traffic by arranging to have a pilot who was not on strike guide ships from the mouth of the bay to Bombay Hook, where the *General Greene* took over for the last leg of the journey. Roach also negotiated with the striking pilots, and on 22 May they returned to work.[42]

After 1794 the Revenue Cutter Service tried to enforce the federal law against the slave trade. Of course, slaves could be imported into the United States until 1808 under the provisions of the Constitution, but an act of Congress dated 22 March 1794 prohibited Americans from carrying slaves from the United States to another country or from another country to a third nation. Oliver Wolcott fully expected customs authorities to enforce the law, and some revenue cutters participated in this work. The *Governor Jay*, sailing out of New York, spoke two vessels at sea that were carrying slaves from Cuba illegally. One was the schooner *Betsy*. This information was passed on to Benjamin Lincoln at Boston, who had her seized for the transgression.[43]

With the end of the Quasi-War with France and the election of Thomas Jefferson, a champion of states' rights and an opponent of standing armed forces, the service was cut to the bone. Its officers were laid off and its cutters sold. The restoration of peace in 1801, of course, reduced the need for large, armed cutters, and the state of the treasury induced Oliver Wolcott to call for limits on federal spending. On 14 October 1801 Jefferson's new secretary of the treasury, Albert Gallatin, explained to Benjamin Lincoln that the president wanted measures "taken to reduce the cutter establishment as nearly as circumstances will permit within its original limits." As a result, Gallatin ordered Lincoln to deliver the guns and military stores of the Boston-based cutter to the navy. After that, Lincoln was to sell the cutter and discharge all of her crew except the master and one mate. Gallatin expected Lincoln to patrol the harbor with a barge manned by a mate and four men until a new cutter of not more than 45 tons was built. When the new craft was ready for service, she would be manned by a master, a mate, and six seamen, including boys.[44]

Gallatin instituted a similar policy in all of the revenue cutter districts. Two of the three cutters retained by the navy at the end of the Quasi-War were sold between June and December 1801. Of the five cutters it returned, only the *General Greene* and the *Diligence* appeared on a list of cutters still in service on 12 February 1802. Of the original ten cutters, only the *Argus* was still in service at the end of the war. Of those retained in the Revenue Cutter Service during the war, the *North Carolina* ended her service in 1798, the *Unanimity* in 1799, the *Maria* in 1800, the *Bon Pére* and the *Massachusetts* in 1801, and the *Governor Gilman* in 1802.[45]

Similar reductions decimated the officer corps. In an incomplete list of officers serving under the navy's jurisdiction between 1797 and 1801, Dudley W. Knox listed fifty-six who served aboard revenue cutters. He was not sure what had happened to twenty of the officers, but seven were known to have been discharged or dismissed, or to have resigned or died before the war ended. In 1801 the government retained eight in the navy and dismissed or discharged another twenty-one. While these figures are incomplete, they indicate a definite policy of discharging men from the Revenue Cutter Service at the end of the war.

There is additional proof. Knox listed sixteen revenue cutter officers who served in the navy during the Quasi-War. In his *Early History of the United States Revenue Marine Service*, Horatio Davis Smith listed the thirty-eight officers who were still in the Revenue Cutter Service on 12 February

1802. Only five of the sixteen who had served with the navy in the Quasi-War were still in the Revenue Cutter Service. It is also noteworthy that the total of thirty-eight officers was two short of the number first authorized by Congress in 1790. And the crews that had been increased when their cutters joined the navy were cut when they returned to the Revenue Cutter Service.[46]

The end of the war and the election of Jefferson may have reduced the numbers of cutters and men in the Revenue Cutter Service, but by 1801 the Federalist administrations of Washington and Adams had formed its essential character. Its primary job was to protect the nation's revenue. That task had dictated the selection of men of good character to command cutters. But the service had also assumed additional responsibilities that included putting out and maintaining aids to navigation, assisting lighthouse operators, charting America's coastal waters, and aiding mariners in distress. During the Quasi-War with France it took on the dual nature of a maritime and naval service; and to its peacetime duties was added responsibility for the safety of America's coastal commerce and shipping lanes in wartime. Most important, the little fleet of revenue cutters had established and maintained respect for the federal government and its laws.

CHAPTER THREE

Jefferson and the Embargo

Historians have aptly described the forty years from 1775 to 1815 as the heroic age of American maritime history. For twelve of those years the United States warred with Great Britain on the high seas, for two, with France. Americans along the coast lived in constant fear of bombardment or invasion. Yankee shipmasters had to maintain careful watch for privateers and warships, and following America's withdrawal from the British empire, merchants had to find new markets for their goods. As Robert G. Albion has pointed out, of all businesses a nation's maritime commerce is most directly affected by international affairs. During the American Revolution and the War of 1812, U.S. commerce came to a virtual halt, to be replaced only by the munitions trade, privateering, and letters of marque.[1] Between the years of fighting, though, American trade flourished.

Independence established the freedom to trade any place in the world where American products were wanted. Americans no longer had to sell their most valuable products to England, or to buy products from the empire at inflated prices. As a result the nation's mariners opened up new trade routes to China, Sumatra, the Sandwich islands, and—more important than the romantic-sounding Pacific—Europe. Although commerce with England dropped off after independence, that with France, Spain, Portugal, and the Netherlands increased. American merchants also found their way back to Europe's West Indian possessions, where islanders needed Yankee fish and timber.

The opening of hostilities between England and France in 1793 gave Americans their chance. France had always kept the profitable long haul between her West Indies colonies and the continent for herself, but because of British dominance on the high seas she had to open it to neutral carriers. This was complicated by Britain's Rule of 1756, which stated that an enemy could not open trade routes to other nations in wartime that it kept closed during times of peace. But France was willing to admit U.S. ships, and Yankee masters adopted the broken voyage to evade the Rule of 1756; that is, they stopped at an American port on their way from the West Indies to nationalize the cargo before continuing to Europe. Profits soared, but at the risk of war.[2] Both the Quasi-War with France and the War of 1812 were outgrowths of this profitable neutral trade.

During eighteen months of peace between 1801 and 1803, American commerce fell off considerably, regaining its momentum only when war was renewed. After that it flourished, and reached a peak in 1807 that would not be surpassed until 1835.[3]

Dark clouds gathered in 1806 and 1807 as both Britain and France passed laws declaring American trade with the other illegal. British and French vessels seized American ships on the high seas, confiscated American cargoes, and impressed American seamen. In the summer of 1807 British cruisers became increasingly insolent, extending their high-handed treatment from merchantmen to revenue cutters and U.S. naval vessels. They opened fire on a cutter with Vice President D.D. Tompkins aboard as it cleared Chesapeake Bay for New York, fired on a naval gunboat as it approached that same city, and insolently boarded and inspected a customs barge. But the deepest humiliation was imposed on the frigate *Chesapeake*. The British *Leopard* stopped her off the Virginia capes, killed and wounded several of her crew, and removed four deserters from her deck. That was too much for the outraged nation.[4]

War threatened to erupt at any moment, and to make sure it was the administration and not individual cutter captains who decided the question of war or peace, Secretary of the Treasury Albert Gallatin proclaimed the government's policy. Cutters were to avoid hostilities by every means possible, for it was "highly desirable that the great question of peace or war should be decided by the Government and not result from petty occurrences in our waters." If attacked, however, cutters were to defend themselves and must not be forced to anchor in U.S. waters under any circumstances.[5]

Seeking to avoid war, Jefferson persuaded Congress on 22 December 1807 to impose an embargo on all American ships bound for foreign ports. Although philosophically opposed to the exercise of federal power to coerce American citizens, Jefferson used his dominance of the legislature to push the bill, which he saw as the only alternative to war, to fruition. In 1801 he had written Robert Livingston that he believed in free ships and free goods, but added that although he considered "the observance of these principles as of great importance to the interests of peaceable nations . . . they are not worth a war."[6] By August 1808 he had admitted to Albert Gallatin that the law was "certainly the most embarrassing one we have ever had to execute," but added that "a continuance of the embargo is preferred to war."[7]

Jefferson thought of the embargo as a way to force Britain and France to rescind their orders and decrees. Instead, it forced him to coerce his fellow citizens, who reacted almost to the point of rebellion.[8]

Under the terms of the embargo, no American vessel was to be cleared for a foreign destination. Boats in the coastal trade and the fisheries were excepted but had to post a heavy bond to assure compliance.[9] After the embargo went into effect, no owner could change his vessel's nationality by selling it. Foreign vessels were still allowed to leave American ports in ballast or with the cargo they had aboard upon arrival, but a customs inspector was put on board until they left U.S. waters to assure compliance with the law.[10]

By Christmas morning the text of the embargo was circulating in New York. John Bach McMaster described the resulting flurry of excitement:

> On a sudden the streets were full of merchants, ship-owners, ship-captains, supercargoes, and sailors hurrying toward the water-front. Astonished at this unusual commotion, men of all sorts followed and by eight o'clock the wharves were crowded with spectators, cheering the little fleet of half-laden ships which, with all sail spread, was beating down the harbor. None of them had clearances. Many were half-manned. Few had more than part of a cargo. One which had just come in, rather than be embargoed, went off without breaking bulk. At the sight of the headings on the handbills, the captains made crews of the first seamen they met, and, with a few hurried instructions from the owners, pushed into the stream.[11]

Nevertheless, as many as 537 to 666 vessels were stranded in port, and no new clearances were being issued.[12]

In a circular dated 31 December 1807, Secretary Gallatin authorized cutters to use force "to detain vessels" suspected of violating the law,[13] and in anticipation of trouble, he canceled all leave for those serving on the revenue cutters and warned their commanders to exercise "the utmost vigilance."[14] On 12 January, Baltimore's collector informed Captain Francis Bright of the revenue cutter *Swiftsure* that he could not take leave during the embargo.[15]

Elijah Cobb, a Cape Cod skipper, was one of the last men to clear from an American port legally, but he was in violation of the embargo by the time he actually left U.S. territorial waters. Cobb had avoided the British Orders in Council—by which England attempted to drive neutral shipping from French-controlled ports—through payment of a bribe to clear the brig *Sally and Mary* from Gibraltar with a cargo of Spanish goods. Arriving safely in Boston, he remained with his family for just a short time before proceeding to New York, where he took command of the ship *William Tell* for Bixby Vallintine and Company. From there he sailed to Norfolk, Virginia, and loaded his ship with flour. According to a book of his, when he asked the collector for clearance, he was told that it made no sense for him to clear his ship because the embargo would arrive the next morning; and even if he cleared her, the collector would send out boats to stop him before he could escape to sea. But Cobb persisted and so the collector granted the clearance, after which Cobb returned to his ship. By nine o'clock that evening he had on board 3,050 barrels of flour and was ready to sail.[16]

At eight o'clock the next morning, Cobb started down river with a fair wind that gradually declined in strength. As a result his progress was slowed, and it was after eleven before he entered Hampton Roads. Putting his glass to his eye at about noon, Cobb saw a boat closing on him under full sail. He feared he would be caught, but then a fresh breeze came up off the south shore and he ordered light sails set. The boat was so near that he could make out the features of the men; within ten minutes of his ship catching the breeze, however, the boat had given up the chase and turned back. Cobb wrote his owners that he had sailed "away from the Embargo" and proceeded to Cadiz, where he sold his flour for $20 a barrel, four dollars more than a barrel had sold for before Cobb arrived with news of the embargo.[17]

Some vessels cleared legally but were stopped before they could escape to sea. The schooner *Juliana*, a Swedish vessel owned by William Israel of St. Bartholemews, cleared from Baltimore with a cargo of herring and sailed down the bay. An inspector found her waiting for a crew at Annapolis and secured her. During the inspector's absence the herring was loaded aboard the *Alligator,* owned by John Dillon of Baltimore. On advice of attorney, the *Alligator* was seized too.[18] Other ships that cleared legally from Philadelphia "proceeded a considerable way down the river," but they too were detained as a result of "the activity and vigilance of the officers of the revenue."[19]

Evidence of the great lengths to which the maritime community would go to avoid the embargo soon poured into Washington. On 4 January 1808, Benjamin Lincoln reported from Boston that he had already seized three vessels and failed in attempts to detain two others. The schooner *Harriet* had been taken while completely provisioned for a voyage and loaded with a cargo of fish, flour, and tobacco. The little sloop *Polly* had been caught with twenty-six barrels of flour, the 25-ton sloop *Packet of Manchish* with rice, flour, beef, pork, tobacco, candles, and sea stores. All were towed to the marshal for prosecution. A few vessels managed to evade the authorities. The *Plough Boy* escaped to sea with a load of cotton, and another craft sailed out of port with a cargo of fish.[20]

Some vessels continued to escape even after the coast was placed under guard. Captain Charles C. Doten of Plymouth, Massachusetts, avoided capture on at least two occasions. On a stormy night he outfitted the schooner *Hannah*, which the collector had stripped, with the rigging of another boat and sailed out of Plymouth Bay. "Later he took the brig *Hope* out of Provincetown in a northeast gale, hotly pursued and fired upon by the revenue cutter; sold vessel and cargo of fish at St. Lucia for twenty-five thousand dollars, and brought it home in the form of Spanish doubloons, sewed into his clothing."[21]

A number of vessels that cleared in ballast for foreign ports were later seized with cargo aboard. The ship *John*, the brigs *Mount Vernon* and *Hiram*, and the sloop *Phebe* cleared from Providence, Rhode Island, in ballast only. Within a month the frigate *Chesapeake* had rounded them up and sent them in to New York for carrying illegal merchandise. Jeremiah Olney, the Providence collector, suspended the inspector of customs who had cleared the vessels and initiated an investigation to determine the facts in the case.[22]

The schooner *Charles*, a sea-letter vessel owned by I. S. Coulson of Baltimore, cleared from that port in ballast. Four days later revenue officers found her down river placed in the charge of a pilot and carrying cargo. Before a customs official could be put on board, someone discharged her cargo at a warehouse belonging to John Barron. The collector ordered the warehouse to hold the goods, but most were removed.[23]

Coastal trade offered the best chance for evasion of the embargo. By posting a bond to guarantee that cargo would be landed in the United

States, "dangers of the sea excepted," skippers could legally clear port on coastal voyages. Throughout 1808 a huge number of ships suffered broken spars and other disasters that forced them to enter Caribbean ports. Once there, of course, cargoes had to be sold to pay for needed repairs to the vessels.[24]

Captain David Porter of the U.S. Revenue Cutter Service reported that there had been four American vessels at Havana when he left that port early in 1808. The schooner *Sea Flower* and the brig *Joseph* had cleared from Baltimore for New York on 26 and 29 December, and the schooners *James* of Norfolk and *Hiram* of New York had both "put in under color of distress."[25] Expecting the Baltimore vessels back soon, the collector ordered Captain Bright, USRCS, to proceed down the bay and intercept them, and he informed Gallatin that two of the gunboats would be useful in the war against smugglers.[26]

Outlying ports soon experienced a tremendous increase in their volume of trade. According to Robert G. Albion, Maine "had always needed some flour from the southward, but suddenly this need seemed to have grown a hundredfold." Coasters now passed up the usual Atlantic ports for Passamaquoddy Bay on the not too well defined border of New Brunswick, and the collector at Passamaquoddy, L. F. Delesdernier, a simple but vigorous and honest man, could not successfully meet the challenge on the border. Perhaps threats to burn his house prompted him to adopt a tolerant attitude. Certainly the threats were real, for smugglers had fired upon revenue boats in the area. In any case shipments of flour, beef, pork, lumber, and naval stores poured into Passamaquoddy in great excess of the legitimate needs of the place. On 22 March 1808 two ships were loaded at Boston with 1,400 barrels of flour for Passamaquoddy. At the other end of the coast, cotton and rice flooded the market at St. Marys, Georgia, on the border of Spanish Florida, whence British ships carried it off. The occasional revenue cutter that visited that port found it impossible to stop "the shameless leakage that went on at Amelia year after year."[27]

Albert Gallatin authorized the collector at St. Marys to employ, arm, and man revenue boats to check smuggling in that southernmost district. Fourteen years later Secretary of the Treasury William Crawford inquired as to why they were there and discovered that they had been authorized in 1808 and again in 1811. He belatedly terminated their use in 1822.[28]

Widespread abuse of the embargo led Congress to enhance the powers of collectors, giving them the authority to detain vessels bound for ports on the border, to refuse clearance to masters who were known smugglers, and to detain vessels on the mere suspicion of intent to violate the law, if bound toward the border with cargoes of cotton, lumber, or naval stores.[29] On 28 December 1807 Gallatin actually allowed Gabriel Christie, the collector at Baltimore, to refuse coasting papers to a vessel on the suspicion of intent to violate the embargo.[30]

Jeremiah Olney of Providence, Rhode Island, vigorously exercised his newly acquired powers. Earlier, on 8 July 1808, a 75-ton sloop owned by Joseph Foot had escaped to sea, probably bound for a foreign port. The owner had loaded his vessel under the guise of using it for storage, and since no sails were bent on, Olney had allowed that use. The sloop then slipped out of town and down Narragansett Bay with two other masters aboard. When they failed to return, Olney knew that he had been hoodwinked and vowed not to allow it to happen again. In subsequent similar cases, he made owners give up their sails to customs officials.[31]

When one Mr. Callahan fitted out the 38-ton sloop *Victory* and loaded her with 500 quintals of dried fish for Albany, Olney had the sloop watched throughout the night. No attempt was made to leave port and Olney had no proof of Callahan's intentions, but he refused to clear the vessel, having the fish offloaded and the sloop's sails stored in the customhouse to assure compliance with the law.[32]

The worst offenders were New Englanders. Both their hearts and pocket books were hurt by Jefferson's embargo, and they justified their outrageous evasions by claiming that it was a partisan policy.

Joseph Whipple, the collector at Portsmouth, had charged the citizens of York, Maine, with intending to violate the embargo when the case of the sloop *Rhoda* confirmed his suspicions. The *Rhoda* was loaded at Portsmouth, but Whipple refused to clear her and her goods were offloaded and taken overland to York. In the meantime, she cleared in ballast for the same port. Whipple responded by sending the revenue cutter *New Hampshire* (Captain Hopley Yeaton) to watch for developments. Yeaton's crew soon learned that the same cargo had indeed been loaded aboard the *Rhoda* at York, so the captain put four men aboard her. Receiving no help from the collector at York, he sailed to Portsmouth for orders. Whipple reported what happened next.

He ordered Yeaton to return to York with a man who was ready to sail immediately and dispatched four more men shortly thereafter. Taking a sleigh at the ferry, the volunteers struggled through deep snow and reached Cape Neddick at one o'clock in the morning. By then forty or fifty men had overpowered the guard on the *Rhoda* and she had gone to sea.[33]

Regretfully, Whipple wrote Gallatin that Jeremiah Clarke, the collector at York, seemed to have been in collusion with the smugglers. But having no proof, Whipple could make no formal complaint.[34]

THE EMBARGO:

DEAR Sirs, it is wrong
To demand a new Song;
I have let all the breath I can spare, go;
With the Muse I've confer'd,
And she won't say a word,
But keeps laughing about the Embargo.

I wish that I could,
Sing in Allegro mood;
But the times are as stupid as Largo;
Could I have my choice,
I would strain up my voice:
'Till it snapt all the strings of Embargo.

Our great politicians,
Those dealers in visions,
On paper, to all lengths they dare go;
But when call'd to decide,
Like a turtle they hide,
In their own pretty shell the Embargo.

In the time that we try,
To put out Britain's eye;
I fear we shall let our own pair go;
Yet still we're so wise
We can see with French Eyes,
And then we shall like the Embargo.

A French privateer,
Can have nothing to fear;
She may load and may here or may there go;
Their friendship is such,
And we love them so much,
We let them slip thro' the Embargo.

Our ships all in motion,
Once whiten'd the ocean,
They sail'd and return'd with their cargo;
Now doom'd to decay,
They have fallen a prey
To Jefferson, Worms, and Embargo.

Lest Britain should take
A few men by mistake,
Who under false colours may dare go;
We're manning their fleet
With our Tars, who retreat
From poverty, floth and Embargo.

What a fuss we have made,
About rights and free Trade,
And swore we'd not let our own share go,
Now we can't for our souls
Bring a Hake from the shoals,
'Tis a breach of the twentieth Embargo.

Our Farmers so gay.
How they gallop'd away.
'Twas money that made the Old Mare go;
But now She won't stir,
For the whip or the spur,
'Till they take off her clog, the Embargo.

If you ask for a debt,
The man turns in a pet,
"I pay, sir? I'll not let a hare go;
If your officer comes,
I shall put up my thumbs,
And clap on his breath an Embargo."

Thus Tommy destroys,
A part of our joys;
Yet we'll not let the beautiful Fair go;
They all will contrive
To keep commerce alive,
There's nothing they hate like Embargo.

Since rulers design,
To deprive us of wine,
'Tis best that we now have a rare go;
Then each to his post,
And see who will do most,
To knock out the blocks of Embargo.

Broadside Satirizing Jefferson's Embargo. (Courtesy American Antiquarian Society.)

Following this incident, Captain Yeaton, who was charged with enforcing the embargo between Eastport, Maine, and Portsmouth, resigned his commission. The first seagoing officer commissioned by the United States under the Constitution, Yeaton had served the Revenue Cutter Service for nearly three decades. Suffering from bad health, he retired to a farm at Eastport, where he spent the last years of his career.[35]

The owner of Brewster Island, located at the mouth of Boston Harbor, delivered a unique challenge to the embargo by sending flour and fish from Boston to Brewster, where the products were loaded onto other vessels for transshipment. When customs officials seized one of his ships on its way to the island with a load of fish, he argued that he was not subject to the embargo because the shipment remained within the harbor. This tactic evidently befuddled Benjamin Weld, the Boston collector; he wrote that he did not know how or whether to respond.[36]

Actions taken by neighboring collectors and the governor of Massachusetts further complicated Weld's efforts to enforce the embargo. Using permits granted by the governor out of ignorance, Bostonians shipped eight or nine cargoes of flour out of the country from Barnstable. Each shipment ranged from 1,000 to 1,500 barrels.[37]

In a case at Cohasset, Weld ordered a revenue cutter to seize a vessel suspected of loading fish for a foreign port. The cutter seized the vessel, escorted it into Boston, and turned it over to the marshal. The next day the vessel's owner obtained a new endorsement and a clearance from the Plymouth collector, and he loaded the ship without anyone from the collector's office present. Once again, Weld seized the ship because it had no presidential clearance. Doggedly pursuing his personal interest, the owner sued Weld and forced him to seek additional guidance from Secretary Gallatin.[38]

Similar harassing suits were brought against Weld and anonymous charges were filed against the Boston office, no doubt in the hopes of discouraging such diligence as was displayed there.[39]

In a third embargo act, 12 March 1808, Congress authorized the president to allow ships to clear in ballast for a foreign port so that property owned by American citizens abroad could be brought home. As expected, the president was flooded with requests. In one instance he greatly embarrassed his administration. As Robert G. Albion tells it, since all foreign voyages were prohibited by the embargo, New York was amazed to learn that the *Beaver* had cleared for Canton. As an act of international friendship, President Jefferson had given John Jacob Astor permission to return a stranded Chinese mandarin to his home. Indignation replaced amazement when New York learned that the mandarin was actually a common

Chinaman dressed for the part. And envy mingled with admiration when the *Beaver*'s returned cargo brought her owner a profit of $200,000.[40]

The policy was a great mistake. Between 22 December 1807 and 30 September 1808 at least 594 vessels were allowed to sail to foreign ports, and by the latter date 137 had failed to return.[41]

Violations were also rife along the Canadian border. Goods prohibited entry into the United States were imported in Canada and then smuggled across the border. Gallatin warned the collectors at Michilimackinac, Michigan, and Sackets Harbor, New York, to be on guard against this practice. He was most concerned about smuggling along Lake Champlain and Lake Ontario, and wanted inspectors appointed at proper places along the St. Lawrence River, especially at Oswegatchie, St. Regis, and Hamilton Mills.[42] Not having much faith in the ability of boats to deter smuggling along the border, he had to rely heavily on men stationed at strategic choke points ashore.

The crisis approached insurrection on Lake Champlain, where a revenue cutter was active. John Bach McMaster tells us that "sometimes a revenue cutter would chase a smuggler up the Orion river and exchange shots, or, as on one occasion, have a pitched battle."[43] In September 1808, the cutter intercepted the bateau *Black Snake* and followed it "up a small river where its crew abandoned ship. The revenue men went ashore and engaged in battle; a citizen was killed, and the captain of the bateau and one of the crew were convicted and executed."[44] Soon after this engagement the militia arrived and violations on the lake did diminish, but it was impossible to close the long frontier.

The Revenue Cutter Service could not always count on superior force at the border; nor was public support assured. When two boats were refused clearance for Sackets Harbor, "the captains went off without clearance. The Collector gave chase in a revenue cutter; but finding the crews armed and ready to fight, he suffered them to go on."[45] McMaster reports that "on Salmon River, in Oneida County, the crew of a revenue cutter behaved so insolently that the people rose, seized them, and put them into jail."[46]

President Jefferson had reduced the size of the Revenue Cutter Service after the Quasi-War with France, but he could not maintain his assault on the service while trying to avoid war by imposing an embargo on American commerce. Enforcing restrictions on 800,000 tons of American shipping engaged in foreign trade required the efforts of a vigorous, effective service.

Prior to the embargo, Jefferson's administration had made just one exception to its generally restrictive policy toward the Revenue Cutter

Service. The Louisiana Purchase was close to the president's heart, and following it he dispatched H. B. Trish to New Orleans to establish a new customs office. Anxious at the outset to stop smuggling in the Gulf of Mexico, Secretary Gallatin authorized Trish to hire men and boats as needed, even if the cost rose to one half of all duties collected.

Hoping to place a cutter on the scene quickly, the secretary attempted to buy a pilot boat already afloat, and when that did not work he contracted with William Parsons of Baltimore to build the new cutter *Louisiana*. Parsons had a good reputation, and as Gallatin described in detail the kind of vessel he wanted, we can probably assume with some confidence that the *Louisiana* was built according to his wishes. If that assumption is correct, the cutter was about 60 tons burden with a 6' draft. She was built of the best wood and materials available, copper-fastened and copper-bottomed, blessed with a good turn of speed, and armed with six 4-pounders. Secretary of the Navy Robert Smith selected Joseph Newcome as her commander. The Treasury Department hired a crew for a year, put aboard $400 worth of provisions, gave Newcome $1,500 in cash, and sent him on his way in early December. After the *Louisiana* reached New Orleans, a boat of from 15 to 20 tons assisted her on Lakes Pontchartrain and Borgne.[47]

Trish realized that the service could not instantly stop all of the smuggling to and from New Orleans. It had flourished there for years and would take some time to eradicate. He was especially concerned about armed vessels smuggling in spirits, coffee, salt, and slaves from New Providence. They were often armed with eight or ten guns and manned by fifty to eighty men. Realizing that a cutter armed in the usual manner would be of little or no value against such vessels, Trish put twenty-seven men aboard the *Louisiana* and armed her with ten guns.[48]

The cutter quickly proved her worth in the Gulf of Mexico. In early April 1805 she sailed from New Orleans to Belize, where she lay for a short time. On the sixteenth, Captain Newcome learned that two privateers operating off the mouth of the Mississippi River had seized the American schooner *Felicity* en route to New Orleans from Campeche, Mexico. That afternoon he went ashore and hired eleven volunteers. Within half an hour, the cutter was under way with every man at his battle station. Overtaking the privateers, the *Louisiana* fired three warning shots, which were ignored, so Newcome ordered a broadside poured into one of the offenders. In the ensuing engagement, the *Louisiana* suffered no damage and handed out a good deal of punishment that forced the privateers to abandon their prize. The rescued schooner and her cargo were worth $35,000, and she carried another $27,000 in cash.[49]

When Congress called for a survey of the Louisiana territory in the spring of 1806, she made another contribution to its development by transporting the surveyor to any part of the coast that he wanted to visit.[50]

In spite of such utility, the *Louisiana* came under fire from Washington. Having been launched without regard to cost, she had shipped a crew at higher salaries than were customary on cutters or even on naval vessels. Such indifference to cost was atypical of the Treasury Department and could not last. Gallatin soon ordered the collector at New Orleans, William Brown, to pay the crew less money. If the men were unwilling to accept a reduction in pay, he was to dismiss them and hire a new crew. To guarantee that the government got its money's worth for expenditures, Gallatin also ordered Brown to make sure the cutter remained in port no longer than necessary to refit and provision.[51]

By September 1807, Gallatin had added queries about Captain Newcome to his concerns about the New Orleans cutter. After ordering a reduction in the size of the crew to further curb expenses, the secretary demanded particulars on Newcome's general conduct. It seems that he believed Newcome to be primarily responsible for the great expense of operating the cutter. More important, two of Newcome's lieutenants had charged him with drunkenness and dueling; in fact, the captain had been shot in a duel and was unable to go to sea when Gallatin's inquiry arrived. Even if he had been well enough to resume his duties, he could not have found officers to sail with him. The president decided to relieve him of command.[52]

Smuggling continued to flourish at New Orleans during the embargo and into the War of 1812. The many bayous and swamps of southern Louisiana combined to make the job of law enforcement difficult. When opposition to customs laws by inhabitants of the Gulf Coast and the City of New Orleans was added, the job of the Revenue Cutter Service became impossible. Between 1810 and 1815 hundreds of smugglers operated along the gulf. Although some goods were seized, and in large quantities, this did not make a real dent in the illicit trade. Not even thousands of troops and sailors from the U. S. Navy who were available for duty could stop it. The emergence, during the war, of Jean Lafitte and the pirates who assisted General Jackson in his victory over the British indicates the dimensions of the problem.[53]

The issue of the Louisiana territory excepted, the administration's policy toward the Revenue Cutter Service changed little during Jefferson's first term. In 1801 the Treasury Department sold the revenue cutter *Governor Gilman* at Portsmouth for $3,110 and discharged her officers and crew. According to Joseph Whipple, the "exorbitant prices demanded for vessels suitable for a Revenue Cutter" held up construction of a replacement; but a new cutter, the *New Hampshire*, built for $3,325, was ready to go to sea by September 1802. Ten months later the department authorized the addition of a mate and two men or boys on cutters wherever it seemed warranted.[54]

The *New Hampshire* sailed on her first cruise under the command of Captain Hopley Yeaton, who set out with a first mate, Benjamin Gunnison, and a crew of four men and two boys. By 1808, the Treasury Department had allowed Yeaton to add one mate and a seaman to his crew because it wanted him to enforce the embargo in Passamaquoddy Bay. In the meantime, Yeaton had asked permission to add four more boys to his crew so that he could train them as seamen, navigators, and pilots. This request shows that he was way ahead of his time on the subject of the training of revenue cutter officers, but like so many forward-thinking people, he was turned down.[55]

Implementation of the embargo also led the Treasury Department to authorize bigger crews for the cutters at Boston and Wilmington, Delaware. Having sailed initially with just one captain and two lieutenants, the Boston cutter added a warrant officer, and the new *General Greene* added a mate and five seamen at Wilmington.[56]

The case of the brig *Rachel* demonstrated a serious need to reinforce the Revenue Cutter Service in the Chesapeake Bay, but an adequate response had to await the embargo. After taking on supplies at Baltimore for a voyage to Hamburg the *Rachel* sailed down the bay, where the surveyor of the port tried to board her, only to be warned off by an intoxicated captain backed up by a foreign crew. Even after Robert Purviance, Baltimore's collector, reported this outrage to the department, just one cutter, the schooner *Jefferson* (Captain William Ham), was assigned to the bay at Norfolk.[57]

At about the same time, Norfolk's collector of customs sought permission to add a bigger cutter at his station, and after considerable correspondence with Gallatin he was allowed to purchase the revenue cutter *Dolly* (Captain Bright) at New York, for $17,817.[58]

The *Dolly* never got the chance to make much of a contribution in the Chesapeake. The service laid her up the winter after purchasing her. The following spring, it fitted her out for a summer cruise, but by then she needed repairs and there was growing concern that she might be too big for the bay. In the meantime, Baltimore repeated a request for a cutter. Gallatin decided that he could not approve the request because the bill that had created the Revenue Cutter Service had called for two cutters in the bay. Gallatin believed that either the service would have to sell one of its cutters at Norfolk or Congress would have to approve an additional cutter before he could add one at Baltimore. Seeing this as a problem for the president, Gallatin sought Jefferson's advice and was told to assign a cutter to Baltimore but to sell one of the two at Norfolk. The service sold the *Dolly* and discharged all of her officers except Captain Bright, who was offered command of the new cutter at Baltimore.[59]

In his request for a cutter, James McCulloch of Baltimore had acknowledged the cutter at Norfolk but argued that smuggling remained a problem in the Chesapeake. He hoped, and claimed to believe, that an additional cutter stationed at his port would pay for itself in saved revenue. His argument was successful, leaving just one unanswered question—what kind of a vessel to build.[60]

McCullock wanted a cutter of 75 tons carpenter measure with a copper bottom (to prevent destruction by worms) delivered complete except for guns for $11,000. He planned to arm her with one large gun and five swivels. In July 1807, the service authorized McCullock to build a cutter of the desired dimensions, as long as she was fast, and ordered Captain Bright to Baltimore to supervise the construction. By the end of September the new cutter, christened *Virginia*, was ready to join the fleet. We can only surmise that she was all McCullock had hoped for.[61]

Sixteen months later, during the embargo, Captain Bright successfully sought two additional small vessels to patrol the many bays, inlets, and rivers of the Chesapeake Bay. The two boats, which measured 30' in length, were hired for periods of from three to six months throughout the embargo and were manned by five or six men who acted under the orders of the captain of the cutter. Thus by March 1809, two revenue cutters and two armed, open boats patrolled the bay as far south as the Virginia capes.[62]

Just a few months after the *Virginia* joined the fleet at Baltimore the department added the new cutter *Gallatin* (Captain Hugh McNeill) at Charleston, South Carolina. She was purchased at Norfolk for $9,434 in early 1808, and started her career in an unpleasantly memorable fashion. On 14 March 1808, a schooner flying Danish colors fired two shots at the *Gallatin* and chased her into the St. Mary's River.[63]

The first indication of a dramatic change in the administration's policy toward the service took the form of instructions to the collector of customs at Boston. Gallatin ordered him to buy a fast new cutter of 100 to 120 tons, armed with suitable guns or carronades and manned by a crew of thirty men. The secretary followed up with a request to Congress for funds enough to purchase ten or twelve fast cutters to enforce the embargo. He thought that cutters of from 70 to 130 tons armed with six to ten 4-pounders or 12-pounder carronades would answer the purpose. He wanted crews of fifteen to thirty men, and he asked that the cutters be coppered and delivered ready for the sea, except for arms, and at a cost of between $8,000 and $12,000.[64]

With a new urgency brought on by the embargo, Gallatin sent a Treasury Department circular to the collectors of customs on 16 January 1809 asking whether or not any fast vessels, not exceeding 130 tons, were immediately available as cutters. If so, the collectors were to hire them for terms of not more than six months, arm them, and send them to sea with officers and crews of fifteen men. Baltimore, which a few years before had encountered difficulty getting authorization to employ one cutter, was told to hire three.[65]

In response to Gallatin's urgent circular, the Philadelphia collector examined the brig *Friends* but found her wanting because of a lack of speed.[66]

In April New Haven's collector, Abraham Bishop, hired the brig *Potomak* from Captain Frederick Lee and sent her to sea under Lee's command with a first and second mate and twenty-five men. She cruised in the eastern part of Long Island Sound and between the sound and Martha's Vineyard.[67]

The schooner *Glee* was offered for service at Wilmington, Delaware, but must have been found wanting because the Revenue Cutter Service built a new cutter at Philadelphia for the Wilmington station in the fall of 1810.[68] She was probably 60' in length of keel and 18' in beam, built by W. Eyre of Philadelphia for $24 per ton.[69]

In the meantime, Congress authorized twelve new cutters averaging 125 tons, carrying from six to ten light guns, and shipping from fifteen to thirty men.[70] Until the War of 1812 the new cutters tried, against overwhelming odds, to enforce the embargo. Subsequently, nine of them, the *Active*, *Eagle*, *Commodore Barry*, *Gallatin*, *Jefferson*, *James Madison*, *Mercury*, *Surveyor*, and *Vigilant*, joined in the conflict with Great Britain.

According to Leonard White, the expert on the administrative history of Jefferson's term, the record of the enforcement agencies during the embargo was highly credible. Most important to our story, White found "no evidence . . . suggesting indifference on the part of the captains of the revenue cutters." In the "Journal of Economic and Business History," W. Freeman Galpin added this positive note: "No better story of loyalty in administrative work can be told—and that under trying circumstances—than that which may be found in the efforts of forgotten revenue and naval officers. While others grumbled, these men worked. . . ."[71]

There were some exceptions among collectors. One district attorney refused to do his job, and one revenue cutter officer, Captain Richard Howard, who commanded the *General Greene* under the supervision of Collector Peter Muhlenberg at Philadelphia, disgraced the service. Under the command of Lieutenant Joseph Sawyer, the *General Greene*'s officers boarded the smuggler *Favorite* in Delaware Bay and found Captain Howard working in the gang illegally discharging that ship. It is not clear what Howard was supposed to have been doing at this time, for he had been absent from his own cutter for over fifteen days when caught aboard the *Favorite*. Wilmington's collector, Allan McLane, brought formal charges against the wayward officer, and Gallatin ordered a complete investigation. The result of this was Howard's dismissal by the President, who replaced him with Captain Thomas Moore. Moore sailed the cutter thereafter under the supervision of Allan McLane at Wilmington.[72]

Honest officials faced two serious problems during the embargo. Juries were reluctant to convict smugglers, and the latter brought malicious, vexatious suits against conscientious officers.[73] One such suit was filed against Benjamin Weld of Boston, "the captain of the revenue cutter and the collector of Barnstable, upon the refusal of the district attorney to libel a vessel under detention and suspected of smuggling flour." Understandably concerned, Weld wrote Gallatin: "I may be involved in law suits that may be perplexing or even serious. Your answer to this is earnestly requested with explicit information of the extent of the [government] support I may expect."[74] But Gallatin had no authority to instruct district attorneys and no way to guarantee the protection of collectors or revenue cutter officers. Dishonest shipowners had found a weak link in the enforcement process.[75]

On 25 April 1808, Congress authorized U. S. Navy gunboats to join revenue cutters in enforcing the embargo.[76] The president ordered Secretary of the Navy Robert Smith to comply with Gallatin's orders in the matter, and Gallatin in turn asked Smith to send north as many gunboats or cruisers as he could spare.[77]

The Navy Department dispatched the *Wasp*, *Argus*, *Chesapeake*, and *Revenge* to the Massachusetts coast. Only three gunboats were available, one each for Newport, New Bedford, and Barnstable. "This," Gallatin wrote Jefferson, "with the revenue cutters, is all we can do, and of course we must remain satisfied with the result, whatever it may be."[78]

Within a week, according to Leonard White, the *Wasp* and *Argus* were dispatched to Newburyport, where a mob was interfering with customs officials; the *Chesapeake* had already seized eight vessels. "On the Georgia coast Gallatin could only send gunboats."[79]

Jefferson actually considered asking Congress for the authority to destroy boats in order to prevent evasion of the embargo. Gallatin wrote Jefferson, "We cannot destroy the boats, & c., at St. Mary's without being authorized by law so to do; and Congress shows so much reluctance in granting powers much less arbitrary, that there is no expectation of their giving this."[80]

Congress did give extraordinary powers to collectors on 9 January 1809, but the movement toward strong federal authority exercised by the president and Congress really signaled the beginning of the end for the embargo. By this time, opponents of the law had moved to open defiance. At Newburyport, Massachusetts, a sloop left port without clearance and was brought back in by a revenue cutter after a ten-hour chase. Shortly thereafter, when a cutter brought a schooner laden with fish back into the same port after another chase, the people "were with difficulty prevented from destroying the cutter at the wharf."[81]

At Providence, Rhode Island, a mob openly interfered with Jeremiah Olney's efforts to do his job as the collector. On 21 January 1809, the 80-ton schooner *Commerce*, owned by William Farrier of Providence, left port without papers for Wilmington, North Carolina. The schooner subsequently froze in the ice, and Farrier agreed to take her back into port, landing the cargo once he got free. Instead, when the ice permitted and the wind blew up, the *Commerce* left the harbor and headed out to sea. Between nine and ten o'clock that night a large body of men assembled at the wharf, where the government held the sloop *Betsy*. The crowd began to break the ice with the intention of running off with the sloop, and a naval officer sent to stop them was simply ignored. The collector then dispatched an inspector to ask the collector at Newport to order the gunboats in his district to stop all vessels leaving the bay without official papers. Before morning, the mob had abandoned the *Betsy*, but only because it could not free her from the ice. To avoid further problems, the collector removed the cargo and the vessel's rudder. He informed Gallatin that the governor had ordered a detachment of the militia to help revenue officers execute the laws. But Olney reported candidly that he did not believe the militia would obey their officers if called upon to fire on their fellow citizens.[82]

Two days later, at eight o'clock in the evening, two to three hundred persons assembled at the wharf and took possession of the *Betsy*. They broke into the public store, seizing her rudder and one of her sails. When the collector called upon the militia to assist the revenue officers in executing the laws, the commanding officer of one of the independent companies of Providence informed the governor of his refusal. The same spirit of opposition existed in many other ports, according to Olney, who advised Gallatin that the embargo had to be rescinded in order to restore faith in the government.[83]

On 1 March 1809, Jefferson reluctantly signed a bill that ended the embargo and substituted nonintercourse, which forbade trade with Britain and France.[84]

The embargo had failed to force Britain and France to rescind their offensive laws, but it had essentially stopped Americans from shipping goods to foreign ports.

The embargo also spelled disaster for most of the maritime community. Shipyards fell silent, fisheries languished, and shopkeepers and artisans faced the future with despair. Most serious was the crisis facing foreign exporters, especially farmers who depended on foreign markets to sell their products. The resultant economic crisis led to panic in the West, where voters elected men to Congress who would in turn vote for war to redeem America's national honor and to redress grievances against Britain for her highhandedness at sea. A desire for British Canada and Spanish Florida also played a part with some who voted for war.

CHAPTER FOUR

The War of 1812

The United States enjoyed spectacular success in single-ship engagements during the War of 1812, as the celebrated destruction of the *Guerriere* by *Old Ironsides* illustrates, but ultimately Great Britain triumphed. Using her superior navy, she clamped a blockade on the American coast that reduced U.S. trade to a mere ten percent of its prewar level. For her part, America resorted to *guerre de course* and preyed on British shipping in hopes of forcing the stronger nation to sue for peace. While privateers succeeded in damaging the British merchant marine, their success did not translate into a military victory. *Guerre de course* ruined enemy commerce in the Napoleonic Wars, the American Civil War, and the First World War, but it has never determined the outcome of a major conflict.[1]

The experience of the Revenue Cutter Service paralleled that of the U.S. Navy in the War of 1812. Nine cutters, the *Active, Eagle, Gallatin, Jefferson, James Madison, Mercury, Surveyor, Vigilant,* and *Commodore Barry* (which also appears in the records as the *Commodore Hull* or the *Commodore Barney*), served with the navy. Although too small to take on all comers, these vessels did seize a number of British merchantmen and privateers in single-ship engagements.

The *Jefferson* (Captain William Ham) enjoyed a number of successes. She made the first seizure of a British merchantman by capturing the brig *Patriot* in June 1812. Ten months later, four British barges ran down the schooner *Flight* and removed Captain Kelly and his crew. A sudden, violent storm then drove the barges into Hampton Roads, where one was surrendered to Captain Charles Stewart of the *Constitution*. While attempting to escape up the James River, the other three were discovered in the roads by the *Jefferson*. Joined by a mail boat, the *Jefferson* took aboard Captain Stewart's rifle company and a detachment of volunteer militiamen. Thus reinforced, she overtook the barges and in the ensuing fight captured one lieutenant, two midshipmen, one boatswain, and fifty-nine seamen, and recaptured Captain Kelly, the supercargo, and the crew of the schooner. In company with the cutter *Gallatin*, the *Jefferson* also participated in the seizure of the brig *General Blake*, the *Active* from London, and the *Georgiana* from Liverpool.[2]

Sailing alone, the *Gallatin* seized the brig *William Blake*. The revenue cutter *Surveyor*, also sailing solo, fittingly captured a valuable British prize from Jamaica on 4 July 1812.[3]

The topsail schooner *Madison* greatly enhanced the prestige of the Revenue Cutter Service during the war. Built in Baltimore in 1807–8, she had a 94′ 4½″ deck, 24′ 7⅛″ beam, and 10′ 6″ depth of hold. Early in the conflict her skipper, Captain George Brooke, fulfilled a boast by taking into Savannah the British brig *Shamrock* of 300 tons, six guns, and sixteen men. Before falling to the British, the *Madison* added to her list of conquests the ship *Snow* and the schooner *Wade*. The latter carried a substantial prize of £20,000 in specie.[4]

Of the cutters the *Vigilant*, built by Benjamin Marble at Newport for $8,500, made the most impressive capture. On the evening of 4 October 1813 the privateer sloop *Dart*, having already seized over twenty merchantmen in Long Island Sound, arrived in Newport Harbor with her latest victims, a ship and a brig. The *Vigilant*'s skipper, Captain John Cahoone, volunteered to give chase if Captain Joseph Nicholson, the navy's commanding officer at Newport, supplemented his crew. Thus reinforced by three sailing masters and a score of men, the *Vigilant* struck out after the *Dart*, which immediately set sail for Block Island; but the cutter proved to be the faster vessel. In spite of being outgunned by the *Dart*'s six 9-pound carronades and six swivels, the *Vigilant* closed with the sloop and gave her a broadside. In a successful boarding operation, the *Vigilant*'s crew killed the *Dart*'s first lieutenant and captured her remaining twenty-four crew members. Two of the *Vigilant*'s men were slightly wounded.[5]

The *Mercury* (Captain William H. Wallace) made her mark in the war in quite a different fashion. Built at New Bern, North Carolina, she sailed out of Ocracoke with a captain, three mates, and a crew of twenty-five. At about nine o'clock on the evening of 11 July 1813, the *Mercury* appeared off Ocracoke Bar and anchored about a mile from the inlet. That night a fleet under Admiral Cockburn was discovered nearby and reported to Thomas Singleton, collector of customs at Portsmouth. Singleton packed the port's money and customhouse bonds into a trunk, which he placed aboard the *Mercury* for safekeeping. As dawn broke, Captain Wallace set sail. At about the same time the vessels of Cockburn's fleet, consisting of one seventy-four, three frigates, one brig, and three schooners, got under way. The *Mercury* cleared the wash a mile and a half ahead of the fleet, which captured the brig *Anacosta* of New York and the letter-of-marque schooner *Atlas* of Philadelphia. Several of Cockburn's ships passed up the prizes for the cutter, because the admiral was anxious to stop her before she could carry word of his fleet to New Bern. After an eight- to ten-mile race through the sound, the *Mercury* made her escape by crowding on all sails and cutting away her long boat. Thus the cutter both saved the custom receipts and prevented Cockburn from proceeding to New Bern with his fleet.[6]

In defeat as well as victory, the story of the Revenue Cutter Service in the War of 1812 parallels that of the U.S. Navy. The *Gallatin* (Captain John H. Silliman) blew up in Charleston Harbor on the morning of 1 April 1813. She had arrived from a short cruise the day before and anchored off the town. After giving his crew orders to clean their small arms, the captain went ashore, leaving about thirty-five men aboard. About ten of the men were on the quarterdeck or in the cabin cleaning the arms when a dreadful explosion hurled the entire quarterdeck into the air. In the words of the Charleston *Courier*, "some of the bodies were thrown nearly as high as the mast head of the vessel; others were driven through the cabin and lodged upon the main deck. The whole stern of the vessel was torn down to a level with the water; the mainsail, which had been hoisted to dry, was torn to rags, and the fragments of broken spars were scattered in all directions." Immediately after the explosion, boats put off from the wharves to render assistance and attempts were made to run the cutter into a dock, but to no avail. Fire quickly spread to the mainsail and through the rigging. As the hull filled with water, wounded men were hurried into boats. The cutter sank stern first a few yards off Blake's

The USRC Vigilant *Capturing the* Dart *off* Block Island, 4 *October* 1813.
(*Oil painting by* Dean Ellis, *courtesy* USCG *Public Affairs Staff.*)

wharf.[7] Three men were never found. Four more were severely wounded, several others slightly.[8]

The Revenue Cutter Service suffered additional losses as Great Britain deployed her fleet along the Atlantic coast. On 12 August 1812, "after a long chase off Savannah," the British frigate *Barbadoes* captured the cutter *Madison*. On 16 January 1813 the American privateer *Anaconda* accidentally fired on the *Commodore Hull*. The cutter survived this encounter, but on 3 August 1814, she ran afoul of the British and was captured. According to some accounts, the Royal Navy subsequently used her as a tender. The *Active* (Captain Caleb Brewster), a chartered vessel turned cutter, was part of the naval flotilla that the British blockaded in the Thames River at New London, Connecticut, in June 1813. The *Surveyor* was captured that same year, and the *Eagle* fell to the British one year later.[9]

Even in defeat, the *Surveyor* and the *Eagle* performed admirably, leaving their mark on Coast Guard history and winning the respect of friend and foe alike.

The British captured the *Surveyor* as she lay at anchor under Gloucester Point at the mouth of the York River on 12 June 1813. Captain Samuel Travis took extra precautions that evening because it was raining and fog was rolling in. He opened the *Surveyor*'s gun ports, ran out her six 12-pound carronades, and prepared for action. As an added precaution, he deployed a small guard boat under the command of his younger brother, Third Lieutenant William L. Travis. But the *Surveyor* was up against Lieutenant John Crerie in a much bigger ship, the frigate *Narcissus*. Crerie sent out a boarding party of fifty men in two boats to seize the cutter. By the time the five men in the *Surveyor*'s guard boat heard the "regular stroke of man-of-war boats," they were under fire from the larger party. When the *Surveyor*'s crew heard the gunfire and realized the guard boat was under attack, it was too late to bring the cutter's guns to bear on the boarding party. Travis responded by ordering each of the sixteen officers and men still aboard the *Surveyor* to take two muskets each and defend their ship. This they did with stubborn courage in a desperate hand-to-hand engagement. Howard Chapelle tells us that "the hoarse cheering of the British men-of-war's men was answered by the shrill, savage yell of the Americans, that became better known as the 'rebel yell' in the Civil War." The Americans killed three British sailors and wounded another seven during the contest, while suffering just five casualties themselves. Finally Travis, realizing that further opposition would lead to more fruitless bloodshed, gave the order to surrender.[10]

The best evidence of just how good a defense the *Surveyor* put up is revealed in the letter that Lieutenant Crerie sent to Captain Travis when he returned his sword to him. "Your gallant and desperate attempt to defend your vessel against more than double your number," he wrote, "excited such admiration on the part of your opponents as I have seldom witnessed, and induced me to return you the sword you so ably used. . . ." His poor men had suffered severely because of the precaution Travis took to prevent surprise and "the determined manner in which the deck was disputed inch by inch." Wishing Travis and his brave crew a speedy parole, Crerie expressed regret that he had no influence over such matters, adding "otherwise it should be forth coming."[11]

The British subsequently manned the *Surveyor* and added her to their fleet at Hampton Roads.[12]

Eleven months later, Travis was set free. The normal complement aboard the *Surveyor* in the summer of 1813 had been twenty-five men, including him and three lieutenants. But on the night of her capture, the *Surveyor*'s numbers were down to twenty-one. Travis had sent three men ashore prior to the engagement, one was ashore on sick call, and the five he had sent out on guard duty escaped in the guard boat. Therefore the British captured only sixteen men with the cutter. Travis, First Lieutenant John Hebb, and two crew members were released at different times, all before 17 May 1814; the rest of the captives remained prisoners at that time.[13]

Following his release from captivity, Travis asked S. H. McCulloch, customs collector at Baltimore, to pay him and his crew whatever the law allowed. Unbelievably, it was not clear to the collector whether or not he could pay the officers and crew for the time they had been held as prisoners of war.[14] The secretary of the treasury informed him that he could make an equitable payment upon such terms as had been adopted in similar circumstances, but the collector could find no precedents. Inquiring into U.S. Navy policy, he found that men were paid for the time of their detention. That seems to have solved the problem for the enlisted personnel, but the officers claimed a different standard. Travis complained that he had served in the Revenue Cutter Service for ten years, during which he had been paid about half as much as he could have made in the merchant marine. He knew that officers of the Norfolk cutter had been paid for fifteen months while their cutter was laid up, yet he and his crew had been discharged after being captured by the British. This had tainted their reputations and thus added to their hardships. Travis wanted a new commission, payment for the time he had been held captive, and compensation for the provisions he had supplied to the *Surveyor* (these were lost with the cutter). Meanwhile, the collector continued to withhold payment from the families of men who had not been released by as late as July 1814. To his credit, he did try to acquire authorization for these payments. Drawing on his own meager resources, Travis provided them with some help.[15]

Personnel of the Revenue Cutter Service first received retirement benefits at the end of the War of 1812, but these were limited indeed. Cuttermen who had suffered casualties while serving with the navy were placed on its pension list and received the same benefits as officers and seamen of that service.[16] Other pensions would not be given out for almost a century.

The government's neglect went farther. The United States chartered revenue cutters during the war without assuming responsibility for them. On 24 July 1812 Gallatin wrote Larkin Smith, the collector at Norfolk, that he could employ Captain Edward Herbert, USRCS, in any way that would be most useful. If Smith thought it necessary he could "charter and equip his vessel, but the risk of capture must not in that case fall on the United States."[17]

Those captured during the war were often kept in distressing conditions and required expensive medical care after their release. They were not alone in their suffering. During the first winter of the war, expenses were unusually high at marine hospitals because of the cost of caring for the many seamen who had been severely frozen and had lost limbs as a result.[18]

The revenue cutter *Eagle*, a schooner of about 130 tons that sailed out of New Haven under the command of Captain Frederick Lee of Guilford, Connecticut, had an active career prior to her capture in October 1814. A year before falling to the British, she sent three brigs into New Haven for trading with the enemy: the *Patriot* of Milford, bound for Liverpool with salt; the *Harriet* of Kennebunk, en route from Bristol, England, to New York with copper; and the *Ann McLane* of Portsmouth, sailing from Liverpool with dry goods. Hearing that a schooner, probably the *Liverpool Packet*, had captured the sloop *Astrea* within sight of New Haven, Captain Lee set sail in the *Eagle* on 30 May 1814 with her usual complement of men and about fifty volunteers. What she discovered in Long Island Sound was the British frigate plus two other British vessels; being no match for that, she put back into New Haven. Over a year later the *Eagle* successfully convoyed the sloops *Astrea*, *Allen*, and *Rising Planet*, loaded with valuable cargo, down the sound to New York.[19]

Then the *Eagle*'s fortunes took a turn for the worse. On 10 October 1814, word reached New Haven that the American merchantman *Suzan* had been captured earlier in the day by a British sloop. A party of forty men from a tender of the frigate *Pomone* (Captain Cartwright) had taken

Captain Frederick Lee. (*Oil painting by George* Sottung, *courtesy* USCGA *Library.*)

the *Suzan* while she was en route from New York to New Haven. After rounding up a crew of forty volunteers from the streets and taverns of New Haven, Captain Lee put two boats with sweeps over the side and towed the *Eagle* to sea in a flat calm. The cutter searched all night long without success, and as dawn broke a mist covered the sea. When it rose, Lee discovered the sloop, the *Suzan*, the brig *Dispatch* (Captain James Galloway) of eighteen 32-pounders, and her two boats. After beating off the two boats, which returned to the *Dispatch* at about eight o'clock, the *Eagle* tried to escape over the shallows. When the *Dispatch* brought her guns to bear, Lee, greatly outgunned, beached the *Eagle* off Friar's Head, a 160-foot-high bluff fifteen miles northeast of Port Jefferson, New York.[20]

After stripping the *Eagle* of her sails and rigging, Lee's crew manhandled her two 2-pounders and two of her four 4-pounders ashore and up the steep bluff. Thus positioned, they kept the British from landing in boats or taking the *Eagle*. Throughout the day and night and into the next morning the *Eagle*'s crew fought bravely in defense of their cutter. When their supply of shot ran out they retrieved spent British rounds and re-

The Defense of the Eagle. (*Courtesy* USCGA *Library*.)

turned them. When they ran out of wadding during the hottest phase of the fight, several crewmen volunteered to return to the cutter for more. Shots carried away the *Eagle's* masts while the volunteers were aboard, and a brave boy erected a flag on her stern. This too was shot away, being "immediately replaced by a heroic tar, amidst the cheers of his undaunted comrades, which was returned by a whole broadside from the enemy." Finally the *Dispatch* sailed over the horizon, whereupon the Americans refloated the *Eagle*, kedged her off the beach, and tried to sail her into New Haven under a jury rig. Unexpectedly, the *Dispatch* reappeared on the scene and forced Lee to surrender. In the meantime the volunteers from New York City, having left Captain Lee and his crew, arrived in New York aboard a sloop from Long Island.[21]

By the end of the war, the Revenue Cutter Service, along with America's navy and maritime community, had suffered tremendous losses. During the darkest hour of the War of 1812, New England merchants grumbled about "Mr. Madison's War" and threatened secession at the Hartford Convention. Overseas, the British shipping community joined its Federalist counterpart in cursing the stupid conflict. Merchants on both sides of the Atlantic had had enough; they joined heartily in celebrating the Peace of Ghent. The war had proven the folly of armed conflict between two trading countries. Unfortunately, the lesson was not a lasting one.[22]

CHAPTER FIVE

Fighting Piracy

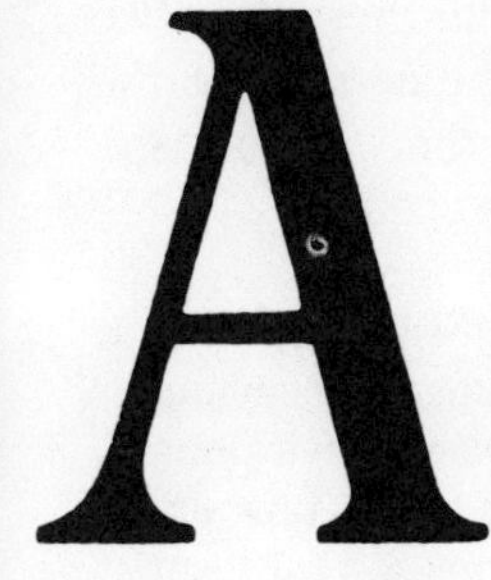

After the Peace of Ghent, America's shipping industry enjoyed a golden age of growth that culminated in the decade before 1857. Congress supported this growth in a number of ways. It tolerated smuggling from the United States to the West Indies, passed the Navigation Act of 1817 banning foreign flag vessels from trading along the U.S. coast, and provided protection for American shipping in the Pacific Ocean and Caribbean Sea. Growth was stimulated as well by the nation's enthusiastic support of a naval war against Caribbean piracy.

This piracy, which was almost as old as that of the Barbary coast, was at its worst between 1818 and 1825. Early nineteenth-century revolts against colonial rule prompted many Latin American nations to offer the protection of their flag to privateers who would raid Spanish shipping. Some Americans who had sailed as privateers during the War of 1812 welcomed the opportunity to continue raiding and took up Latin American colors. Their attacks on Spanish merchantmen succeeded, and as the number of targets declined they attacked ships of other nations, becoming in time no better than pirates and being joined by freebooters swarming out of Cuba, Puerto Rico, the Bahamas, and other Caribbean haunts.[1]

As this outrage spread northward into New Orleans, St. Marys, Georgia, and Baltimore, it posed a serious threat to U.S. shipping. A great number of vulnerable little sloops and schooners sailed from U.S. ports to Cuba and the West Indies, or through the Straits of Florida to ports in the Gulf of Mexico. Whereas only twenty-two ships fell to the Barbary pirates during a thirty-year period, five hundred vessels worth $20 million were taken in the West Indies.[2]

The Caribbean pirates were a vicious lot. They progressed from robbing their victims to raping, torturing, and murdering them. It is not necessary to review all the awful stories that appeared in the newspapers of the day; one that Robert G. Albion recounted makes the point with spine-tingling clarity. The coasting schooner *Mary* was bound from Philadelphia to New Orleans when she was attacked by pirates off the southern tip of Florida. One boatload of men was stopped by her guns, but the crew of another succeeded in boarding her. During the assault they killed two of the schooner's crewmen, and once aboard bound the narrator to the mainmast because he looked too "well-dressed" to throw overboard. Thus restrained, the poor man was forced to watch this scene:

> Over my left shoulder, one of our sailors was strung up to the yardarm, and apparently in the last agonies of death; while before me our gallant captain was on his knees and begging for his life. The wretches were endeavoring to extort from him the secret of our money; but for a while he was firm and dauntless. Provoked by his obstinacy, they extended his arms and cut them off at the elbows. At this human nature gave way, and the injured man confessed on the spot where he had concealed our specie. In a few moments it was aboard their own vessel. To revenge themselves upon the unhappy captain, when they had satisfied themselves that nothing else was hidden, they spread a bed of oakum on deck, and after soaking it through with turpentine, tied the captain on it, filled his mouth with the same combustibles, and set the whole on fire. The cries of the unfortunate man were heart rending, and his agonies must have been unutterable, but they were soon over. . . .
>
> On casting my eyes towards the schooner's stern, I discovered that our boatswain had been nailed to the deck through his feet, and the body spiked to the tiller. He was writhing in the last agonies of crucifixion. Our fifth comrade was out of sight during all this tragedy; in a few minutes, however, he was brought upon the deck blindfolded. He was then conducted to the muzzle of the swivel and commanded to kneel. The swivel

was then fired off, and his head was dreadfully wounded by the discharge....

The wealthy passenger's turn came next, but fortunately a sudden squall sent the raiders back to their own boat. Although they scuttled the *Mary*, a passing ship saved the narrator before she sank beneath him.[3]

To protect American seamen against such wanton attacks, the Navy Department established the West Indies Squadron under the command of David Porter in 1822. The son of the second skipper of the revenue cutter *Active*, which had sailed out of Baltimore, Porter faced a difficult task. Piracy in the Gulf of Mexico and Caribbean Sea was decentralized, and small craft easily found refuge in the many harbors where Porter's seventeen bigger warships could not navigate safely. Thus he added to his fleet nine schooners, five twenty-oared barges, and the Connecticut River sidewheel steamer *Sea Gull*—the first steamer used in active service as a warship.[4] Porter's plight also led the administration to augment his squadron with revenue cutters, modifying precedents in which the navy had been called upon to assist the Revenue Cutter Service.

A combination of smuggling, slave trading, and privateering overwhelmed the nation's law enforcement officers at New Orleans in 1812. Two pirates who fitted out at the Crescent City escaped from the revenue cutter *Louisiana* (Captain A. O. Fraser). From the Plaquemine River, Fraser reported that he had exchanged shots with the pirates, who had escaped using their superior speed and the approach of darkness. A few days later one of the freebooters landed $8,000 or $10,000 of silver. Then the two anchored at Cat Island, about one hundred miles to the west of Belize, at the southeast pass of the mouth of the Mississippi. Once again the cutter closed in on the pirates and forced them to cut their cables, only to have them escape, "as usual," on the strength of their "superior sailing."[5]

In the wake of these failures Theodore H. Williams, the collector of customs at New Orleans, informed Albert Gallatin that naval assistance might be necessary. A series of subsequent disasters confirmed the collector's worst fears. In August a hurricane destroyed the *Louisiana*. Shortly thereafter the pirates of Lake Barataria, sailing under French colors, raided Spanish shipping in violation of U.S. law, and all that Williams could do was send cuttermen after them in open boats. In the resulting skirmish, government forces suffered a number of casualties. With no other recourse open to him, Williams requested permission to use the naval units in the area, and on 24 August 1813 that authorization was granted.[6]

Five years later, with increased smuggling in the Chesapeake Bay, the navy ordered the U.S. schooner *Non Such* to cruise with the cutters there. Acknowledging the Revenue Cutter Service's superior experience in such matters, Secretary of the Treasury William Crawford instructed the collectors at Norfolk and Baltimore to order cutter commanders to provide *Non Such* with all the information she would need to do her duty.[7]

The nation had suffered two years of abuse before issuing those orders. On 8 November 1816 Baltimore's collector of customs, James McCulloch, reported that a South American privateer had anchored off Annapolis to smuggle goods. Since the revenue cutter *Active* had already sailed down the bay, McCulloch ordered her commanding officer, Captain Alexander Beard, to seize the privateer and bring her into Baltimore. The captain took the collector aboard at Annapolis and sailed to the Chester River, where the privateer was known to be operating. The *Active* overtook the vessel and fired a shot across her bow, but the latter, ignoring the warning, ran for Annapolis. When Beard overtook her again and again tried to board her, soldiers armed with fixed bayonets stopped him, even though the colors of the U.S. Revenue Cutter Service were flying from the *Active* and the collector of customs from Annapolis was standing by Beard's side.[8]

Early in 1818, McCulloch wrote that he was humiliated to have to report the ease with which privateers flying Latin American colors accomplished their objectives in the bay. Obviously, he wrote Crawford, "the little Cutter of one gun and eight men" could not by herself restrain privateers. Thus he requested the assignment to the bay of an additional bigger cutter or a naval vessel. He preferred the cutter, he wrote, "as the service is not relished by the officers of the Navy, nor are their vices or knowledge favourable to it, nor can they perhaps under their own regulations be brought to report to the Collectors and be directed by them." Nevertheless, in March McCulloch did finally accept assistance from the navy, as noted above.[9]

Cooperation between the Revenue Cutter Service and the navy continued off and on until 1819, when it culminated in a concerted effort against West Indian piracy.

The *Louisiana* and the *Alabama* were the most important cutters in this struggle. Built in New York for $4,500 each in 1819, they were an extreme type of Baltimore clipper designed by the veteran naval constructor William Doughty, who had had a hand in the design of the forty-four-gun frigates *Constitution*, *United States*, and *President*. He had also designed 31-, 51-, and 80-ton cutters for the service. The *Louisiana* and the *Alabama* were 51-tonners, measuring 56.8′ on deck, with a 17′ 4″ beam and 6′ depth of

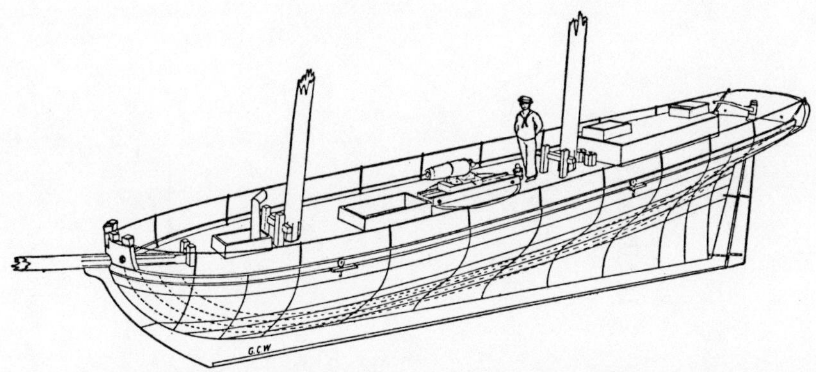

A U.S. *Revenue Cutter of* 31 *Tons,* 1815, *designed by* William Doughty. (*Courtesy Smithsonian Institution.*)

hold. Rigged as fore-topsail schooners, they had fine lines, square sterns, raking masts, and light rails in place of heavy bulwarks. Doughty's cutters were armed with 12- or 18-pound carronades or with long nines, twelves, or eighteens. They were designed to carry a pivot gun amidships, which was supposed to have been the heaviest gun carried, but the *Louisiana* did not have a pivot gun when she first went to sea, a shortcoming that caused her captain, Harris Loomis, a great deal of anxiety.[10]

Because of a similar concern William Johnson declined the command of the *Louisiana*'s sister ship *Alabama*.[11]

The Treasury Department knew, of course, that it had to replace the cutters lost in the War of 1812, and the rise of piracy accented the need for speedy action. As a result, Secretary of the Treasury Alexander J. Dallas wrote the customs collector at Philadelphia, asking when and on what terms the shipwrights in his district could "build and completely fit with Sails, Rigging, anchor, Cables & s including also two Boats, one or more Schooner-rigged Cutters" of the 51-ton Doughty design. Dallas wanted them "constructed of the best materials & coppered to the bends."[12] It is safe to assume that similar letters went out to other collectors, for a number of cutters were built or acquired shortly thereafter, and all but one of them were built from Doughty's plans.

In addition to the aforementioned *Alabama* and *Louisiana*, the *Search*, *Wasp*, and two *Detectors* were probably 51-tonners. The cutters *Detector* and *Search* were built in 1815 by Charles Gyles and Clark Cooke at Newport, Rhode Island, for the Boston and Portland stations respectively, costing a total of $12,500. As for the second *Detector* and *Wasp*, although Howard

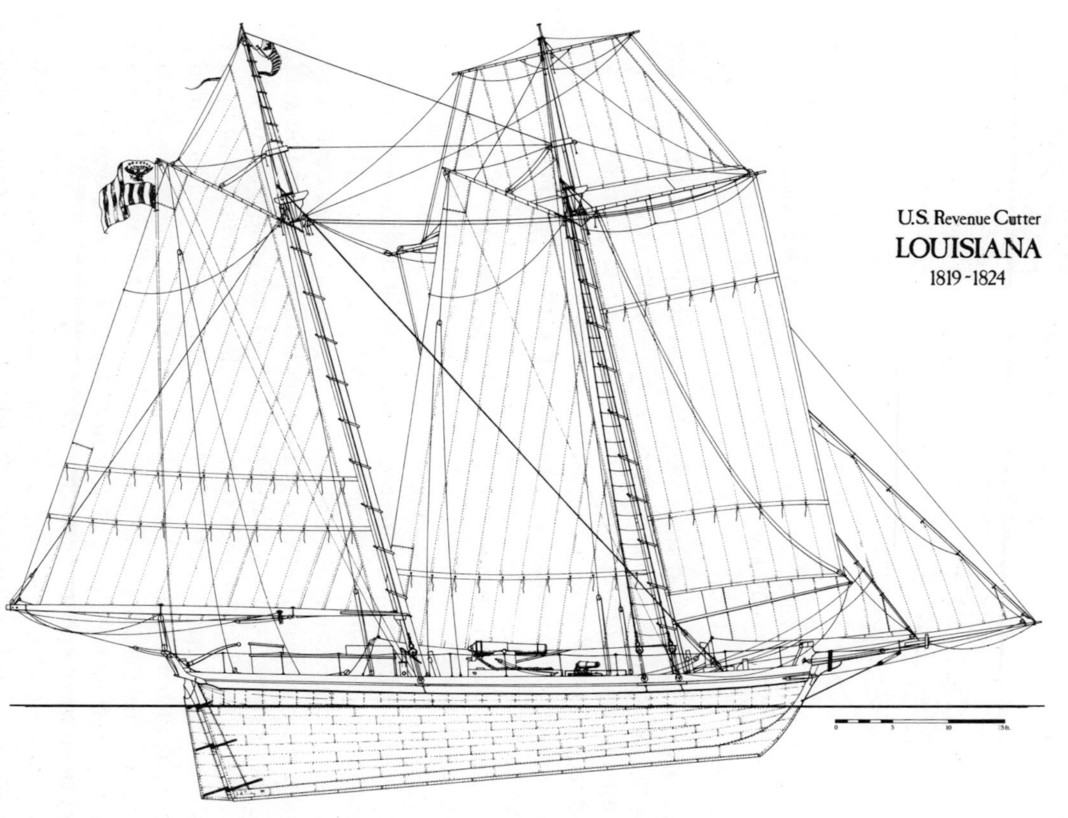

The USRC Louisiana, 1819–24. (*Drawing by* John A. Tilley, *courtesy* USCG *Public Affairs Staff.*)

Chapelle claims they were built at Portsmouth, the *Record of Movements* and the correspondence of the secretary of the treasury clearly indicate that they were built at Portland, Maine. The department contracted with Messrs. Fisher and Webster to build the cutters under the supervision of Captain R. Drinkwater in 1815. Captain John C. Jones went to Portland to sail the *Wasp* to the Norfolk station. The government paid Fisher and Webster $1,825 for the completely furnished *Detector.*[13]

Three cutters were probably built from Doughty's 80-ton plan, and another four were probably built on one of the two larger plans. The 80-ton cutters, the *Surprise*, *Dallas*, and *Crawford*, were all constructed in New York, the *Surprise* in 1815 for the Charleston station, and the *Dallas* and the *Crawford* in 1821 for the Savannah station. The *Surprise* was finished and completely equipped in less than ninety days. Because her draft was too deep for the water around Charleston, she was transferred to Norfolk in 1817. The *Crawford* was assigned to Savannah, where she worked until her loss off St. Marys on 19 February 1822; the *Dallas* succeeded her on that station. Built on one of Doughty's two bigger plans were the *Gallatin* at Baltimore in 1816–17, the *Eagle* at New York in 1816, the *Monroe* at Norfolk in 1817, and the *Alert* in 1818.[14]

Soon after the War of 1812 the service purchased one additional cutter that Doughty did not design. The 38-ton *Active* was bought at Baltimore for $1,300 on 22 August 1816.[15]

Sailing from their home bases in the Gulf of Mexico, the Doughty-designed cutters *Louisiana* and *Alabama* made an important capture on 31 August 1819. While cruising north of the Dry Tortugas, they sighted three sails. Because the winds were light, Captain Taylor of the *Alabama* and Captain Loomis of the *Louisiana* ordered all their sails set and wetted down. Sweeps were brought into play and the cutters gave chase. While two of the vessels bore away, the third made for the cutters and was stopped by a shot fired across her bow by the *Louisiana*. A boarding party from the *Alabama* discovered that the vessel was a victim of the *Bravo*, a pirate ship mounting one brass 6-pounder. When the cutters first appeared on the scene, the *Bravo* had left this vessel to fend for herself and started sailing off with another of her prizes, the Spanish flour schooner *Filomena*, which she had captured earlier off the coast of Cuba. The *Bravo* was owned by Jean Lafitte, the pirate who had helped Andrew Jackson win the battle of New Orleans, and was sailed by Jean Defarges, Lafitte's successor.[16]

Expecting Defarges to make a run for safety, Taylor and Loomis were surprised when he changed course, hoisted his pirate flag, and stood toward them. The *Bravo* opened the engagement with a volley of musketry that wounded the *Louisiana*'s first mate, Daniel Hazard, and three crewmen. While the *Louisiana* engaged the *Bravo* in musket fire, the *Alabama* maneuvered into position and fired a broadside that drove the freebooters below deck. Boarding parties from both cutters then scrambled aboard the *Bravo* and captured eighteen men, including Defarges and his lieutenant, Robert Johnson. At least two pirates, and possibly as many as six, were killed in the fray.[17]

Twelve of Defarges's prisoners, who had been robbed of all of their possessions, even the clothes off their backs, were set free. Most were black, suggesting that the *Bravo* was active in the illegal slave trade.

The *Bravo*'s survivors were taken into Bayou St. John from Lake Ponchartrain to await trial before a U.S. District Court, which sentenced all of them to die by hanging.[18] Before the execution could take place Jean Lafitte tried to win their release by starting a reign of terror in New Orleans, but volunteers thwarted his efforts by conducting night patrols of the city. Lafitte then went to Washington, where he won a sixty-day reprieve from President James Monroe. In spite of the delay, the government hanged Defarges and Johnson "from the yardarm of a U.S. naval vessel moored at the foot of St. Ann Street" on 25 May 1820. One member of the crew was later pardoned, but the fifteen remaining crewmen were executed early in 1821. President Monroe allowed the executions because of "a case of peculiar atrocity" in which Defarges had killed several persons during a raid on a ship at the mouth of the Mississippi River.[19]

Secretary of the Treasury William H. Crawford praised Captain Loomis's conduct in the fight with the *Bravo* and authorized the collector at New Orleans to retain control of both the *Louisiana* and the *Alabama* if he would continue the fight against piracy. Such praise and promise of support should have been rewarded, but alas this was not the case. Soon after his triumph Loomis insisted that the *Louisiana* needed an additional 9-pound swivel gun and two 3-pounders.[20] This demand reflected a lesson learned in his recent fight with the *Bravo*, but that was not the only reason he made it. Shortly after the engagement threats had been made against the *Louisiana*. When one of her officers was killed, instead of receiving the additional guns, Captain Loomis was hauled before a justice of the peace on charges of piracy. Although he was found innocent, he resigned his commission and returned to New York early in 1821.[21]

Shortly thereafter, the *Louisiana*'s crew of fifteen men plus officers was reduced to just two men and a boy. While her sister ship, the *Alabama*, had sailed with a crew of ten seamen, two boys, one cook, and a complement of officers, the *Louisiana* had sailed initially with a larger crew because of her service in a region of rampant piracy.[22]

In spite of her difficulties, the *Louisiana* continued to campaign against piracy. She sailed under Loomis until early in 1821 and then, following his resignation, temporarily under First Lieutenant Daniel Hazard. In September of the same year, Captain John Jackson stepped aboard as her new skipper. During this same period, Captain Taylor of the *Alabama* died and was replaced by Hazard, who was in turn replaced by Captain Francis Cartigan.[23]

On 16 April 1820 the *Louisiana*, under Loomis, and the *Alabama*, under Cartigan, destroyed a rendezvous of pirates on Breton Island. Twenty-five well-armed men landed on the island and set fire to everything—houses, wood lots, and buildings. Having completed this task, they sailed westward to break up additional pirate's haunts.[24]

While cruising 250 miles west of Belize just two months later, the *Louisiana* netted four pirate craft, $4,000 of dry goods, and a number of black prisoners.[25] She subsequently captured another five ships of between 80 and 100 tons each. Captain Jackson burned two of them and sent the other three to New Orleans as prizes. He captured just one of the ship's crews; the rest made good their escape.[26]

The *Louisiana* was joined at Havana by the U.S. sloop of war *Peacock* and the British schooner *Speedwell* in 1822. On a single cruise the *Peacock* captured five pirate ships. One was reclaimed at Havana, two were burned, and the others were sent to New Orleans along with eighteen captured buccaneers.[27]

In need of extensive repairs, the *Louisiana* was sold out of the Revenue Cutter Service on 24 March 1824 for $1,040.[28] She was replaced with another *Louisiana*, which continued the fight against picaroons into the mid-twenties. On 7 May 1827, the new *Louisiana* seized the Colombian privateer *Bolivar* in the southwest pass of the Mississippi Delta. The *Bolivar* had sailed into Mobile, Alabama, armed with three guns and carrying a crew of thirty-seven under the command of Captain François Reibaud, who was warned by the local collector not to molest the schooner *Antoinette* because both the ship and her cargo were American. Reibaud remained at Mobile himself but sent the *Bolivar* to sea under Lieutenant Auguste Chirot, who seized the *Antoinette* while she was en route from Mobile to Tampico, Mexico, with a valuable cargo. Chirot took her into Tampico where he tried to ransom her, but failing in this, he sailed back into U.S. waters and attempted to smuggle her cargo into New Orleans.[29] While the privateer was anchored off the southwest pass, the schooner *Isabella* ran up river on her return run from Brazos de Santiago, Mexico, to New Orleans with a cargo of specie worth $35,000. Chirot hailed the *Isabella*, and when she refused to stop, the *Bolivar* opened fire without effect. Being the swifter vessel, the *Isabella* fled up river pursued by Chirot's vessel. During the chase the privateer ran aground and stuck fast in the mud. Under the cover of darkness the *Isabella* doubled back and sailed into Belize, where her skipper, Captain Thomas Byrne, related his encounter to Captain Jackson of the *Louisiana*. Jackson got under way immediately and at about four in the morning on 7 May discovered the *Bolivar* still stranded. Meeting no resistance, Jackson "took her officers and crew into custody, put a prize crew on the privateer, . . . and carried the whole assortment—men, boats, and all—to New Orleans where they were delivered into the hands of the United States Marshal."[30]

The Court of Admiralty condemned the *Bolivar* for violating the laws of the United States and for firing at the *Isabella*. In passing sentence, the judge condemned Chirot to four years' imprisonment, his lieutenant to three, the petty officers to two, and all but one of the crew members to one. For some unknown reason he sentenced one man, Aristide Delanaux, to just one month. The underwriters and merchants of New Orleans were delighted with the outcome, for they were sure the *Bolivar* intended to seize every vessel that she encountered with specie aboard.[31]

Captain Reibaud escaped virtually unscathed from this escapade. In 1841 a New Orleans newspaper accused him of piracy, but at the time he was a U.S. naval officer and a resident of New Orleans and so, according to another source, his "honor was upheld by a score of respected citizens." During the Mexican War, he commanded a U.S. Navy fleet headquartered at Merida, Mexico. He served for a time as the consul general of Mexico in New Orleans and died in that city's French Quarter in 1861. Although he had not been on the *Bolivar* expedition, "he unquestionably was its promoter."[32]

Although few of the cutters rivaled the *Louisiana* in exploits, the cutters in the Chesapeake Bay and along the southern coast of the United States saw a good deal of action. The *Active* of Baltimore lived up to her name. Under the command of Captain Steven White, she began a year of intense activity on 22 August 1816 by taking possession of a Spanish brig in the Patuxent River. Earlier, an American ship had seized the brig as she left the bay and sent her into the Patuxent to await a new crew. When the Spanish consul sought help from the Baltimore collector, he immediately dispatched the *Active* to seize the vessel. Captain White put six men aboard the brig to hold her until the courts could decide her fate.[33]

When the *Active* returned to Baltimore, collector James McCulloch faced a series of disturbing personnel problems. He had to remove Captain White from command because "of an unhappy derangement of faculties." Shortly thereafter, charges were brought against Captain Alexander Beard, White's replacement. An experienced sailor, Beard had been a master in Commodore Barney's flotilla for the defense of the bay and had commanded merchant ships sailing out of Baltimore. While we do not know the nature of the charges brought against him, we do know that President Monroe dismissed Beard because of the charges and the whispering campaign that followed upon them. He might have been the victim of revenge wreaked by a drunken mate who had previously been dismissed.[34]

Beard clearly believed that the administration had treated him unfairly, and he reacted accordingly. As captain, he had provided the *Active* with furniture from his own allowances and contracted for her provisions himself. When he left the cutter he took both furniture and provisions with him. His successor had to replace even knives and dishes. Understandably furious, Secretary Crawford demanded an accounting from McCulloch. The main thrust of McCulloch's defense was that the *Active* had been bought and fitted in a hurry because of pressure to stop smuggling in the bay, and while the skippers had been chosen in haste, they had come highly recommended. McCulloch nevertheless revealed a great deal of anxiety about the case, perhaps because he had been guilty of nepotism in appointing a neighboring collector's son to command.[35]

In spite of her troubles the *Active* continued to be a productive cutter. Nine months after Beard took command, he forced a South American privateer posing as an armed merchantman to leave the Chesapeake Bay. On 12 August 1817, while temporarily under the command of Captain Henry Cahoone, the cutter captured the ship *Margaret* after she departed New York for Amelia Island with the intention of joining the pirates there. In the midst of this operation, the *Active* was ordered to stand by and provide President James Madison with transportation if he should need it on a trip he was taking to the north and the west.[36]

In 1818 there was no relief for the *Active*. The year began with orders to seize the heavily armed brig *Regent*, a South American privateer that had put into the Patuxent River to take aboard a crew recruited in Baltimore. We do not know whether or not the cutter was able to break through the ice to reach the *Regent*, but we do know that on 18 July the *Active* sailed into Baltimore with the *India Libra*, a fine brig of ten guns whose crew had mutinied, put their officers ashore, and set off for a life of piracy.[37]

The year ended badly for the *Active*. On 17 September she took possession of the Chilean privateer schooner *Hornet*. After fitting out at Baltimore, the *Hornet* had left port without formal clearance and the collector ordered the *Active* to pursue her. She seized the *Hornet* in Patapsco and put Lieutenant Philip M. Marshall aboard with orders to take the schooner into Fort McHenry when the winds were favorable. Next morning the brig *Puerrydon* of Buenos Aires came down river; as she passed the *Hornet* the latter's officers and crew gave her three cheers, which were returned. In defiance of orders, First Lieutenant Beaty of the *Hornet* then got the schooner under way and proceeded down river. When Lieutenant Marshall tried to speak a vessel on the way out to sea, the pirates simply carried him below. They released him at the Virginia capes before escaping to sea.[38]

The following spring the *Active* seized the pirate brig *Irresistable*, a Spanish man-of-war that had been taken over by mutineers while most of the crew was ashore. The *Irresistable* had plundered a number of vessels, including the *Superior* of Baltimore and ships of both French and British registry, before anchoring off New Point Comfort, where the *Active* made her seizure. The cutter returned to Baltimore with twenty-two of the mutineers in irons, and it was assumed that more would soon be arrested at Norfolk.[39]

During a cruise in the fall of 1823 the *Active*'s second officer, Richard Evans, successfully met the moral challenge presented by the offer of a bribe. Captain J. A. Webster, a worthy and patriotic officer, put Evans ashore at a spot where vessels from abroad often stopped before proceeding up the bay to Baltimore. Soon thereafter, Evans boarded the schooner *Cherub* of Baltimore and discovered that she had offloaded part of her cargo on or near a small island. Her officers claimed that she had gone aground and had to be made lighter, but crew members evaded some of the questions put to them. As it turned out, the vessel that had received the cargo had carried it up a creek to a farm that was an equal distance from the nearest port but harder to reach. Evans had the cargo returned and took the *Cherub* into Vienna, where she cleared customs. There were blank manifests aboard, and a new set with false particulars about the cargo surely would have been made had Evans not intervened. The decisive factor in the ensuing case was that the captain of *Cherub*, who was a part owner, had "offered two hundred dollars to Mr. Evans to conceal his knowledge of the landing of the goods." Using Evans's deposition as his principle evidence, McCulloch initiated a prosecution.[40]

That same year, 1823, the *Vigilant* replaced the *Active* at Baltimore. The *Active* had needed repairs as early as 1819, when McCulloch started a campaign to acquire a new cutter. He submitted a survey to the Treasury Department before proceeding, and although in it he proclaimed the cutter's condition to be deplorable, the department ordered McCulloch to repair her, if she could be saved, for further service in the bay. Thus in

1819 the *Active* acquired a new suit of sails, anchors, and chains. Next year the department ordered extensive repairs to her planks, timbers, and sails. A violent storm that did a great deal of damage drove her aground in 1823, but as a result of the foresight of the cutter's second officer, she was hauled off the beach without damage. The following year, five years after McCulloch had begun his campaign for a new cutter, the department finally authorized the purchase of a replacement.[41]

The *Vigilant* had the honor of replacing her. She received little attention in the correspondence of the Baltimore collector, being built when Captain Isaiah Doane arrived at Baltimore to supervise the construction of the *Marion* and the *Pulaski* for the Florida station, a project that occupied his attention. We do know that the *Vigilant* was about twice as big as the *Active*, that her lead ballast weighed between 15 and 18 tons, and that in addition to cannon she was armed with twelve muskets, six to eight pairs of pistols, a dozen swords, and eight to ten boarding pikes.[42]

Doane proved to be an energetic and capable man who wanted the best of everything for his new vessels, which was a source of great worry to McCulloch throughout 1825. Doane's cutters were bigger than planned, owing to the freedom allowed carpenters, and their cabins were finished in mahogany with a good deal of brass and ornamental work.[43] McCulloch's letters to Secretary Richard Rush had expressed reservations about the size, cost, and luxury of Doane's cutters, but after inspecting them himself he wrote that they were "the most complete vessels of their class ever presented to my view." All reservations were forgotten, for they were of the best material, of the neatest workmanship, and the best suited to their intended service. "In short," he wrote, "the whole appearance of these vessels is such that I could not on inspection find it in my heart to wish anything otherwise."[44]

McCulloch was a good judge of vessels. The *Pulaski* and the *Marion* proved to be every bit as good as he had thought they would. The *Pulaski* was a fast and hearty sea boat. Unfortunately, both vessels were 115 tons burden and drew 9½′ of water, which was too much for the Florida station. As a result the *Pulaski* was transferred to Delaware Bay for a short time in 1827–28. Needed at Key West, she was soon returned to that port in spite of her draft.[45]

Concern for the health of the crewmen assigned to Key West dominated the decision to station the *Pulaski* there in 1828. The Treasury Department made its decision after a few of the seamen on the revenue cutter *Florida*, stationed at Key West, died from drinking bad water that had been taken aboard at Havana. The *Florida* was small and lacked the space to carry both sufficient water and provisions and an adequate crew for the station. Thus she had to put into Havana on occasion for water. In contrast, the *Pulaski* was a big cutter that could be fitted out with a wrought-iron tank in place of the usual water casks; she did not have to take on water at Havana. This difference was so important that the department assigned the *Pulaski* to Key West and transferred the *Florida* to Philadelphia.[46]

Because of fear of contagious diseases entering Key West, local authorities placed a quarantine on ships arriving from Cuba. Anyone who boarded a vessel from that island before the health inspector had lifted the quarantine faced a fine of $300. Nevertheless, in some cases officers had to board at once to prevent smuggling, for all too often fishing vessels entered Key West with illegal sugar and glass concealed in small bags. In one such case, on the night of 10 August 1832, a small boat from Cuba anchored close to the wharf at Key West. After determining that there was no sickness on board, customs officers boarded the boat to collect the revenue. City officials subsequently prosecuted them for violating the law and forced the collector to appeal the decision to the Treasury Department.[47] Although the department's response has not been found, one would assume that federal law prevailed in the case.

The *Active* and the *Vigilant* did not sail the Chesapeake Bay alone. The revenue cutter *Monroe*, built at Norfolk in 1817, cruised with them. On 22 October 1818 the *Monroe* seized the armed brig *Columbia*. The brig's master and eleven members of his crew had cut her out of a Venezuelan fleet at Grenada and sailed her to the United States with the intention of taking her into Baltimore. As they entered the Virginia capes the *Monroe* took possession of the brig, which the government of Venezuela subsequently claimed as its own.[48]

In the summer of 1818 the *Dallas* (Captain John Jackson) seized a shipful of pirates off the harbor of Port Royal, South Carolina. Word that a ship and a schooner were hovering off that city had reached the *Dallas*'s home port, Savannah, on 17 June. His suspicions aroused, Captain Jackson dispatched two boats under Lieutenant Hubbard to investigate. Hubbard found the pirate ship *Young Spartan* (Captain Ralph Clintock) and her prize, the *Pastora*, which had been seized en route from Caronne to Havana with boxes and bale goods. The *Pastora*'s captain was missing—the pirates claimed that they had put him and his crew adrift in open boats. Taking possession of both vessels and the sloop *Firefly* of Beaufort, whose crew had assisted the *Young Spartan* in offloading some of the stolen cargo, Hubbard proceeded into Savannah. Through the vigilance of the *Dallas*'s officers and crew some of the stolen goods were recovered, and the *Young Spartan*'s officers and crew were put into jail. While the entire story is not known, it is clear that they had killed the *Pastora's* captain rather than putting him adrift and committed outrages on his vessel. They had also plundered a Dutch ship from Amsterdam bound for Havana with a cargo of Holland gin. These offenses caused the *New York Evening Post* to call for the execution of the pirates. On 21 December 1819, Captain Clintock of the *Young Spartan* was convicted of piracy at Savannah.[49]

In June 1820 the revenue cutter *Diligence* (Captain Joseph Burch), sailing out of Wilmington, North Carolina, seized a number of mutineers from the Buenos Aires privateer *General Rondeau*. Captain Miles of the *General Rondeau* was a successful privateer, but he had treated his men with such severity that they mutinied and killed the first officer, put Miles and the crewmen who remained loyal to him into the ship's cutter about eight miles from Grenada, and then made sail for the United States. En route they put some dissatisfied members of their party onto a Boston-bound vessel. Still more men were landed at Georgetown, South Carolina, before the privateer proceeded to the waters off Wilmington. There the cutter *Diligence* sighted the *General Rondeau* and gave chase. The eight men still aboard, the leaders of the mutiny, finally scuttled their vessel near the coast of North Carolina. They were arrested along with their comrades at Boston and Georgetown and confined to await trial for piracy.[50]

The revenue cutter *Gallatin* (Captain Benjamin Mathews), cooperated with the schooner *Revenge* in seizing nineteen Americans as they attempted to join the crew of the Colombian privateer *Wilson* at Charleston in the summer of 1820. The cutter and schooner set out after the *Wilson* as she left the harbor with her Spanish prize *Santiago*. Unable to overtake the privateer, the *Gallatin* and the *Revenge* returned to Charleston empty-handed the following day.[51]

On 11 October 1817, far to the north, the *Vigilant* returned with the brig *B* of Bristol to her home port at Newport. The brig had sailed from Newport on the second and cleared from Bristol for Puerto Rico the following day. According to her manifest, she had cleared from port with a cargo of apples and potatoes, armed with one gun and manned by fifteen men; when she was taken in Vineyard Sound, she mounted five guns and was manned by a crew of forty-six. Captain Cahoone found an additional four guns stored in her hold along with twenty casks of powder, a quantity of shot, and enough provisions for a long cruise. The U.S. District Court at Providence libeled the vessel and condemned it for violating American neutrality laws.[52]

That same day Captain Cahoone seized the Spanish brig *Belle Corunnes* off Block Island. She had been captured by the Buenos Aires privateer

Puerrydon while sailing from Tarragona, Spain, with a cargo of brandy and silks. The captors were trying to smuggle the goods into the island port of New Shoreham when Captain Cahoone, his crew greatly strengthened by the addition of twenty men from an artillery detachment at Fort Wolcott, overwhelmed them. The *Vigilant* captured twenty-five of the brig's crew, and another eleven surrendered soon thereafter. The *Belle Corunnes* ran aground, but she was refloated by the cutter's crew and subsequently sold for the benefit of the libelants and captors.[53]

The war against piracy and privateering had essentially been won by 1825, but it did not end completely. On 24 June 1826 the revenue cutter *Marion* (Captain Josiah Doane), sailing out of Charleston, seized the *Brilliant* after that sloop wrecked off the Bahamas. The *Marion* took her into St. Marys, whence she was sent to St. Augustine for adjudication. In April 1829 the *Marion* (Captain John Jackson) returned from a cruise along the coast of Cuba in search of a pirate schooner that had taken four American vessels and killed their crews. As late as October 1837 the revenue cutters *Gallatin*, *Andrew Jackson*, and *Roger B. Taney* sailed in search of a pirate that had captured the packet *Susquehanna* near Cape May, New Jersey.[54] According to Samuel Eliot Morison, pirates remained active in the Caribbean as late as 1840.[55]

CHAPTER SIX

Winter Cruising

By the time piracy had been brought under control, New York emerged as the leading port in the nation. The construction of the Erie Canal, which made the Midwest into a market and a hinterland for New York, the introduction of an auction into the sale of goods at New York after the Peace of Ghent in 1815, and an excellent natural harbor all played a part in the rise of the port. With the inauguration of the Black Ball Line in 1817, New York added to its advantages packets that sailed on schedule. Other lines began operating to Liverpool, Le Havre, and America's southern and gulf ports, and soon all the cotton trade of the nation was flowing through New York.[1] When the ports of Boston, Philadelphia, and Baltimore realized what had happened, they had to "struggle on in a futile stern chase." They did this by, among other things, starting their own coastal and transatlantic packets. The price of competition could be high, as Bob Albion points out: "The trip from New York to New Orleans was reckoned as more risky than that to Liverpool, London or Havre and almost as dangerous as the route halfway round the world to China."[2]

Because of the dramatic increase in U.S. coastal trade that followed the establishment of dependable packet service, Secretary of the Treasury Louis McLane introduced a policy of regular winter cruising for revenue cutters. Prior to the winter of 1831–32, cutters in northern climes enforced customs laws as weather conditions permitted. The Revenue Cutter Service laid up vessels for the winter months and let most crewmen go. In mid-December 1831 that changed. McLane spelled out the details of his new winter cruising policy in letters to collectors who controlled the *Swiftsure*, *Morris*, *Portsmouth*, *Hamilton*, *Wolcott*, *Alert*, *Rush*, *Gallatin*, and *Dexter*. He ordered each cutter to add to her usual duties "that of assisting vessels found on the coast in distress, and of ministering to the wants of their crews," and each commanding officer to furnish without delay "such quantities of provisions, water, wood, and other necessary supplies, as [could] be conveniently stored in the vessel and . . . to cruise on his assigned station . . . keeping as close to the mainland as [was] consistent with the safety of the vessel."[3] He directed captains to stay at sea and cruise along a specific section of the coast until forced into port by the "stress of weather or want of supplies." The captain was to speak every vessel approaching the coast and to offer any aid or relief that was needed and within his power to give. All supplies furnished under this authority were to be accounted for and sold at cost. The money due the government was to be collected from the owners, at their convenience.[4]

McLane realized that revenue cutter officers could probably claim salvage rights to many of the ships they assisted under his orders, but he insisted that they not demand such rights, for he wanted the actions of cutters to be strictly humanitarian.[5]

Ignoring McLane's wishes, Captain Farnifold Greene of the revenue cutter *Dallas* claimed $250 for aiding the schooner *Capital Game* at New Bern, North Carolina, in March 1833. When the schooner's captain refused to pay up Captain Greene threatened to libel the vessel. In response, a complaint was filed with the Treasury Department. McLane ordered an investigation and suspended all judicial proceedings against the *Capital Game*.[6]

The early cutters were not always large enough for the strenuous work of winter cruising. Within a month of McLane's order, the revenue cutter *Rush* was "wrecked on Long Island, high and dry at low water and 'bilged.' Anchored in Huntington Bay, she had parted her chain in a 'huricane,' dragged her hemp cable, and run ashore."[7]

Surprisingly, a few of the northern cutters enjoyed an uneventful first winter. The *Dexter* sailed out of Norfolk in December 1831, and although she was "a dull sailer and an old vessel," there was "no doubt of her doing essential Service."[8] She reported no unusual problems. In January 1832 the *Morris* (Captain Henry D. Hunter) put to sea from Portland with a typical winter cargo—five barrels of ship bread, five barrels of beef, one cord of wood, and six hogsheads of water—and cruised between Mount Desert Rock and Cape Elizabeth without any unusual difficulty.[9]

None of the northern cutters had the honor of being the first to cruise regularly in the Atlantic during the winter. At least as early as the winter of 1830 cutters were cruising between Charleston, South Carolina, and Key West. In February of that year the *Marion* and the *South Carolina* sailed the same cruising grounds, one bound for Charleston and the other for Key West. Each boat sailed her station at least once every seventy-five days, visiting waters off the ports of the area, boarding foreign vessels, and placing officers in charge of any ship operating under suspicious circumstances.[10] But, of course, McLane's winter cruising was carried out primarily to assist mariners in distress, regardless of weather conditions; for this reason it was a new and notable service.

Before 1831, one northern cutter did go to sea during the winter, but there is no evidence that she did so on a regular basis. In February 1830 John Chandler, Portland's collector, ordered Captain William A. Howard to cruise with the *Detector* between Portland and Passamaquoddy Bay. Her main cruising ground was between Portland and the Sheepscot River; now she was to cruise as far as Mount Desert at least once every twenty days, and occasionally to sail down east to Passamaquoddy. On these trips the cutter sailed into as many of the rivers and harbors as possible, afforded aid "to persons at sea in distress," and preserved "property found on board wrecked vessels." Chandler instructed Howard to follow the orders of the secretary of the treasury on these cruises, acting "as well with discretion as with vigilance and firmness."[11]

Several cutters proved inadequate to their tasks. The *Hamilton*, a fast, beautiful ship, had been a superb cutter before the advent of winter cruising but was found wanting when ordered to cover the grounds between Cape Ann and Cape Cod in the cold months. With low decks and heavy spars, she was in great danger when iced up. Moreover, being a sharp ship, she could not carry adequate provisions for extended cruising.[12]

Similar problems plagued the *Portsmouth* during her cruises between Portland and Cape Ann. Originally built as a pilot boat, she was a small, sharply built vessel of 60 tons burden with a narrow deck and a 10′ draft. In the winter of 1831, Captain Thomas Shaw had to take her into port every night because of heavy ice on her rigging. On 3 January, while coming into Portsmouth, she was so unmanageable that the collector of customs, William Pickering, reported a disaster would surely have struck had she been blown offshore. Local shipbuilders agreed with the collector's assessment and Captain Shaw asked for a new cutter, but to no avail; the *Portsmouth* continued to cruise along the coast that winter.[13]

So did the *Alert*, which sailed out of New York against her captain's better judgment. She left for her first winter cruise on 22 December 1831. Nine days later Samuel Swartwout, New York's collector, relayed to Secretary McLane Captain Bell's assertion that she was unfit to cruise on the coast in the winter, an opinion confirmed by all the captains Swartwout had spoken with. But the *Alert* was forced to stick with her task; and on 9 January 1832 Swartwout informed the secretary that she would leave on a cruise immediately, in keeping with orders received on the fifth. Although the *Alert* did have to sail out of New York that winter, the department eased her burden somewhat by assigning her to southern ports in subsequent years.[14]

The *Gallatin* and the *Rush* also sailed from the port of New York in the winter of 1831–32. As noted above, the *Rush* was wrecked on Long Island, and the *Gallatin* returned from a cruise in January leaking so badly that she required a survey and major repairs.[15]

Sickness and injury plagued the crewmen on winter cruises. The *Swiftsure* (Captain Howard) was authorized ten men and four boys, who worked as boatswains, gunners, carpenters, sailmaker's mates, cooks, and stewards, leaving just four men and four boys to perform the ship's and boat's duties. In January 1831, the Treasury Department allowed Howard to hire an additional two men and two boys for the winter. The following spring Howard asked permission to retain these crew members, noting that, owing to the severity of the weather, two or three men had been on the sick list all winter.[16]

When David Henshaw, the collector at Boston, received McLane's winter cruising orders, the *Hamilton*'s officers and crew were so sick with influenza that the ship could not go to sea. Captain Samuel Trevett, her commander, had been confined to his bed for months. Second Lieutenant Penn Townsend and the warrant officer, Mr. Thomas Stoddart, had been confined to their houses ashore for about ten days, and three crew members were under the care of a physician. First Lieutenant Lewis Girdler was the only officer aboard, and he was too sick to perform sea duty. Under the circumstances, Henshaw recommended that the cutter go out for a short cruise as soon as possible and that he be allowed to add men to the *Hamilton*'s crew to relieve those suffering from frost and hard service.[17]

Before 13 January 1832, Captain Richard Derby reported aboard as the *Hamilton*'s new skipper. He took the cutter to sea on the nineteenth. Lieutenants Girdler and Townsend, still sick, were replaced by Josiah Sturgis and Jacob Williams. Other substitute crew members had been hired, but some of the old crew members had deserted and replacing them was difficult because Derby had a reputation as a tough disciplinarian. Thus he left Boston shorthanded, planning to put in at Gloucester or Marblehead to enlist more men if that should prove necessary.[18]

Derby's troubles had just begun. Before the month was out, Carpenter's Mate James Patrick fractured his thigh and was put ashore.[19] By 11 March the *Hamilton* was riding at anchor because Derby could not hire a crew. When their enlistments were up on 1 May all but one of the seamen left the cutter, choosing to ship as merchant seamen for eighteen dollars a month rather than accepting the fourteen that Derby could pay. Derby requested higher salaries for his crew, but the Treasury Department turned down his request. We know this because his successor, unable to match the wages of sixteen to seventeen dollars a month being paid to seamen on first-rate ships, could not hire a full crew in the spring of 1833.[20]

By that spring the *Hamilton* was sailing with a crew of just two seamen, a sailmaker, a cook, a steward, and two boys.[21] Her officer corps had changed completely: Derby had suffered a shock and could not resume command, Townsend had resigned, and Girdler had taken command temporarily. His replacement, Captain William Coody, was too sick to go to sea, so by March of 1832 the *Hamilton* had been rendered inactive once again.[22]

When Captain Andrew Mather of the revenue cutter *Wolcott*, stationed at New Haven, received orders to cruise between Montauk Point, Long Island, and Point Judith, Rhode Island, he and two or three crewmen were under a doctor's care in New London. The *Wolcott* took on wood, water, and provisions and set sail from New London on 22 December 1831 without her captain. By 4 January Mather was feeling better, and he assumed command of the cutter on her second winter cruise. Since she was an uneasy sailer, especially in a fresh blow, Mather shipped three additional seamen.

The *Wolcott* was fitted out with one chain cable and one somewhat worn hemp cable that did not work well together. This made Mather nervous; feeling that he needed two chain cables, he requested a new chain and capstan.[23]

In the "Rough Copy of Directions for Building a Revenue Cutter, 1829," from Samuel Humphreys's *Offset Book*, builders were told to provide two anchors, each weighing 500 pounds, one with a 9″ hemp cable and one with 60 fathoms of 1″ chain.[24] Such tackle was found wanting by most captains, who returned from their winter cruises also feeling the need for two chain cables. Hard use was pointing up weaknesses that future designers, builders, and outfitters would have to take into account.

Some sign of change was evident in the contract for the revenue cutter *Roger B. Taney*. It required the builders, Isaac Webb and John Allen, to provide two 700-pound anchors, one with 75 fathoms of 9″ hemp cable and the other with 60 fathoms of ⅞″ chain cable.[25] While two chain cables were not requested, the size of the anchors was increased by 200 pounds each.

Despite such problems, valuable services were rendered to ships in distress during that severe winter of 1831–32. Throughout December, January, and February, the *Swiftsure* carried out the treasury secretary's orders in an efficient and satisfactory manner, affording necessary aid to both U.S. and Canadian vessels.[26]

Congress finally recognized the great value of winter cruising by making it law on 22 December 1837, six years after cutters first sailed regularly throughout the winter months.[27] The act authorized the president to order public vessels to cruise the coast during the cold months and offer assistance to mariners who needed it.

Records of early winter cruises were scanty until Alexander Fraser took office as the first military commandant of the Revenue Marine Service. He augmented them by ordering skippers to track their cruises on charts and enter into journals notes on soundings, water depth, and holding ground. The commanding officers also kept records of what ships were boarded and where, and what assistance was rendered. On the first day of each April they sent an abstract of the information to revenue marine headquarters. Fraser used the material in his 1846 annual report, leaving a good record of the difficulties of early winter cruising in small sailboats and of services performed.[28]

According to him, such cruising was a duty "embracing great privation and hardships, as well as exposure; and taken with the small uncomfortable class of vessels then in use, rendered the life of officers in the revenue marine anything but luxurious and pleasant."[29]

Fraser continued to assign additional crewmen to cutters during the winter, hoping thus to ease the seaman's lot. In 1843–44 he added five men to the crew of each cutter, and subsequently he asked for the authority to employ medics on cutters. "There are now living upon the cold charity of the world," he wrote, "several men who have lost limbs in the Service by frost during the winter, or other casualties, in the execution of their duties, when beyond the reach of assistance from the shore. However meritorious the cause which has deprived them of the means of gaining a livelihood, no pension is provided, nor any other refuge left them than the almshouse affords."[30] Despite the logic of this appeal, the government turned down his request. It assigned no medics and still granted no pensions.[31]

Cuttermen received the same medical care as others who earned their living upon the sea. On 2 March 1798, Congress instituted a medical program for sick and disabled seamen. Under the provisions of the law, the government deducted twenty cents a month from the wages of merchant seamen, naval officers, marines, and revenue cuttermen. Ships' captains delivered this revenue to designated customs collectors, who administered the funds and saw that medical care was made available in marine hospitals or other suitable institutions. The first such hospital opened its doors in Norfolk, Virginia, in 1800.[32]

Collectors were expected to run the hospitals with these sums, and those seamen entitled to use the medical facilities were expected to do so. If they chose instead to seek other care, the government paid the doctor of their choice such a sum as would have been taken from the hospital fund for the same treatment.[33]

Captain John A. Webster of the revenue cutter *Vigilant* at Baltimore was sick throughout the 1820s. His physician, Dr. Joseph Allender, attended him eighteen days in 1820, forty days in 1821, forty-two days in 1823, and thirty days in 1826. Having regularly paid the tax on seamen, Webster was eligible for care in a marine hospital, but he had chosen instead to go to Allender and the doctor wanted to be reimbursed for his services. At the time, the government paid $0.50 a day for treatment in a marine hospital. Treasury Secretary Rush decided that the cost of Webster's care, had he gone to a marine hospital, would have been between $60 and $75 and therefore authorized a payment of $60 to Allender.[34]

Webster had incurred additional medical expenses for treatment of an accidental wound received during a cruise in 1825. The government also paid this bill out of his hospital account.[35]

Captain Webster might have selected his own physician because of the poor quality of care at marine hospitals. That offered in Ocracoke, North Carolina, certainly left a lot to be desired. On Christmas Eve, 1827, Treasury Secretary Rush wrote Joshua Taylor, customs collector at Ocracoke, that medical care should be made available to the seamen of his district. He asked Taylor to find out how much per year a responsible person would charge for room, board, nursing, medicine, and medical assistance.[36] In response to Rush's initiative, three bids to establish a marine infirmary were sent to the Treasury Department. The best offer came from Dr. John W. Potts, who agreed to establish a hospital for $1,500 a year. His contract with the government began on 1 April 1829, and he was paid quarterly by a draft drawn on the collector at New Bern.[37] Potts soon learned that his expenses exceeded expectations, and within eighteen months he asked permission to discontinue the contract.[38]

About that time, a Mr. Dudley visited Ocracoke looking for a school for small children and volunteered to take over the medical contract from Dr. Potts. The government had no intention of renewing with Dudley, for as Joseph B. Hinton, who volunteered to succeed Potts in1831, observed in a letter to Treasury Secretary Ingham, seamen were reluctant to seek treatment: "Their condition, when sick in our little towns, is truly distressing. If they live in the filthy brothels into which they are generally placed, neglect and suffering is their certain doom: if they die, they die alone, or among the outcasts from Heaven and earth."[39] Hinton, though he did not know how sick seamen fared "in regards to diet, cleanliness, nursing or medical assistance," described in some detail the marine hospital at Ocracoke. It was a small rented house measuring 16′ to 18′ by 20′ to 22′, without plaster or glass windows. Its furnishings were "about six cots, a pine table or two, & a few benches or chairs." The building stood 2′ above sea level on a barren island with neither trees nor shade. There was no cistern for fresh water, just "a hole about a foot in depth in the sand—and such brackish and hot stuff as filters into such hole is the Hospital water."[40] Hinton wanted the hospital moved to the lighthouse at Ocracoke, a cool brick structure.[41]

Surviving evidence indicates that arrangements for the care of sick and disabled seamen at Ocracoke did not change as a result of Hintons' exposé.[42] In a letter to Ingham, Ocracoke's collector, Joshua Taylor, claimed that Hinton's treatise was meant to deceive rather than to inform. According to Taylor, the hospital was as good as could be expected under the circumstances. It was, he said, "as eligibly situated . . . as any other on this Island . . . , having a passage and two comfortable rooms below and a spacious room above with glass windows."[43] The only real change since Dr. Potts had run the hospital was that it cost about a thousand dollars less per year to operate. As regards Dr. Dudley's medical qualifications, Taylor argued that he had practiced medicine at Plymouth, North Carolina, before moving to Ocracoke, that he had assisted Dr. Potts, and that the people of the town used his services. Taylor concluded his letter with this revealing admission: "In selecting Doctor Dudley to take charge of sick an[d] disabled seamen, I had no choice; there being no other person who practiced medicine, nearer than fifty miles of the place."[44]

Those who could not perform their duty because of job-related injuries received fair treatment from the government as long as they were only temporarily incapacitated. In 1830, when Lieutenant Ezekiel Jones could not accompany the cutter *Crawford* on a cruise from Norfolk because of injuries suffered in an accident, he was paid his usual wages. The service even allowed him to remain at Norfolk with his family after it was determined that indulging his preference would cause no problems for any other officer.[45]

Treatment was dramatically different when a seaman was permanently disabled. In 1821 the cost of operating the marine hospital in Philadelphia exceeded the sum collected. Secretary Crawford investigated the cause and learned that this hospital and the one in Baltimore admitted those who were permanently disabled, while the New York hospital sent them to the place of their birth or their last residence. As a result, Crawford ordered collectors to refuse admission to the incurably ill.[46]

In 1805 the collector in New Orleans, where there was no marine hospital, requested a surgeon for the local cutter. Secretary of the Treasury Gallatin turned down the request as contrary to law. If a revenue cutter crewman required medical care, he was to be relieved of duty just like any other seaman.[47] This decision was consistent with practice in the Revenue Cutter Service. In the fall of 1802, medical expenses incurred for a crewman who died of yellow fever aboard the Philadelphia cutter had been paid out of the marine hospital fund, but it appears that the captain of the cutter had obligated the government in the case. Gallatin wrote Peter Muhlenburg, the collector in Philadelphia, that in the future the captain was not to enter into any agreements without previously obtaining authority from the Treasury Department.[48]

In 1812 Gallatin ruled that Dr. Shaw could not be paid for treating the crew of the revenue cutter at New Orleans; they were to be assisted from the hospital fund like other seamen.[49] Sixteen years later George Baylor, an army doctor, treated some of the *Louisiana*'s crew at Bay St. Louis, where there was no marine hospital. When Baylor asked for payment and had the cutter's acting commander, James Nicholson, certify that treatment had indeed been given, the New Orleans collector refused.[50]

In contrast, when a seaman attached to the *Campbell* at Baltimore was too sick to be removed to the marine hospital, the Treasury Department allowed the collector James Mosher to pay him fifteen dollars, the amount the fund would have been charged by the hospital.[51]

There was no rehabilitation program for seamen in the early nineteenth century. In 1831 William Bloodworth, a warrant officer and the pilot aboard the *Campbell*, was charged with drinking on duty, sleeping on watch, and sleeping in a stupor when he should have been piloting the cutter. The department simply ordered Bloodworth to resign his commission.[52] Others who were generally good men but had difficulty with alcohol were similarly dismissed from the service.[53]

The department's denial of requests for medics to sail with the cutters and the inadequacy of medical care for sick and disabled seamen did not excuse the service from winter cruising. Between 1 December 1845 and 1 April 1846, twelve cutters sailed 26,354 miles during the winter and boarded 1,264 vessels. The cutters saved hundreds of lives and millions of dollars' worth of property, safely escorted to port eighty-nine vessels, and reclaimed cargoes valued at four times the cost of operating the service for the year.[54]

As mentioned earlier, Fraser attached detailed accounts of cutter cruises to his annual report, and any congressman who read them would have appreciated the great worth of the Revenue Cutter Service. Prior to being dismasted in a storm, the *Wolcott* boarded and offered help to thirty-one vessels. The *Morris* (Captain Green Walden) cruised the Maine coast where the schooner *Globe* got into trouble while bound from Harrington to Fall River with a load of lumber. She lost her deck cargo, was blown off course, and split her sails. Captain Walden provided the *Globe* with blocks and rigging. A few days later the *Yarico*, sailing out of Thomaston with a load of lime, caught fire. The *Morris*'s crew hauled her in toward shore and sank her. When the *Morris* came upon the disabled *Orbit*, Captain Walden provided her with sails, provisions, and three crewmen to help sail her into Owl's Head.[55]

The *Ewing* (Captain Gay Moore) compiled an impressive record. She sailed over three thousand miles, spoke and boarded sixty-two vessels, and provided relief and supplies to seven. She piloted the bark *Trinidad*, bound from Trinidad to New Haven with a cargo of coffee, into New London. When the bark *Waban* from Rio "lost her anchors, sails, and spars" and sprung her masts, Captain Moore provided the crippled vessel with water and provisions and towed her into New London, some three days' sail away. When the *Louisa Benton* ran "aground on the east end of Gull Island," the *Ewing*'s crew floated the ship free by placing casks under her and towed her into port.[56]

The *Forward* (Captain H. B. Nones) rendered assistance to the bark *Ohio* as she was en route to Philadelphia from Bordeaux with brandy and wine and was found to be in need of bread and beef. In another, more serious incident, the *Forward* came to the aid of the ship *Commerce*. Her crew had mutinied at Newcastle, Delaware, while she was preparing to sail for Liverpool with a cargo of flour. Captain Nones quelled the mutiny, put the mutineers in irons, and delivered them to jail.[57]

The revenue cutters *Crawford* and *Legare* put down at least two mutinies at the same time. The efforts of twelve of the *Legare*'s officers and men were required to quell a disturbance aboard the British ship *York*. The crew was placed in irons on board the *Legare*, whereupon the *Legare* and the *Crawford* worked the *York* and one other offending vessel into port.[58] Not all the hazards of winter cruising were caused by the elements.

Several cutters were commanded by naval officers when McLane introduced winter cruising. The U.S. Navy gave its officers only half pay when they were ashore during the nineteenth century. This put pressure on the service to obtain sea duty for its officer corps and partially explains its quest for control of the Coast Survey founded by President Jefferson, who wanted scientific studies made of the coast. Other exploratory and scientific expeditions attracted the navy's interest for the same reason.[59]

The search grew more active at the end of wars and during periods of economic constraint. After the War of 1812, when the navy was looking for seagoing assignments, the Revenue Cutter Service felt the impact. In 1818 the navy succeeded in taking control of the Coast Survey from civilian scientists. Two years later the Treasury Department ordered the captain of the revenue cutter at Ocracoke to place himself and his cutter at the disposal of naval officials for the duration of the survey.[60]

Between 1830 and 1832 naval officers even took officer's billets in the Revenue Cutter Service. While on duty with cutters, they were furloughed from the navy and made subject to the orders of the secretary of the treasury. On 4 January 1830 Secretary Samuel D. Ingham wrote William A. Howard, USN, ordering him to report to John Chandler, the collector at Portland, and take command of the cutter *Detector* at that port.[61] Howard was followed by others, including Lieutenant Charles H. Bell, who assumed command of the cutter *Alert* at New York, and Lieutenant Oscar Bullis, who took command of the cutter *Rush* at the same port. The *Rush*'s first and second lieutenants were Passed Midshipman John S. Glasson and Midshipman Stephen C. Rowan.[62]

Customs collectors did not welcome these assignments. In May 1830 Chandler wrote Ingham that Lieutenant Richard W. Meade had left the *Detector* for Washington, presumably to resign his commission; Chandler refrained from recommending a replacement because he did not know whether the secretary planned to assign an officer from the navy. By August, Chandler had recommended Second Lieutenant Green Walden for first lieutenant but had made no recommendation for second lieutenant on the assumption that a midshipman from the navy would be appointed. However, he pointed out to Ingham, he did not believe it was in the "interest of the Government to place those young Midshipmen in the Cutter Service. Although there is smartness enough about them, still I do not think they have as much discretion as is necessary; and I fear that parade and show will cost the government more than it will be worth to them."[63]

A number of problems soon became evident. Naval officers disliked their duties, resented taking orders from civilian superiors, and continued to wear naval uniforms, resisting assimilation by the Revenue Cutter Service.[64]

On 23 January 1832 Secretary of the Treasury Louis McLane sent out a Treasury Department circular terminating the assignment of naval officers to cutters and revoking all commissions of naval officers in the Revenue Cutter Service after 30 April. Experience, he wrote, had shown the practice to be objectionable. "With a view to greater efficiency in the Cutter Service," he wrote, "future vacancies will be filled by promotion from among the Officers in that service."[65]

Soon thereafter recommendations arrived at the Treasury Department for persons to fill vacancies when the naval officers were discharged.[66] There were, however, fewer openings than anticipated, for thirteen naval officers chose to take commissions in the Revenue Cutter Service rather than return to the navy.[67]

CHAPTER SEVEN

The Morris Class of Cutters

The Revenue Cutter Service built a new class of bigger, faster, and more heavily armed cutters in the 1830s. David Henshaw, the Boston collector, had been trying to get permission to replace the *Search* since 1815. He persuaded Commodore William S. Bainbridge to visit the Treasury Department in 1818 in support of his cause, but that did not produce results. Then in the summer and fall of 1829 he hit upon an argument that carried weight. He pointed out that the *Search* was a small boat and a dull sailer, and that a large percentage of the wood and lumber coasters on her station outsailed her, rendering her completely unsatisfactory as a cutter.[1] Although many of the other, older cutters were fast enough, they shared with her the problem of being too small for the extended cruising now required of them.

Winter cruising, moreover, revealed weaknesses in vessels that had been perfectly good cutters when sailed only during the milder seasons. New York's collector of customs described the *Alert* as a fine seakeeping boat that was perfect for trips between Montauk Point and Delaware Bay. Six months later, her

The USRC Hamilton. (*Oil painting by* Robert Salmon, 1840, *photo by* Mark Sexton, *courtesy* Peabody Museum *of* Salem.)

skipper recommended repairs at a cost that almost equaled the price of a new cutter. The *Alert*, a 122-ton cutter that measured 80′ in length and 20′ in beam, was "almost proverbial for the admirable symmetry of her model and her remarkable velocity in sailing." Such praise led the Treasury Department to repair her at considerable expense. Subsequently McLane introduced winter cruising, and Captain Charles H. Bell, her new skipper, had to acknowledge that she was unfit for it. Although outraged by this turn of events, the department transferred the cutter to a more moderate climate and built a new cutter for the New York station.[2]

Howard I. Chapelle wrote in *The History of American Sailing Ships* that "the usefulness of the cutters as dispatch-boats and as naval auxiliaries in time of war was recognized" at this time, "so the new cutters were to be large and powerful enough to serve these purposes as well. . . . The trend in regard to revenue cutters was away from the small pilot-boat type of 1815 toward the naval schooner type of 1798."[3] Many naval architects influenced the design of these new cutters, including the famous Samuel Humphreys. Secretary Ingham asked Boston's collector, David Henshaw, to furnish "the draft of a model for a cutter," and on 19 March 1830 Henshaw submitted a model made by H. Churchill and approved by Captain Josiah Barker, a naval architect at the Charlestown Navy Yard. Henshaw also sent along a model of a 130-ton yacht built for John Crowninshield of Salem, which the builder wanted returned.[4] And Isaac Webb and John Allen of New York designed and built the revenue cutter *Taney*.[5]

The service built the new cutters in the New York and Washington navy yards and in private yards under contract. It had intended to have all the construction done at navy yards, but they were backed up with work and very expensive.[6] Other problems arose with the privately owned yards. The service had planned to build the *Hamilton* in a private yard but wanted to withhold a quarter of the purchase price until the cutter proved to be a fast sailer. Not surprisingly, the builder was unwilling to make such an agreement, for he had not designed the boat and some who had seen the model thought it would be a dull sailer. Boston's collector reported this to the Treasury Department and noted that, not being a competent judge, he did not know what to do.[7]

Ultimately, the New York Navy Yard built the *Hamilton*, *Morris*, and *Gallatin* under the supervision of Captain Richard Derby.[8] The *Morris*, the class boat, was a beautiful fore-topsail schooner of the Baltimore clipper type. She displaced about 112 tons, measured 73′ 4″ between perpendiculars, and had a 20′ 2″ molded beam, 20′ 6″ extreme beam, and 7′ 4″ depth of hold. She had an unadorned pilot-boat stern, as some of the others did. Her sister ship *Hamilton* was built with a billet-head, and probably all of the class were similarly fitted at some point.[9]

The *Morris* was fitted out in style. Brass hand railings adorned her cabin and wardroom stairs, and carpets covered her cabin and wardroom floors.[10]

She initially mounted two "very large and clumsy double fortified six pounders." In 1832 her skipper, Captain Henry Hunter, asked the Treasury Department to replace them with two brass 6-pounders, such as some other cutters carried, for they were lighter and easier to manage than the guns issued.[11] A sister ship, the *Wolcott*, carried in addition to the two cannons a dozen each of muskets, pistols, and cutlasses.[12]

The *Hamilton*, an especially fast and beautiful boat, was the pride of her skipper, Captain Josiah Sturgis. According to Howard Chapelle she, like her sisters, "was a very fine sailer and was used as a supreme test of any schooner claiming a reputation for speed. In races with opium-smuggling schooners, fast pilot-boats, fishermen, coasters and yachts, few vessels passed her either on or off the wind."[13]

The firm of Webb and Allen built a number of the new cutters, including the *Roger B. Taney*. The firm agreed to allow the government to hold back one quarter of the purchase price pending proof of the *Taney*'s performance, and the government assured Webb and Allen that they could design the cutter and change her masts and rigging as required to increase speed.[14]

Samuel Swartwout, the collector at New York, signed the *Taney* contract with Webb and Allen. It called on the builders to deliver a fully equipped cutter for $8,500, but the *Taney* ran over budget and cost $10,914.[15] In spite of this, the firm competed successfully for other contracts because it built good cutters for a fair price. In addition to the *Taney*, Webb and Allen built the *Louis McLane*, *Samuel D. Ingham*, *Richard Rush*, and *Dexter*, and possibly the *Oliver Wolcott*. All these cutters were launched in 1832. The next year they built the *Jefferson*, renamed *Crawford* in 1839. They repaired the cutters *Alert* and *Pulaski* and built a number of revenue boats.[16]

Isaac Webb, the *Taney*'s designer, made a unique contribution to shipbuilding, training his son William and also Donald McKay, who between them dominated the industry in America for two decades before the Civil War. McKay built many of the great clipper ships, including the *Flying Cloud*. William Webb built both clipper ships and steamers, and produced more tonnage than any other American before 1860.

In 1831, Webb and Allen built an unusually big revenue boat. It was a time when most of those used along the coast were small and cost only $75 to $200 each. Theirs was an 11-ton boat, constructed for the Cape Florida lighthouse at a cost of $1,100. It measured 35' in deck length, 8½' in width, and drew 4½' of water.[17]

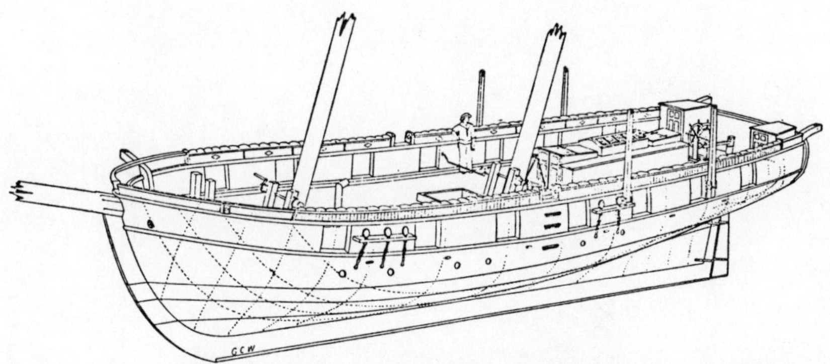

The USRC Morris. (*Courtesy Smithsonian Institution.*)

Most revenue boats were transported to their stations as deck cargo on a cutter or some other vessel, but because of her size the Cape Florida boat was sailed, by Captain Joseph Twiler of the revenue cutter *Pulaski*. On her way south, the boat was wrecked near St. Augustine. Her loss is worth mentioning because there is an extant itemized list of articles she was carrying:

> One revenue ensign, one revenue pendant, one small compas [*sic*], two tin kits, one tin pan, one tinder box, one hand pump, one ball lamp wick, one chart, one binacle [*sic*], one binacle lamp, one campboose [stove], one hawser & kedge, main-sail, fore sail & Jib worm, rigging complete worm, four fifteen gallon Breakers for water . . . (from boat *Georgia* to be returned in the *Marion*), one lantern, one ax, one hatchet, two Buckets, Shipping articles and quarterly accounts in Blank.[18]

The cutters that Webb and Allen built gained a reputation for speed and beauty. After she was finished, the *McLane* sailed to Washington, where a number of congressmen made visits and marvelled at her beautiful lines and fine finish.[19] In *The History of American Sailing Ships* Howard Chapelle wrote that she was considered the "fastest of the class" and "the most beautifully built. Webb and Allen had constructed her with unusual attention, her gun carriages and deck fittings were fine examples of cabinetwork and her brass guns and metal work were highly polished. The inside of her bulwarks were panelled and she was a yacht in finish, inboard and out."[20]

In his praise of the *Dexter*, Samuel Swartwout was even more effusive. When she left New York on 11 December 1832, he wrote Secretary McLane that Webb and Allen had "more than fulfilled their contracts in the

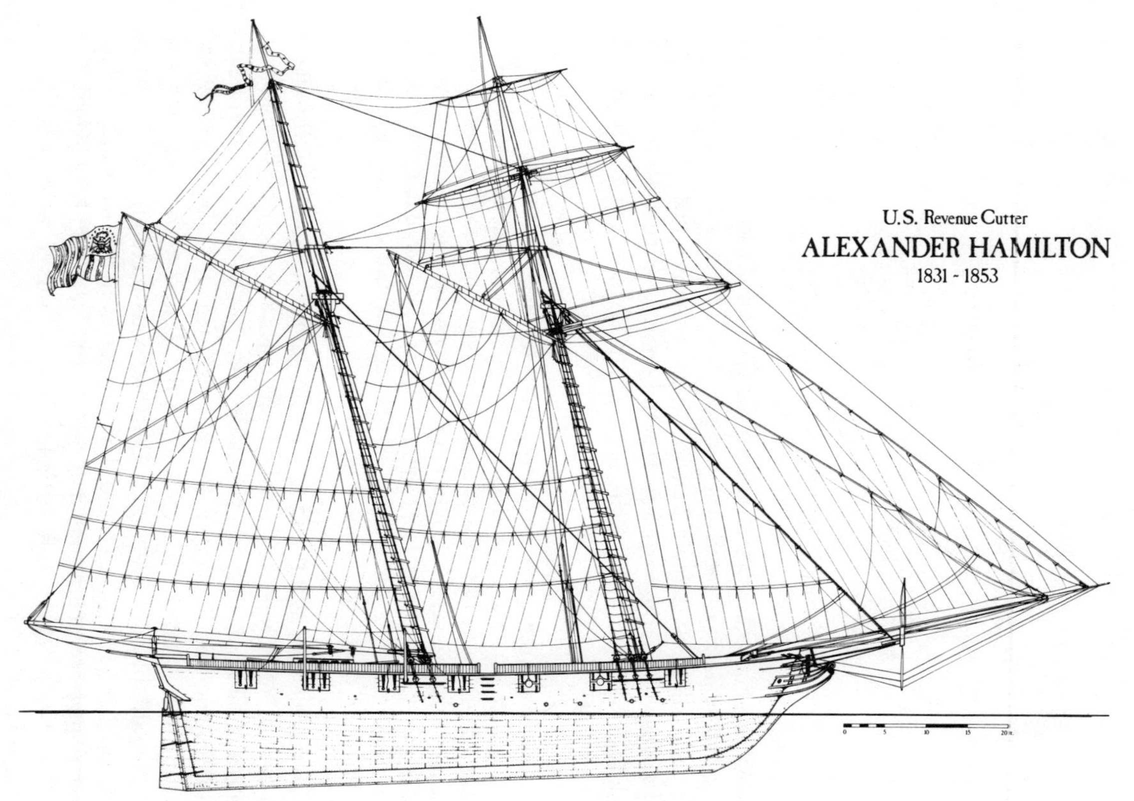

The USRC Alexander Hamilton, 1831–53. (*Drawing by John A. Tilley, courtesy USCG Public Affairs Staff.*)

building of this class of vessels. They are admitted, by judges, to be superior to any, not only in the United States, but in the world, of their tonnage and class."[21] Swartwout added a word of praise for Captain Howard, who had supervised the *Dexter*'s construction. The collector had "never known a more prompt, active, and enterprising officer. . . . The arrangements of the Cabins, quarters and fixtures of the *Dexter* are most judicious; and the tasteful manner in which she has been fitted and furnished . . . is . . . in the highest degree creditable to his taste."[22]

In addition to the cutters already mentioned, the class included the *Campbell*, built in New York, and the *Andrew Jackson*, built at the Washington Navy Yard. In 1833 the *Madison* was built at the Washington Navy Yard under the supervision of the famous constructor William Doughty, and the *Washington* was built at New York. These were followed by three cutters built at Baltimore: the *Levi Woodbury* in 1836, the *Washington* in 1837, and the *Van Buren* in 1839.[23]

Two of the Morris class, the *Crawford* and the *Hamilton*, were lost at sea. The *Crawford* was an especially tough-luck cutter. In an accident on her maiden voyage, she suffered so much damage that she had to return to port for repairs. A second serious accident caused $1,800 worth of damage. Finally on her way to New London, Connecticut, on 15 July 1847, she was lost at Gardiner's Point.[24] The *Hamilton* was destroyed on Charleston Bar because of the stubbornness and stupidity of her skipper, Captain T. C. Rudolph of Georgia. When Rudolph failed to get under way on schedule, he was reprimanded by the collector who controlled his cutter. Rudolph responded angrily and vowed to "go to sea that night or go to h–." True to his word, he departed and lost his cutter. A lone seaman survived by lashing himself to a boat and drifting until he was picked up by a passing steamer.[25]

A third cutter of the class, the *McLane*, capsized and sank off Hadley's Harbor in a tornado on 30 August 1837. She was salvaged and repaired at a cost of $2,000.[26]

The only cutter of the 1830s that was not of the Morris class was the 65-ton *Erie* built at Presque Isle in 1832.[27] Constructed under the supervision of Captain Daniel Dobbins for service on the Great Lakes, she was launched in the spring of 1833.[28]

The *Erie*'s finest hour came four years later. Chafing under British restrictions on self-government, a small group of inland Canadians led an easily suppressed rebellion. When fighting erupted along the New York border, many New Yorkers sympathized with their Canadian neighbors and smuggled arms to them across the Niagara River. Others formed so-called patriot bands and made plans to join the Canadian rebels. The secretary of the treasury responded by ordering Captain Dobbins to proceed to Buffalo with the cutter *Erie* and enforce U.S. neutrality laws.[29]

The *Erie* sailed from the city after which she was named on 15 January 1838 and arrived at Buffalo the following day. By three o'clock that afternoon, she had stood down the Niagara River to protect the steamer *Barcelona*, which a British schooner was threatening. As the *Erie* came to opposite the British vessel, the *Barcelona* proceeded up river ahead of the cutter.[30]

Responding to intelligence received by the collector at Buffalo, the *Erie* spent the next few days patrolling this area to keep the steamboat *New England* from reaching Navy Island with troops and arms.[31]

First Lieutenant Douglass Ottinger played an important role in the events at Buffalo. For two weeks in January and February he served aboard the steamer *Robert Fulton*, which sailed with American troops. Then on 25 February the collector sent him and an armed detachment from the *Erie* to Hamburg, located eight miles up the lake from Buffalo. Upon arrival, Ottinger discovered that an armed mob had taken ammunition from the militia guard. In support of the deputy marshal, he gave chase and succeeded in recovering the ammunition. When he returned to Hamburg Ottinger learned that approximately one hundred patriots had seized powder and cannon from twelve militia guardsmen. Exercising his force of will, Ottinger recovered the weapons and took them to Comstock, where they were placed under guard. A crowd of fifty men that grew to one hundred during the night tried to retake the ammunition, but the cuttermen held on.[32]

At daylight on 27 February Ottinger loaded his men into a sleigh and accompanied the collector, the marshal, and some militia guards onto the lake. At seven o'clock that morning, about five miles from shore, the party drew up before a shanty that housed seventeen patriots. They surrendered and gave up three pieces of artillery and about two hundred stands of arms. On his return to shore Ottinger met Lieutenant Thomas of the U.S. Army, who was going out to destroy the shanty. He accompanied Thomas on his mission and then returned to Erie.[33]

During the spring of 1839, the *Erie* returned to her home base and played a more leisurely role in the protection of U.S. neutrality. She stood by for some time to assist General Brady in case of an emergency, then under Ottinger's command sailed to Detroit. During the greater part of the summer she cruised between Erie and Detroit or west of Detroit, always staying in close touch with Brady.[34]

The career of Captain Dobbins, who supervised the construction of the *Erie*, illustrates better than any other how political patronage affected the lives of nineteenth-century revenue cutter officers. From the service's inception, it had played an important role in their selection, promotion, and assignment, in Dobbins's case to the point of absurdity. Born near Lewiston, Pennsylvania, on 5 July 1776, Dobbins spend most of his life in Erie. Before the War of 1812 he commanded merchant ships on Lake Erie. As a sailing master in the navy during the war, he was "the organizer, initial superintendent, and general 'trouble shooter' for the construction of Commodore Oliver Hazard Perry's famous fleet. . . ." Dobbins resigned from the navy in 1826 and three years later joined the Revenue Cutter Service.[35]

At that time there was just one revenue cutter on the Great Lakes, commanded by Captain Gilbert Knapp. During the scandalous presidential election of 1828, Knapp campaigned against President Jackson with these vitriolic words: "I consider General Jackson a cut-throat and murderer, and his wife a strumpet, and if he should be elected I never will hold an appointment under him." As soon as Jackson took office, he dismissed Knapp and replaced him with Dobbins. During the rebellions in Canada, Dobbins played an important role on the lakes, but success afforded no protection against political change. Following the inauguration of the Whig president William Henry Harrison in 1841, Dobbins was fired without cause and replaced by Knapp. Four years later, James K. Polk returned the Democrats to office and reinstated Dobbins. Zachary Taylor, a Whig, won the election in 1848, and on 9 May 1849 Dobbins was removed from command for the last time. He died as a private citizen in Erie on 29 February 1856.[36]

CHAPTER EIGHT

The Second Seminole War

Between 1836 and 1842, the Revenue Cutter Service employed the *Morris*-class vessels in the Second Seminole War. Begun because the Seminoles refused to obey the federal government's orders to leave their homes in Florida, the war lasted until just a few hundred Seminoles survived. The conflict was basically a land war, but eventually the Indians resorted to guerrilla warfare and retreated into the swamps of southern Florida. Because the swamps were surrounded on three sides by salt water, naval forces were brought into action, and the Revenue Cutter Service joined the fray along with the navy and Marine Corps.

Revenue cutters and naval vessels of the West India Squadron were interchangeable during the war. General Duncan L. Clinch, the first army commander in Florida, asked to have a revenue cutter assigned to cruise along the west coast of Florida. He wanted it to carry orders to the Seminoles, who were to report to Fort Brooke on Tampa Bay and from there be embarked on their journey west. Washington moderated Clinch's request and ordered Commodore Alexander J. Dallas, USN, commander of the West India Squadron, to provide the ship. The Seminoles heard the orders and responded on 28 December 1835 by ambushing an army unit under the command of Major Francis L. Dade, killing Dade and 105 of his 108-man party. By mid-January the Seminoles had killed the Indian agent Wiley Thompson, burned the Cape Florida lighthouse, and so frightened the citizens of Florida that they flocked to the more populous centers of St. Augustine, Jacksonville, Tallahassee, and Fort Brooke. Throughout the first half of 1836 the army tried to crush the Seminoles in western Florida, but they proved difficult to locate and bring to battle. When, as a result, naval vessels were called upon for assistance, revenue cutters were as likely to be called upon as the vessels of the West India Squadron.[1]

Nine cutters participated in this war: the *Dallas*, *Dexter*, *Jackson*, *Campbell*, *Washington*, *Jefferson*, *Madison*, *Van Buren*, and a second *Jefferson*. Some historians have mistakenly reported ten, counting the *Madison*, which fought in the war at two different times, twice.[2]

During the early phase of the war, the United States had no basic naval strategy. Single ships or a handful of vessels simply did whatever the army officers in charge asked of them. This usually amounted to carrying out scouting expeditions, transporting military personnel, harassing the enemy, or operating a blockade. Revenue cutters participated in all of these activities, but since there was no clearly defined strategy, the story of their participation in the early part of the war lacks coherence.

The revenue cutter *Dallas*, stationed at New Orleans under the command of Captain Farnifold Greene, was the first to enter the fray. Following the destruction of Major Dade's expedition, the collector at New Orleans ordered Greene to report to the collector at St. Marks and provide the city with protection. The *Dallas* arrived at St. Marks with her crew, Mrs. Farley, the widow of one of the troopers who died with Dade, Lieutenant Casey of the army, and three Indian chiefs with their interpreters. In addition to protecting the city, a landing party of six men led by Lieutenant C. B. Beaufort took possession of an empty guard boat that they found on the beach.[3]

The *Dexter* also entered the war to protect a city. Reports of a large number of Indians at Pensacola reached Master Commandant Thomas T. Webb, commander of the navy's *Vandalia*. He immediately set out for west Florida, ordering Captain Thomas C. Rudolph of the revenue cutter *Dexter* to return part of Lieutenant Edward T. Doughty's expedition to Tampa Bay while he, Webb, was gone.[4]

In the meantime, army Major General Edmund P. Gaines led a large detachment against a band of Seminoles who moved down the west coast of Florida to escape the expedition. Gaines ordered Captain Ezekiel

Jones of the revenue cutter *Washington* to cut off their retreat. Because Jones's crew was small, he augmented it with navy Lieutenant William Smith, Assistant Surgeon Charles A. Hassler, and fifteen seamen. Thus reinforced, the *Washington* sailed to the Manatee River on 16 March. That night Smith and Jones led twenty-five men ashore, where they found evidence of an Indian encampment. The next day the seamen marched ten miles into the interior without catching a single person, but they did turn up evidence that the Seminoles were moving south toward Sarasota.[5]

Lieutenant Smith discovered an encampment of Indians at the mouth of the Myaca River just eleven days later. Counting twenty-two people in the camp and a number of fires nearby, he realized that his little party was outnumbered and sent two Indian guides to find out how strong the opposition was. The Seminoles met them with leveled guns, and the guides returned without information.[6]

General Winfield Scott, who had recently taken command of the army in Florida, ordered forty crewmen aboard the cutter *Washington* and a barge and, reacting to the recent information about Indian movements, had the vessels proceed to Charlotte Harbor to stop the Seminoles from escaping south into the Everglades. The crew fought a number of skirmishes around Charlotte Harbor in April. They found the body of Dr. Henry B. Crews, the customs inspector, who had been murdered, and took a number of Indian prisoners. The prisoners were put aboard the revenue cutter *Dallas*, which had been sent to reinforce the *Washington*.[7]

Returning to Tampa Bay, Captain Greene of the *Dallas* informed Scott about the concentration of Seminoles inland from Charlotte Harbor. Scott in turn ordered Colonel Persifer F. Smith to proceed to the harbor with his Louisiana volunteers; the *Dallas* and the *Vandalia* were given the job of transporting Smith's expedition. After the ships went aground three miles short of the intended anchorage, the crew made the final leg of their journey in ship's cutters and Indian pirogues. At Charlotte Harbor Smith's Louisianans joined Lieutenant Levin M. Powell, USN, in a search for the Indians that was fruitless but nonetheless important, for it revealed the capabilities of the revenue marines. Colonel Smith praised both Powell and Greene for their handling of the small craft, saying that "when they left their boats they rivalled the best soldiers."[8]

Such abilities might have influenced the decision to order the cutter *Washington* to protect St. Marks in June, where Governor Call of Florida expected a raid by a combined force of Creeks and Seminoles. As a result, the *Washington* augmented her crew with Lieutenant Henry A. Adams, USN, and sixty men from the *Concord*, and on the second sailed for St. Marks to prevent the union of Indian forces and protect the city. The anticipated raid never took place, so after two weeks the *Washington* returned to blockade duty.[9]

The *Washington* and the cutters *Jefferson* and *Dexter* simultaneously carried out a blockade along the west coast of Florida and afforded protection to a number of communities on demand.

Aware of the possibility of arms smuggling during the war, Commodore Dallas of the West India Squadron took action to prevent it. By June of 1836 he had issued orders to three cutters to cruise along the west coast from Anclote Key, located north of Tampa, to Key West in the south. The *Washington* cruised between Anclote Key and Charlotte Harbor, about midway between Tampa and the Everglades. The *Jefferson* covered the area between Charlotte Harbor and Tampa, and the *Dexter* cruised between Charlotte Harbor, Key West, and Indian Key. In October the *Jefferson* extended her cruising grounds southward as far as Key West.[10]

In addition to trying to intercept supplies intended for the Seminoles, the *Jefferson* guarded the coast to prevent the exportation of slaves to Cuba.[11]

Frequently, the cutters were called away from blockade duty to answer the requests of local communities for protection against expected Indian raids. In June 1836, Commodore Dallas ordered Captain John Jackson of the cutter *Jefferson* to provide protection to St. Joseph for as long as it was needed, and the *Dexter* was ordered to stay at Indian Key because of great apprehension about an attack there.[12]

Sometime before June, Secretary of the Treasury Mahlon Dickerson had asked Commodore Dallas to return the cutters to the Treasury Department. But, thinking the Indians might attack along the Florida Keys by canoe at any time, Dallas retained the cutters. There was, he told Dickerson, no time since the cutters had been under his care that they had been more needed than at that moment.[13]

In fact, the cutters remained totally occupied during the Seminole War. Winslow Foster, who succeeded Captain Jackson as skipper of the *Jefferson* on 28 October 1836, wrote the secretary of the treasury on 31 July 1837: "Since I assumed command of the *Jefferson* she has been almost constantly on the move at sea; twice to the West Indies, several times up and down the whole coast of Florida, and on the last expedition to Mexico, and of the one hundred days preceding the 9th instant was actually at sea 73."[14]

Commodore Dallas complained bitterly about the skipper of the *Washington*, who himself was grumbling about how busy his cutter was and how inadequate his crew: "If the Cutters are continued in my command and this Gentleman is not more on the alert, I shall suspend him from his Command and put one of my Lieut. on board. . . ."[15] His observations were unjustified. Captain Ezekiel Jones of the *Dallas* had been extremely active since arriving in Florida, and he and the skippers of the *Washington*, *Dallas*, and *Dexter* were praised by Captain Thomas Webb of the *Vandalia* for their "prompt and ready cooperation with the Army," which had "called forth the highest commendation from the commanding generals who take occasion to eulogize the services rendered by the *Vandalia* and Revenue Cutters." It seems likely that much of the problem between Dallas and Jones resulted from the cutters being ordered to serve with both the army and the West India Squadron, as conditions might warrant.[16] And, of course, cutter captains had additional obligations to the Treasury Department, which meant they often suffered unjustly the wrath of one or another of their superiors. Even contemporary historians sometimes criticize them on this score, pointing out that the communication and command system was complicated by the presence of cutters.[17] While this may be true, it was not the fault of cutter captains that they had so many bosses.

Fortunately, cooperation was more typical of the relationship between the seagoing services. When in July 1837 the treasury secretary requested the return to his department of the cutters *Jefferson* and *Dexter*, the latter was returned in September with Commodore Dallas's "thanks for the promptness, celerity and cheerfulness" with which Captain Rudolph had "discharged the mane and arduous duties" imposed on him and men under his command.[18] The *Washington* had already returned to her cruising grounds at Key West by this time.[19]

An important development occurred during the Seminole War before the cutters were called back into action. In late 1837 and early 1838, Lieutenant Powell took the first steps toward creating a combined riverine force. He recommended a drive into the Everglades by units composed of the regular army, army volunteers, and sailors who would take the war directly to the Seminoles. In many ways, the effort resembled the search-and-destroy missions of the Viet Nam War, except that instead of helicopters small, shallow-draft boats carried the soldiers. Powell hoped that such units would be effective on land or water and that they would be able to use the rivers and waterways of Florida to reach the enemy. His first efforts failed but were significant for leading to the formation of additional combined forces that would make use of revenue cutters.[20]

At about the time Lieutenant Powell questioned the policies of the armed forces, General Thomas S. Jesup stated his conviction that arms and supplies from Havana and New Providence were reaching the Seminoles. He "was convinced that the West India Squadron's blockade was ineffective." In response, Commodore Dallas assigned the schooner *Gram-*

pus to sail off the southern tip of Florida and the cutters *Jefferson* and *Jackson* to cruise along the west coast.[21]

Indian raids against the captain of the Carysfort Reef lightship and along the shore between Key Biscayne and Key West resulted in the assignment to Florida waters of still more cutters. The *Madison* (Captain William A. Howard) arrived at Pensacola for service with the West India Squadron in March 1838. Two months later the *Campbell* and the *Madison* reported for duty to the new army commander, General Zachary Taylor, who had replaced General Jesup.[22]

Taylor planned to isolate the Seminoles by driving them south of the line from Tampa Bay to St. Augustine and cutting them off from the outside world. Cutters cruised out of Cape Sable along both sides of the Florida Peninsula to carry out the second half of Taylor's plan. At the same time, they offered assistance to American merchantmen in Florida waters.[23]

In a series of heavy gales along the Florida coast in September 1838, many an unfortunate mariner fell victim to both the storms and the Seminoles. One gale drove ashore the brig *Alma* of Portland, Maine, bound from Santiago de Cuba to Boston; three fishing sloops, the *Alabama*, *Dread*, and *Caution* from Mystic, Connecticut; and the French brig *Courier de Tampico*. While the Seminoles left the Frenchmen alone, they massacred seventeen fishermen and a number of down-easters. The revenue cutter *Campbell*, commanded by first Lieutenant Napoleon L. Coste, and the naval vessel *Wave* made their way to the scene of the disaster. At five o'clock in the morning Second Lieutenant John Faunce, USRCS, led twenty-three officers and men from the cutter and thirty of the *Wave*'s crew ashore, where they discovered the burnt fishing boats and spotted the *Alma* eight miles away. Manning their boats, they sailed for the *Alma*, where they confronted fifteen Indians in three canoes. Faunce ordered his men to charge, and the sailors tried to cut off the Indian's retreat. After suffering five casualties, the Seminoles deserted their canoes and fled into the swamps. A month later, near Bears Cut, the *Campbell*'s crew killed two Indians who bore "powder pouches decorated with eleven scalps which had been taken from the castaways of the September gale."[24]

Following these attacks, General Taylor increased the number of vessels patrolling Florida waters and refused a Treasury Department request to return the *Campbell* to revenue duty, employing her instead in the blockading force. Thereafter, oared barges carried out the blockade in the bays and inlets at the southern tip of Florida. The schooners *Wave*, *Otsego*, and *Campbell* patrolled along the reef, the sloops-of-war *Boston* and *Ontario* farther offshore.[25]

In 1839 and 1840 the Mosquito Fleet, assembled by Lieutenant John

T. McLaughlin, USN, went on the offensive with great success. The unit, composed of soldiers, sailors, and marines, entered the Everglades in canoes and small boats. Led to the Seminoles by guides who knew the area, McLaughlin's men carried ammunition and supplies for sustained operations.[26]

Prior to 1839, the naval effort had essentially been defensive. The commander of the West India Squadron, in charge of naval affairs, had emphasized seagoing operations. What seemed to be needed was a commander who would aggressively pursue the Seminoles in the Everglades, and hope was kindled in 1839 when all the forces fighting them were placed under one separate command.[27]

As the Mosquito Fleet prepared to take the offensive in 1841, it was doubled in size. Plans called for an enlarged naval force to cut the Seminoles off to the south as the Mosquito Fleet entered the Everglades. This

Combined Operations in the Florida Everglades against the Seminoles. (Courtesy U.S. Naval Historical Center.)

required the employment of revenue cutters, and the Treasury Department offered the services of the *Jefferson* (First Lieutenant Richard Evans), *Jackson* (First Lieutenant John McGowan), and *Van Buren* (Captain H. B. Nones). The army accepted all but the *Jackson*, which was judged unsuited to operate in Florida's coastal waters because of an 11′ draft. The department substituted the *Madison* (Captain J. J. Nimma).[28]

Before their assignment to cruising stations, the crews of the cutters underwent intensive training along the Florida reef. Meanwhile, five detachments of sailors and marines, including a detachment from the *Van Buren* under the command of Lieutenant John B. Marchand, entered the Everglades in support of an army unit already there.[29]

When Lieutenant McLaughlin came to the area at the end of 1841, "he assigned the *Phoenix* and the *Otsego* to cover the passes of the west coast along Biddle's Harbor; the *Madison* and the *Wave* were to cruise along the

reef; the *Jefferson* and the *Van Buren* were sent to patrol the east coast; the *Flirt* was to remain at Key Biscayne acting as a depot for the expedition."[30]

Because the crews of the *Van Buren* and the *Flirt* had been on patrol in the Everglades since their arrival in Florida, McLaughlin gave them a brief rest in Havana in late December. By 13 January they were once again exploring the area around Cocoanut Island, along with a marine detachment under Lieutenant Marchand.[31]

In February, Colonel William J. Worth estimated that there were no more than 300 Seminoles left in Florida, of them perhaps 140 in the Everglades. Believing that he could not bring so few in by force, he wanted to terminate the war, but his wishes were frustrated and so once again a detachment of men from the *Madison* and the *Jefferson* entered the cypress swamp east of Lake Okeechobee. For two fruitless months they lived in dugout canoes that measured 30' by 4', under conditions that compared unfavorably even with those of men digging the nation's canals at the time. Rogers reported pulling the canoes over "floating grass and weeds, so strongly matted together that the men stood upon the mass and hauled the boats over it," while others commented on the acrid smell of the swamp.[32]

The objective of the operations was to keep pressure on the Seminoles, never allowing them to settle down for planting or harvesting. If this could be accomplished their capacity to fight would be destroyed. During the last two years of the war the raids, though few in number, were successful, keeping the Indians on the move and reducing them to a hungry, poorly supplied ragtag band.[33]

The effectiveness of the Mosquito Fleet's blockade is harder to measure. It is true that no supply ships were seized, but by April 1842 the Seminoles had just five kegs of powder left, and they were forced to hunt with bows and arrows and fire their guns only in combat.[34]

John Spencer, the secretary of war, finally authorized an end to hostilities on 10 May 1842. On 19 July the *Jefferson*, *Van Buren*, and *Madison* sailed into the navy base at Norfolk, ending the Florida expedition for the Revenue Cutter Service. By the end of October all three cutters were back on station enforcing U.S. revenue laws—the *Van Buren* at Charleston, the *Madison* at New London, and the *Jefferson* at Key West.[35]

The concept of riverine warfare, while it was slow to develop during the Second Seminole War, did develop fully. At the outset of the conflict the navy simply ran a passive blockade and carried out harassing raids against the Seminoles. As mentioned earlier, by the end, combined navy, army, marine, and revenue cutter forces were carrying the conflict to the enemy in operations very much like the search-and-destroy missions of the Viet Nam War. At the same time, three-deep blockading patrols shut the enemy off from the outside world.[36] In this conflict, the Revenue Cutter Service was needed by the nation for operations in the shallow water of southern Florida. Over a century later, the Coast Guard would be called upon to supplement naval units under similarly trying circumstances in the coastal and riverine environment of Viet Nam. In both cases the service proved its flexibility and its great worth to the nation.

CHAPTER NINE

The Reforms of Alexander Fraser

At the end of the Second Seminole War Congress launched an attack on the Revenue Cutter Service. This was the result of a number of developments. The cost of operating the service had risen during the war, while, because of the Compromise Tariff of 1833 and the Panic of 1837, the revenue it brought in had declined. When Secretary of the Treasury Walter Forward predicted a national deficit of $14 million, Congress undoubtedly felt that the service should increase its collections and operate more efficiently. An additional problem was that some officers were being assigned for their own convenience rather than for the good of the service.[1]

A power struggle between the executive department and Congress complicated matters. Congress realized that its power of the purse was weakened when it lost or failed to exercise the right to appropriate money for specific executive functions annually. Leonard White wrote in *The Jacksonians* that the Committee of Public Expenditures had "discovered what it thought a dangerous situation in the revenue cutter service." The committee reported

> a naval force springing up amongst us, controlled by the Secretary of the Treasury, accountable to no one but him, extended at will by him, supported by him out of the revenue before it gets into the Treasury, and [which] may cost the country whatever he shall direct. He appropriates and pays, without the sanction of Congress, and even without its knowledge. The country knows nothing of the expenditure, unless called for by either House. The collectors of the ports pay the expenses of this Treasury navy, and the Secretary of the Treasury approves or rejects the expenditures. The crews, ships, and boats, are subject to their order, for pleasure, interest, or public service.[2]

Secretary Forward responded to this criticism by instilling a spirit of enterprise in the service and promoting economy in its operations. In a circular letter dated November 1842, he reminded officers that they must remain at sea intercepting foreign ships approaching the United States. He noted that special vigilance was necessary because Congress had just passed a new protective tariff. Simultaneously he called for a reduction in cutter expenditures, limiting government-funded furnishings to one mahogany table and one oilcloth carpet for each cabin and wardroom. The cabin could have four cane-seat stools, the wardroom six. Lights were allowed, and cutters north of Charleston could have a sheet-iron stove. Officers were to pay for any other comforts out of their own pockets.[3]

Just three months after censuring officers for inactivity, Forward went to their defense because the very existence of the service was threatened. Congress had charged the Senate Commerce Committee with investigating the expediency of abolishing the Revenue Cutter Service and employing the navy to perform those of its tasks still deemed necessary. When Senator J. W. Huntington, the chairman of the Commerce Committee, asked the Treasury Department for an opinion on the notion, Forward opposed it unequivocally. Collecting revenue was properly a Treasury Department function, he argued. Having the navy assigned to such work would create problems: his department could not discipline naval officers, and past experience had shown that they were not suited to revenue work. Forward defended the officers of the Revenue Cutter Service on the grounds that they were "generally . . . faithful, competent and vigilant in the discharge of their duties. . . ."[4]

With Forward's support the service did survive, but it underwent substantial changes as a result of congressional scrutiny. Forward's successor, John C. Spencer, led the reforms. By nature a stern, indeed frightening, man, Spencer was not popular. He grew up in Hudson, New York, and attended Union College, from which he graduated with high honors in

1806. After graduation he became a brilliant, self-reliant lawyer who rose rapidly in his profession, serving as a member of the New York house, speaker of the New York assembly, and special prosecuting attorney in the famous Morgan case. For his revision of the statutes of the State of New York Spencer gained a reputation as one of the ablest lawyers of his day. He was an early member of the Anti-Masonic Party in New York, and in 1842 President John Tyler appointed him secretary of war. His success in that post played a role in his selection as secretary of the treasury.[5]

Upon entering office in March 1843, Spencer found that it was impossible to exercise control over the personnel or expenditures of the Revenue Cutter Service. "The clerks," he noted "could not be expected to be seafaring men. . . ."—that is, the persons in Washington charged with supervising the service did not know enough about its operations to do the job. Spencer reorganized the service under the provisions of a law passed in 1843 and strengthened centralized administrative control in Washington. Then, to "take charge of the business," he assigned to its Washington headquarters the first captain commandant of the bureau, Alexander V. Fraser. Second Lieutenant George Hayes was to be Fraser's assistant.[6]

Spencer's actions began half a century of confusion about the Revenue Cutter Service's name. In almost all government documents and correspondence before 1843, the organization was referred to as the Revenue Cutter Service or the Revenue Service, the cutters as revenue cutters or cutters. Moreover, the 1843 law did not establish an official name for the service but rather added to the old ones the names Revenue Marine Service and Revenue Marine. Finally in 1863 Congress officially sanctioned the designation Revenue Cutter Service. But that did not solve the problem, for Revenue Marine Service continued to be used along with Revenue Cutter Service until the mid-1890s, when Revenue Cutter Service began to hold sway. For convenience I am going to continue to use Revenue Cutter Service in this book.

To return to Fraser, he brought to his assignment a rich seagoing background. After attending the Mathematical, Nautical, and Commercial School in New York City, where he learned navigation and astronomy, Fraser sailed as a mate and then a master in the West Indies Trade. In 1832 President Andrew Jackson commissioned him a second lieutenant in the Revenue Cutter Service. He first cruised aboard the *Alert* during the Nullification Controversy, in which South Carolina challenged the authority of the federal government to enforce tariff laws, when the winter cruising program was still young. From 1833 to 1835 he lobbied for a promotion to first lieutenant. In spite of support from the *Alert*'s skipper, former Treasury Secretary Dallas, and the Democratic Club of the City of

Captain Alexander Fraser. (Oil painting by Irwin D. Hoffman, Claire White-Peterson photo, courtesy USCGA Library.)

New York, he failed to win promotion, and returned to merchant shipping as skipper of the *Himmaleh*. Between March 1836 and March 1838 he sailed to Japan, China, and the Malay Archipelago, and on returning home learned that he had been promoted during his absence. As a first lieutenant he sailed once again aboard the *Alert*. In 1841 Captain Nicholas Bicker retired, and Fraser gained command of the cutter. With the support of New York marine insurance officials he was finally promoted to captain in 1842, whereupon he took command of the *Ewing*, a new cutter built the year before at Baltimore.[7]

The team of Spencer and Fraser greatly improved the Revenue Cutter Service. Spencer brought to the job from his past service as secretary of war administrative experience, and Fraser added a knowledge of the sea.

The commandant probably suggested most of the reforms, which he might have presented to Spencer in detail. The latter made sure they were put into practice.[8]

Fraser's duties were broad-ranging and important. He carried on a voluminous correspondence with customs collectors and cutter commanders. Control of accounts and of the service's property were his responsibility. He watched over the construction, repair, and maintenance of all cutters and he assigned their cruising grounds. He also appointed all officers and investigated all charges against revenue cutter personnel.

One of Fraser's first acts as commandant was to survey the condition of the service, and so on 9 January 1844 he issued the first annual report of the Revenue Cutter Service. According to the report, there were then 493 men on active duty: 80 commissioned officers, 45 petty officers, 30 stewards, 15 cooks, and 323 seamen. Fifteen schooners, ranging in size from 60 to 170 tons, made up the fleet, which sailed out of Eastport, Portland, Boston, Newport, New London, New York, Delaware Bay, Baltimore, Norfolk, Charleston, Savannah, Key West, Mobile, New Orleans, and Lake Erie. Two cutters, the *Duane* at Mobile and the *Erie* on Lake Erie, were worthless, and the *Nautilus* at Key West belonged to the Coast Survey. Five important stations had no cutters: New Bedford, Portsmouth, Lake Ontario, eastern Maine, and Florida between the Dry Tortugas and Pensacola. The cost of operating the service in 1843 was $205,854.[9]

Fraser and Spencer were successful with their personnel policies. They started a merit system for the appointment and promotion of officers, and they hired the service's first engineering officers. Beginning in 1843, new officers entered the service as third lieutenants, between eighteen and twenty-five years of age. By 1845, promotion beyond second lieutenant required the approval of an examining board, proof of navigational ability and seamanship, and positive character references from two captains in the service. That same year the service assigned to each steam cutter a chief engineer and an assistant engineer, both inferior in rank to all deck officers.[10] Chief engineers received the pay of first lieutenants, assistant engineers that of third lieutenants. Never were engineers to be left in charge of a ship, and when not running machinery they could be called on deck to trim sails, wash decks, and perform other tasks.[11]

Fraser and Spencer improved the lot of enlisted men. They issued new regulations that ended the practice of officers shipping personal slaves to act as servants or crew members and keeping their salaries, and they placed restrictions on flogging. In this, Fraser may have been influenced by the example of Captain Josiah Sturgis of the *Hamilton*, of whom the nautical editor of the *Boston Morning Post* wrote:

Captain Josiah Sturgis. (Oil painting by George Sottung, Claire White-Peterson photo, courtesy USCGA *Library.)*

> Capt. Sturgis has now on board men who have sailed with him many years, and the crew, to a man, with whom we have conversed, consider the cutter a floating paradise, and her captain as their best friend. Let it always be remembered by the despots who manufacture discipline with colts and cats, that this state of things on board the cutter has been accomplished by kindness. Flogging is unknown on board of her, yet a better regulated crew or a neater vessel cannot be found upon the bosom of the ocean.

In addition, petty officers, boatswains, gunners, and carpenters, who had formerly held their ratings at the pleasure of the captain, were given warrants issued by the secretary of the treasury, and their pay was increased from twenty to thirty dollars a month.[12]

Secretary Spencer reported the results of these changes, one would assume, with a certain sense of pride. "The officers and men," he wrote, "feel that the service has been elevated, and a corresponding zeal in the discharge of their duty has been strikingly exhibited."[13]

When Fraser assumed command the service needed a new fleet of cutters, so in his first annual report he called for the construction of new iron steamers. The impetus for steam cutters came from the New York customs office and the shipping interests of the nation. In 1829 Samuel Swartwout, the New York collector, recommended replacing the revenue cutter *Richard Rush* with a steamer to cruise in Long Island Sound. "The commerce of the East & much of the West Indies trade," he wrote, came "down the Sound. All the plaster Vessels from Nova Scotia enter[ed] by that route." The cutter could not make any heading when the wind was adverse, and at times it continued for ten days from the east, confining her to the mooring. This afforded great opportunity for smuggling. No amount of effort could force the vessel against the wind or allow her crew to detect frauds carried out within fifty miles of their anchorage. "No other species of force [than steam cutters]," Swartwout concluded, ". . . can ever prove effective in the Sound."[14]

After a long delay because of the estimated cost, construction of iron steamers finally went ahead under the direction of Secretary Walter Forward. In 1839 he ordered two steamers built, the *Legare* and the *Spencer.* Thus when Fraser assumed command R. and G. L. Schuyler in New York was already building the *Legare,* which was to be driven by an Ericsson screw propeller, and the West Point Foundry Association was building the *Spencer* and fitting her with a Hunter wheel.[15]

In his 1844 annual report, Fraser advocated building additional iron steamers. He wrote that smugglers were operating at an advantage on the Great Lakes, where steamers were running away from sailing cutters, in the Gulf of Mexico, where strong currents favored steamboats, and along the Atlantic coast, where smugglers ran goods into shore with ease. He argued that steam cutters were needed to restore some edge to the service. Steam would be of great utility in operations around headlands and for penetration of bays and inlets under all weather conditions, and, he claimed, erroneously as it turned out, it would not be much more expensive than sail. The *Legare* and the *Spencer* would perform as well under canvas as any sailing cutter, so steam could be used solely as auxiliary power. To further conserve it, commanders could be held strictly accountable for its use.[16]

Fraser endorsed iron, which he felt was superior to wood. It was no longer doubted that iron vessels would float; he pointed out additionally that they were stronger than wooden vessels and thus could better stand the shock of grounding on a bar. As for cost, they were cheaper when maintenance expenses for a twelve-year period were added to the price of construction. He figured a 350-ton iron steamer would cost $50,000, a wooden sail boat of the same size, $62,500. Iron would also outlast wood, and be safer from fire and leaking. With iron hulls, marine borers would cease to be a problem and copper bottoms would not be needed. Red lead would deter rust and corrosion, and marine paint would protect the hull.[17]

Captain Fraser was undoubtedly right to advocate iron and steam, but he failed to anticipate the enormous difficulties that would confront the service during the transition from wood and sail. Nor did he take into account the primitive state of marine engineering, the difficulty of combining sail and steam, or the problem of selecting a proper propulsion system.

The service was not setting any precedents by starting the construction of steam cutters in 1839, and Fraser was not blazing new trails in his 1844 annual report. The application of steam power to ship propulsion had started before the War of 1812. The successful operation of Robert Fulton's *Clermont* in 1807 saw the first major advance in marine technology in more than two hundred years. In 1838 the *Sirius* and *Great Western* crossed the Atlantic using steam power alone. Five years later the *Princeton* went to sea as the first propeller-driven steamer and the *Great Britain* as the first screw-propelled, iron-hulled steamer.[18]

In 1839, the problem for the service was to decide between two experimental systems. Efforts were made to sell the service a screw propeller designed by the famous Swedish engineer John Ericsson and a wheel designed by Lieutenant William H. Hunter of the U.S. Navy. Construction was already under way on one of each when Fraser took the helm. The *Legare* was being fitted with an Ericsson screw and the *Spencer* with a Hunter wheel. Unfortunately for Fraser and the service, the decision was made to proceed with several ships propelled by the Hunter wheel.

The reluctance of the Revenue Cutter Service to adopt the Ericsson screw is not so surprising in light of the record of the British navy. During the 1820s and 1830s it rejected steam altogether because paddles were vulnerable to shot. In 1837 the tugboat *Francis B. Ogden*, which was fitted with an Ericsson screw, actually "towed the Lords of Admiralty in their own barge at the rate of ten miles per hour. The submerged screw was the obvious answer to the vulnerability of the paddle." Nevertheless, the

Admiralty accepted then-current theories that the screw could not work and, denying its own observations, rejected the screw. It was then that Ericsson and his screw "were snapped up by Capt. Stockton of the U.S. Navy and vanished to America." Perhaps the knowledge that experimentation with the screw could be carried out by the Revenue Cutter Service made the decision to press ahead with it easier for the U.S. Navy.[19]

When the navy did proceed, it went with the Hunter wheel. Lieutenant Hunter designed a propulsion system that featured paddle wheels mounted horizontally on the hull of a ship. He first tried to sell his system to the service. After it turned him down, he convinced the navy to give his wheel a chance. The navy then built an experimental steamer, the *Union*, which led the service to reconsider its earlier decision. Captain William A. Howard sailed aboard the *Union* and reported that under steam power alone she sped along at well over ten miles an hour in smooth water and make eight knots with ease in a heavy sea with fresh breezes dead ahead. "Close hauled under canvas alone," Howard reported, she sailed "remarkably fast, in fact is a match for almost any pilot boat . . . and will beat any vessel I ever saw." Without hesitation he concluded that the *Union* could "compete with any vessel in the world, either under steam or canvas, particularly in heavy weather."[20]

With such a glowing report from the officer assigned to evaluate the propulsion system, the service contracted on 20 April 1843 to install Hunter wheels in four of its first steamers. Only after he began to supervise their construction did Howard realize his mistake and recognize the obvious inferiority of the wheel to the screw propeller. Belatedly he tried to reverse his decision , an action that resulted in his firing by Secretary of the Treasury George M. Bibb. It was at this stage that Fraser assumed responsibility for the construction of the Hunter cutters.

Shortly thereafter, the first two steam cutters finally went to sea and the inferiority of the Hunter wheel was confirmed. Captain Howard assumed command of the *Spencer*, which had a Hunter wheel, at New York. The *Legare*, equipped with an Ericsson screw propeller, was assigned cruising grounds between Tampa Bay and Cape Florida. After the two cutters had been at sea a short time Fraser reported that the *Legare* had covered the seventeen miles between the Narrows and Sandy Hook in an hour and fifty-six minutes, while the *Spencer* took over two and a half hours to cover the same course. Furthermore, some of the *Spencer*'s belts and metal had melted. Her blowoff pipe tore away from its fastenings and "the arches of the boiler settled."[21] To make matters worse, three more Hunter-wheel cutters were building: the *McLane* at Boston (Cyrus

Alger), the *Dallas* at Buffalo (Stitmann-Strotton), and the *Bibb* at Pittsburgh (Freeman, Knap and Tatten).

By 1845, the Franklin Institute had reported the Hunter wheel to be a total failure and Captain Fraser was calling for sidewheel steamers. What accounted for this development in part was the *Bibb*'s maiden voyage. Following her completion at Pittsburgh, she headed down the Ohio River toward New Orleans. Packing in her wheel casings, which was impossible to get at, began to leak badly. The skipper had no choice but to run the *Bibb* aground in order to keep her from sinking. She was subsequently pumped out and towed to Cincinnati, where her Hunter wheels were removed and their recesses boxed over. Sidewheels were then installed, and the *Bibb* joined the Hunter-wheel cutters *McLane*, *Spencer*, and *Dallas* in a conversion to either sidewheels or propellers.[22]

Captain Howard, who had convinced the service that it should build the Hunter-wheel cutters, was subsequently given command of the *Spencer*, and then the *Bibb* and finally the *McLane*. He continued to rail against the Hunter-wheel and tried desperately to get off the ships that he had earlier promoted. Treasury Secretary R. J. Walker responded to his requests with a letter that dispensed pure justice:

> Experience has long since convinced this Department of the entire failure of these vessels to meet its reasonable expectations. Expectations founded chiefly upon your own assurances and representations, before their construction was commenced.
>
> Annexed is an extract from a letter addressed by you to this Department dated June 1st 1843, to which it is well to direct your attention at the present moment. The charge of their superintendency was placed under your entire control, and it was not until the vessels were completed, the outfits furnished at a cost far exceeding the most extravagant expectations, and their services required, that the announcement of their failure is made by you.
>
> Having therefore been mainly instrumental in inducing the adoption of plans, in which all the rules of Naval Architecture as well as Mechanics are denied, it is but just that the opportunity should be afforded to you, to realize by practical experience, the lasting injury which has thus been inflicted upon the service, as well as the injustice which has been done to the Government.[23]

While the Hunter-wheel cutters were a disaster, they were not kept in regular service for very long. The *Bibb* and the *Dallas* were transferred to the Coast Survey, and the latter, which had cost the government $82,952 to build, was then taken to New York, where she sold for $3,000. The *McLane* and the *Spencer* served out their lives as lightships, the *McLane* at Ship Island shoal in the Gulf of Mexico, the *Spencer* at the entrance to Hampton Roads.[24]

Two of the new steamers, the *Legare* and the *Jefferson*, were 140′-long screw-driven steamers designed by John Ericsson. Built in New York by R. and G. L. Schuyler, both cutters performed well under steam power alone but proved to be poor sailers—they were too narrow to carry sail effectively. The *Legare* proved her worth by racing the British sidewheel merchant ship *Great Western* from the Battery to Sandy Hook. After giving the *Great Western* a thirty-minute head start, the *Legare* beat her under bare poles, covering the eighteen-mile course in one hour and twenty-seven minutes.[25] This victory helped to confirm the superiority of the screw propeller.

Two additional steam cutters, the sidewheelers *Polk* and *Walker*, were poorly built and turned out to be complete failures. J. R. Anderson built the former at Richmond, J. Tomlinson the latter at Pittsburgh.[26] The service changed the *Polk* into a bark and used her as a marine hospital at San Francisco before selling her out of the service. The *Walker*, run down, foundered off Barnegat.[27]

Additional problems plagued the iron steamers. Their hulls fouled badly. Officers' and crew's quarters were unsuitable and uncomfortable. Boiler after boiler burned out. In all, the experience was a disaster. The service built eight steamers at a total cost of $620,000, and not one proved adequate as a cutter.[28] Even the *Legare*, the most successful of the early steamers, ended her life as a lightship at Pass Mary Ann. The service understandably reverted to wooden sailing ships and did not go back to steam cutters until it built the *Harriet Lane* just before the Civil War. The navy did not enjoy much success with its first steam warships either, although the fact was of little comfort to the Revenue Cutter Service.

After 1838, the Revenue Cutter Service worked to enforce U.S. laws regulating steamboats at sea. The first call for action arose in the House Committee on Commerce after a number of disastrous explosions in 1824 and 1826. The committee reported the danger as follows: "From habitual impunity the engine workers disregard the danger, and rather than suffer a boat to pass them, will increase the pressure of the steam to a dangerous extent. In addition to this risk, accidents may occur from carelessness, inattention, or drunkenness."[29]

Realizing that the nation was in no mood for regulation, committee members approached the issue cautiously but still proposed that every steamboat be licensed and every boiler inspected and fitted with two safety valves. While such regulations seem reasonable today, they were declared totally unacceptable by the Jeffersonians. Secretary of the Treasury William H. Crawford disposed of the matter in a sentence: "I am of opinion, that legislative enactments are calculated to do mischief, rather than to prevent it, except such as subject the owners and managers of those boats to suitable penalties in case of disasters, which cannot fail to render the masters and engineers more attentive, and the owners more particular in the selection of those officers."[30]

The failure to act was costly. Explosions destroyed fourteen percent of all steamers operating in 1832 and killed a thousand persons in the process. In 1838 and 1839 many new and nearly new steamers were totally lost. The *Motto* sank in three minutes when her boilers blew up off the coast of Texas, and the *Wilmington* went to the bottom north of Cape Florida. The disaster of the year occurred on 14 June when the *Pulaski*'s boilers exploded, resulting in the loss of over one hundred lives.[31]

The *Pulaski*, considered one of the finest vessels of her type, was a new sidewheel steamer that measured 260′ in length and 25′ in beam, and displaced 680 tons. Her steam plant could generate 200 horsepower. On 13 June 1838 she left Savannah with ninety passengers aboard. She stopped overnight at Charleston, where she added sixty-five more, and on 14 June left Charleston heading north toward Baltimore. After passing Cape Romain, she changed to a more easterly course. The wind came up from the east, causing the steamer to pitch and roll uncomfortably. Her skipper took her well out to sea past Cape Fear and Frying Pan Shoals. Thirty miles off New River, North Carolina, her starboard boiler exploded and blew her midships to pieces. Almost one half of those aboard were "drowned, scalded to death, or crushed by falling masts and spars" in the first forty-five minutes after the explosion. Only fifty-nine of the nearly two hundred aboard were saved. Fifteen survived in the *Pulaski*'s two yawls, six made it to shore in her small boat, and eight floated ashore on small sections of wreckage. Captain Davis in the schooner *Henry Camerdon* picked up thirty people who had spent four awful days adrift on the bow section and a small raft.[32]

Following the loss of the *Pulaski*, Congress finally took action to regulate all ships propelled by steam. Legislation dated 7 July 1838 created the Steamboat Inspection Service, which would be responsible for checking hulls and boilers in steamboats, employing skilled engineers to stand watches, and equipping steamboats with lifeboats, fire pumps, and hoses.[33]

From the beginning, the Revenue Cutter Service enforced the law at sea for the Steamboat Inspection Service. During routine boarding operations, cutter personnel examined certificates of compliance and checked on required safety equipment. In 1942, during World War II, the successor to the Steamboat Inspection Service, the Bureau of Marine Inspection and Navigation, would be temporarily transferred to the Coast Guard; in 1946 the transfer was made permanent.

Under Fraser's leadership, the Revenue Cutter Service made its first effort to consolidate control of two other government agencies that also ultimately came under the Coast Guard umbrella: the U.S. Life-Saving Service and the U.S. Lighthouse Service.

Although formerly cutter personnel had spent most of their time collecting revenue and enforcing U.S. revenue laws, they always served the maritime community in other ways as well, for example working aids to navigation and assisting collectors responsible for the Lighthouse Service. During Fraser's tenure they continued to perform such tasks, and occasionally the duty was hazardous. The revenue cutter *Massachusetts* (Captain John Foster Williams) helped Benjamin Lincoln to supervise the construction of a beacon on Boon Island off the coast of Maine. While attempting to take a carpenter and two of his assistants off the island, Williams's boat was swamped and the men drowned. Undaunted, Williams proceeded to the mainland where he hired a boat and crew, then returned to the island and removed additional workmen without further incident.[34]

A quarter of a century later, when the Boon Island lighthouse needed repairmen, the *Detector* (Captain William A. Howard) transported them. Although the service had Howard return to his cruising grounds immediately after delivering them, it is significant that he was ordered in the first place to go out of his way in assisting the Lighthouse Service.[35]

Collector John Chandler of Portland assigned broader tasks to Lieutenant Green Walden, who replaced Howard as captain of the *Detector*. Walden had to visit the lighthouses at Franklin Island, Pemaquid, Monhegan Island, White Head, Matinicus Rock, Bakers Island, Petit Manan, Libby Island, Mount Desert Rock, and Moose Peake, all off the coast of Maine. He delivered letters to the keepers and returned their communications to the collector. Each light was inspected and Walden noted any repairs that were needed, along with their probable cost.[36]

Cutter captains routinely transported supplies and provisions to lighthouse and lightship keepers. In one instance, an officer may have profited from this service. In July 1826, the *Vigilant* (Captain John Webster) carried a lighthouse keeper, three or four women, and provisions from Baltimore to the Dry Tortugas. Many of the passengers suffered from sea sickness en route, and when the cutter arrived at its destination, and Webster

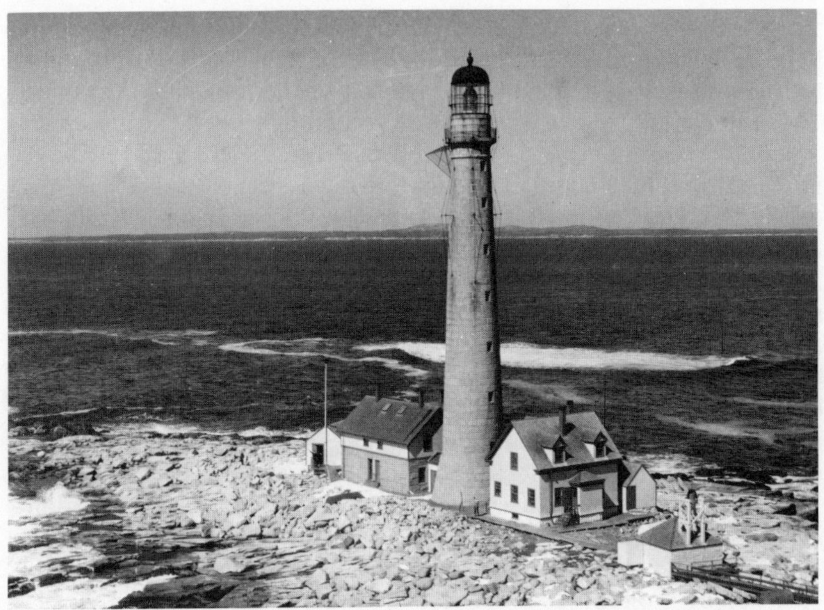

Boon Island Light Station, Second Tower, 1855. (U.S. *Coast Guard official photo.*)

learned that the keeper had not brought along his own provisions, he provided him with $150 of articles. These included some that Webster had shipped as a private "adventure for profit at those places he was bound to where a scarcity of such usually prevails." This author has found no other reference to a private venture by a revenue cutter officer, and although Collector J. H. McCulloch mentioned the details of the case in a letter to Secretary Rush, he did no more than note that he had accepted Webster's bill subject to the secretary's direction.[37] Unfortunately, no response from Rush has been found, so we do not know his official policy in the matter. Nor do we know if Webster was paid for the articles he supplied.

Four years later Joshua Taylor, the collector at Ocracoke, asked Webster, now commanding the revenue cutter *Dallas*, to transport two spar buoys and a contractor to the North and South Inlet near Federal Point. The buoys had not been installed because Taylor was unable to deliver them at a reasonable cost. Webster refused, saying he could not provide transportation without special instructions. Taylor appealed the decision to Secretary Ingham, arguing that because his work required him to go to New Bern, and because the lightboat was unavailable, Webster should transport the buoys and contractor himself. Taylor's appeal bore fruit; in June 1830 Ingham ordered Captain Webster to transport the buoys to the North and South Inlet, and in the future to perform similar duty under Taylor's direction.[38]

Ingham's decision did not end the controversy. When the Cargsford Reef lightboat *Florida* needed oil, Collector W. A. Whitehead of Key West decided to obtain a small amount from Havana and ordered the *Pulaski* (Captain Joseph Swiles) to take him to the island, if that would not conflict with instructions from the Mobile collector who usually supervised the cutter. Swiles agreed to get the oil but refused to take Whitehead aboard, claiming that to do so would violate his orders. In the meantime, the *Marion* arrived in port from a cruise, and to avoid conflict Whitehead decided to sail aboard her. He did, however, inquire about his rights in the case, and as Ingham was still secretary of the treasury he probably won the support he sought.[39]

Cutter captains continued to write sailing directions for the nation's coastal waters. On 5 September 1832 John Chandler, the collector at Portland and the superintendent of lighthouses in Maine, ordered Captain Henry Hunter to proceed in the revenue cutter *Morris* "with as little delay as possible, . . . to the Light House, on Brown's Head, at the Western entrance of the Fox Island thoroughfare, and take such observations and bearings of the Light House, from some of the most prominent objects in its vicinity, as may be necessary to give the most satisfactory information to mariners navigating that part of the Coast."[40]

Cutters also continued to set buoys in coastal waters. Four different kinds were in use by 1808, but two were so expensive as to be almost obsolete. Those worked by the cutter *Massachusetts* were circular, less costly, and well constructed, of seasoned white pine, without sap, which was put into a baker's oven after the bread had been removed. The staves, which were fitted for use, were 5′ long. The buoys measured 4′ in diameter at the largest head and 8″ at the smallest. Each buoy was set up and hooped with eight double-riveted hoops of iron and stapled. A chain of 6″ links was fashioned to the small end of the buoy, which was painted and moored to the bottom by a 2,500-pound sinker. Smaller buoys were used in the harbor, but Boston's collector, Benjamin Lincoln, had had no success with them in shoal water where coasters caught them on their rudders and carried them off station before they could be cleared from the vessel.[41]

Sporadic inspections of aids to navigation had been made prior to Fraser's tenure. As early as 1829, the New York collector Samuel Swartwout recommended that cutter officers be instructed to observe the manner in which lighthouses were kept and report their findings from time to time. Two years later the revenue cutter *Morris* (Captain Richard Derby) carried out a general examination of the coast, inspecting both cutters and their cruising grounds. The *Roger B. Taney* followed up with a special inspection cruise between Maine and Texas in 1834. Acting under pressure from Congress, the fifth auditor of the treasury, Stephen Pleasanton, appointed Lieutenant Napoleon L. Coste in 1837 to survey the Chesapeake Bay's southern coast to determine whether additional lighthouses were needed. Sailing in the *Campbell*, Coste initiated a project to erect a light at Bodie Island, North Carolina, which was placed in operation in the spring of 1848. In May 1846, H. D. Hunter cruised the entire coast of the United States in the revenue cutter *Jackson*, inspecting cutters, their stations, and lighthouses. Within the year he sailed the *Levi Woodbury* to New Orleans, and he stopped at various points along the way to inspect buoys and perform other tasks.[42]

But on 10 May 1843 Fraser institutionalized the regular inspection of lighthouses and aids to navigation by revenue cutter officers. Two years later, on 19 February 1845, Secretary George M. Bibb ordered that thereafter all correspondence about lighthouses be directed through the chief of the Revenue Marine Bureau, thus essentially placing the Lighthouse Service under the control of the Revenue Cutter Service. Although collectors continued to supervise the lights in their districts, revenue cutter officers took over their inspection.[43]

Fraser also started a movement to cooperate with the Life-Saving Service, surely one of the most noble organizations ever run by the U.S. government. Following the loss of the Black Ball liner *Albion* on the coast of Ireland in 1822, which resulted in a great loss of life, two men demonstrated a life-preserving dress in the waters around Governors Island, New York. Apparently life preservers were subsequently sold to any passengers who cared to buy them, but they were not widely used until after a wreck off Hatteras in 1837, when passengers wearing them "were among the few survivors." They seem to have been provided thereafter only to coastal steamers, and a very long time passed before the government required operators to provide them for all passengers.[44]

In the winter of 1836–37, two shipwrecks on Long Island increased interest in the construction of lifeboats for use from shore as well as on shipboard. The New York boatbuilder Joseph Francis designed and built a lifeboat with watertight compartments around 1837. In 1839 a New Orleans packet advertised its intention to sail with his lifeboat, which it was claimed could sustain all passengers. The next day an editorial remarked that lifesaving devices were of much greater importance "than damask tablecloths, silver forks, or anything which is merely intended to please the eye." Nonetheless, many lives were lost over years of sailing before adequate life preservers or lifeboats were provided for passengers.[45]

Lifeboats were becoming increasingly common at shore stations. Volunteers at Rockaway had one by the end of 1837, and newspapers began to urge their use all along the New York and New Jersey shores. The Massachusetts Humane Society, which after incorporation in 1791 had built small unmanned huts on the outer beaches of Massachusetts, crude one-story buildings that housed a stove and food for use by shipwrecked mariners, erected the first lifeboat station at Cohasset in 1807. By 1845 it operated eighteen lifeboat stations and many huts of refuge.[46]

A national rescue organization had to await the shocking loss of life that attended the flood of immigration after the Irish potato famine of 1846 and the unsuccessful revolution of German states in 1848. Most of the merchant ships carrying immigrants to America arrived at New York, the busiest port in the nation, and as the ships piled up along the New Jersey and Long Island beaches many were tragically lost. Between 1818 and 1848 an average of ninety were destroyed each year. Several of the wrecks resulted in the loss of more than a hundred lives off the coast of New York.

In 1847 Congress responded by appropriating $5,000 for the rescue of shipwreck victims. Because marine disasters often occurred near lighthouses, whose keepers had traditionally offered assistance to mariners, the department initially assigned the job of lifesaving to them. Pushed to do more by Congressman W. A. Newall of New Jersey, Congress passed the Newall Act, which created the U.S. Life-Saving Service in 1848 and appropriated $10,000 for the purchase of lifesaving equipment to be used at stations along the approaches to New York Harbor.[47]

At first, the work was done by volunteers. Persons living near a station were given the responsibility of caring for boats and equipment and responding to crises as they developed. Not surprisingly, most stations fell into a dilapidated state and service was spotty at best.[48]

Before the Civil War, the Revenue Cutter Service had limited contact with the Life-Saving Service, though Captain Douglass Ottinger did purchase equipment for the stations, "surfboats, corrugated iron life-cars, mortars (for shooting lines from shore to stranded ships), blue flares, and odds and ends of ship-chandlery."[49] The only unique piece of equipment purchased by Ottinger was the life car, a metal boat shaped like a football with a hatch on top and a big ring at each end. A simple device that untrained volunteers could haul through the surf to and from a wreck,

A *Joseph Francis Life Car in Operation.* (*Copied from* Harper's New Monthly Magazine, *June* 1851, *Claire White-Peterson photo, courtesy* Eastern Connecticut State University.)

the life car was successful on the occasion of its first use, saving 201 of 202 persons from the wrecked immigrant ship *Ayrshire.*[50] But the device filled with water, a serious defect, and eventually had to be replaced by the better-known breeches buoy.

The equipment purchased by Ottinger was placed in eight small life-saving stations built under the provisions of the Newall Act, the first going up at Spermacetti Cove near Sandy Hook, New Jersey. The stations were "little more than crude one-and-a-half-story frame boathouses, 16′ wide by 28′ long. The single room on the first floor housed the surf-boat and other rescue equipment while a small loft above was used for storage. On the outside, each was covered with two or three layers of shingles on the walls and roof and painted or whitewashed."[51]

During the next six years many more stations were established. Although most were in New York and New Jersey, the service did expand into Rhode Island, North and South Carolina, Georgia, Florida, and Texas.

Construction of additional stations along the Atlantic coast and the Great Lakes followed. Still there were problems that prevented the development of an effective organization. To address them, Congress appointed superintendents and assigned paid keepers at each station, but the regulations for keepers were inadequate and accountability was wanting. No further Revenue Cutter Service involvement was forthcoming before the Civil War. The nation had to wait until after that war for improvements.

However, as Dennis Means has pointed out, "it is clear . . . that in spite of poor organization, mismanagement, general neglect, and scanty support, the early service accomplished noble work. Manned only by makeshift crews as each occasion of shipwreck demanded, the stations proved valuable in preserving life and property from storm and sea." In his annual report for 1872, Sumner Kimball, superintendent of the Life-Saving Service, acknowledged that no records of disasters had been kept before 1855 and only irregular ones after that, but he estimated that at least 4,163 lives and $716,000 of property had been saved by the service. The figures, he believed, would have been much higher had accurate records been kept.[52]

In contrast, the results of professional supervision of the Revenue Cutter Service were good. Secretary Spencer reported that "order and system" had "been established. Economy in expenditures and efficiency in service have been greatly promoted. . . . And, above all, the department now knows what is done and what is neglected. . . ."[53] Fraser agreed. Control of the cutters was concentrated in Washington, journals were kept on all cutter cruises, officers were assigned to stations for the good of the service, and no lack of enthusiasm in the discharge of their duties was tolerated. Junior officers were selected with great care.[54] Engineers were brought into the service, and the union of the Revenue Cutter, Life-Saving, and Lighthouse services had begun.

CHAPTER TEN

The Mexican War and Expansion to the Pacific

During Fraser's last years as commandant the United States fought a victorious war with Mexico. Texas had declared her independence from that country in 1836. Nine years later the United States annexed Texas, setting off an international conflict over the location of the border. Loan defaults, cultural misunderstandings, and President James K. Polk's attempts to wrest California from Mexico ensued, all of which led to the outbreak of war in 1846.

The United States extended her revenue laws to the new state of Texas, and as soon as Congress declared war Secretary of the Treasury Robert J. Walker concentrated a squadron of cutters between the Rio Grande and Mississippi rivers. The squadron sailed with orders to protect the economic interests of the United States and to cooperate with other armed forces in the area. The steamers *Legare*, *Spencer*, and *McLane* and the schooners *Woodbury*, *Ewing*, *Forward*, and *Van Buren* set sail with instructions to follow the directions of the commanding general of the U.S. Army, who was to employ the cutters to transport men, supplies, and intelligence, and if necessary use them in combat. Orders to the commander of the cutter squadron complicated matters considerably: he was to obey the commodore of the naval forces in the Gulf of Mexico, if the two forces should chance to meet and if the commodore's orders did not conflict with those of the army general in charge.[1] No organization could hope to satisfy the demands of so many masters, especially when those masters were likely to have conflicting interests and when the chain of command was so poorly defined.

To command the squadron, Walker chose Captain John A. Webster, a man of "acknowledged ability, intelligence, and zeal." Webster had logged enough time in the Revenue Cutter Service to qualify for the job. He also enjoyed a reputation for discretion, and had performed with gallantry during the recent Seminole War. Orders in hand, Webster sailed from Newport, Rhode Island, where he had earlier commanded the revenue cutter *Jackson*, to New Orleans, for his squadron was to rendezvous at the mouth of the Mississippi River. Once there, he chose the *Ewing* as his flagship. She was painted black with a white streak, the standard cutter colors during Walker's tenure as secretary.[2]

Webster's authority extended to all of the ships in the squadron. Each cutter sailed with sealed orders that were opened at sea. They directed each captain to obey all orders issued by Webster. All correspondence and requests had to go through him, and he was authorized to fill all vacancies on his own authority.[3]

Webster commanded the squadron until December 1846, when he contracted a fever. After being relieved by Captain Winslow Foster, he went home and regained his strength. Subsequently he returned to active duty and served his country until October 1865. Then at the age of seventy-nine he retired on duty pay, a status retained until his death in 1876.[4]

The first cutter to join the conflict with Mexico was the *Woodbury* (Captain Farnifold Greene), which began to cruise between Chandeleur Island and the Sabine River in March 1838.[5] By mid-June 1845 Captain Foster had replaced Greene as the *Woodbury*'s commander, and he was employed carrying messages and making reconnaissance runs for General Zachary Taylor, commander of the army of occupation. Next March the *Woodbury* took on supplies for the army at Aransas Pass and convoyed General Taylor's transports to Point Isabel. Responding to this move into disputed territory, the Mexicans attacked Taylor's army and the Mexican War started. After offloading Taylor's supplies, Foster sailed to the mouth of the Rio Grande to set up a blockade of Matamoros.[6]

Five steamers and six schooners ultimately made up the cutter squadron that sailed for New Orleans about the first of June. Two of the steamers burned out their boilers and had to return home; the *Spencer* got no farther than Charleston before she had to go back to Philadelphia, while the *Legare* reached the site of the fray before heading back north. The *McLane*, *Bibb*, and *Walker*, the most heavily armed of the cutters, also experienced difficulty with their machinery, but they were able to participate in the action. The *McLane* probably carried four 12-pounders, one long 18-pound pivot gun, and two lesser guns, the *Bibb* one long 18-pounder and four 32-pounders, and the *Walker* one long and two short 32-pounders. Although not as heavily armed, the schooners proved to be more valuable because of their shallow draft and reliability. The *Woodbury*, *Wolcott*, and *Van Buren* carried only four 12-pounders, while the *Ewing* carried six. The *Morris* was armed with six 6-pounders, the *Forward* with four 6-pounders or possibly with four 9-pounders.[7]

Not all of the schooners reached their destination without delay or difficulty. While the *Van Buren* was sailing past the Charleston lighthouse her fore royal mast was hit by lightning and she was forced back into port to refit. Within just a few days, she was repaired and on her way. Along with the other schooners, the *Van Buren* did yeoman service once she reached Mexican waters.[8]

The Revenue Cutter Service earned praise for its speed in preparing the cutters for war. Two weeks after orders were issued, every one was at sea, and one was ready to sail within just three days. Captain H. B. Nones took the *Forward* into Philadelphia for a quick overhaul, "tarred down her rigging, . . . painted her topmasts, . . . had her copper repaired, . . . ordered a new suit of sails . . . and took on provisions and stores." The job progressed so smoothly that Wilmington's collector sent a note to Secretary Walker complimenting the crew "for their untiring exertions in getting her ready for sea in so short a time."[9] The *Ewing*'s crew went to work with similar enthusiasm and put to sea within six days of receiving orders.[10]

The cutter *Morris* (Captain Green Walden) met disaster upon entering the conflict. She sailed from Portland to Key West, where she picked up orders to protect merchant shipping. On 11 October 1846, while carrying them out, she ran into a violent hurricane that drove her onto the Florida reef three miles northwest of Key West.[11]

Captain Lewis C. Fatio was at Mobile, Alabama, when he received orders to transport a navy purser and a message to Commodore David Conner. Since Conner was sailing in the brig *Lawrence* somewhere off the coast of Mexico, Fatio fitted out the *Wolcott* with provisions and munitions and set sail. But he never arrived at his destination, for on 19 January 1846 his ship was "driven ashore and dismasted in Pensacola Bay." It cost

$877 to repair her. The damage to Fatio's career was irreparable; on 1 September Secretary Walker dismissed him from the service for failing to carry out his orders.[12]

The cutters that reached the war zone spent most of their time carrying intelligence, dispatches, mail, and supplies from New Orleans to Conner's gulf squadron or to Taylor's army depot at Brazo Santiago.[13] They served on blockade duty, scouted for the army, and performed convoy and towing services, and transported troops. Most importantly, just before Taylor's great offensive victory in the battles of Monterey and Buena Vista, the cutters *Legare* and *Ewing* carried one thousand rifles to Taylor at Point Isabel.[14]

Off Brazos on 26 July, the crew of the *Woodbury* (Captain William B. Whitehead) put down a mutiny on the troop ship *Middlesex*. Several Indiana volunteers on the *Middlesex* had died and many more were ill when on the twenty-fifth Whitehead gave his medicine chest to the officers of that ship. During the night the men of the *Middlesex* mutinied and threatened to kill their captain, perhaps holding him responsible for the illness. Whitehead responded by sending over Lieutenant McLean, a petty officer, and five men of the *Woodbury*, who "restored order and landed the troops."[15]

The navy's primary role in the Mexican War was the less than glamorous job of blockading ports in the Gulf of Mexico. Following the declaration of war, Secretary of the Navy George Bancroft instructed Commodore Conner to blockade Mexican ports and secure the seas so that the United States could transport troops and supplies to Mexico. At the beginning Mexico owned just a few small craft, which sought refuge at Alvarado or Tampico. She had another two steam warships under construction in Britain, but they had not been paid for and so were later turned over to the British merchant marine. Taking command of the seas, therefore, required very little effort on Conner's part, and because Mexico made but a feeble effort to send out privateers, the U.S. Navy concentrated on blockading her gulf ports.[16]

Carrying out the blockade was both monotonous and troublesome. The gulf had two seasons, summer, when yellow fever and malaria ran rampant, and winter, when some of the most vicious storms known to mariners in the northern hemisphere hit the coast. Furthermore, most of Mexico's ports were inside shallow-mouthed rivers, which precluded big warships from entering. Since it was often impossible for ships to stay on station off the coast, Conner needed small vessels. His fleet initially included two frigates, three sloops of war, two steamers, five brigs, and just one schooner. Most of the ships available to the navy had been built for a blue-water war with European navies. The navy subsequently commandeered the light-draft steamers *Vixen* and *Spitfire* and the schooners *Bonita*, *Petrel*, and *Reefer*. The latter, built for the Mexicans by Brown and Bell of New York, proved to be valuable to Conner.[17] So, too, did the ships of the Revenue Cutter Service.

During the first year of the war, Commodore Conner made two attempts to attack Mexican warships in the Alvarado River. The initial action, in July 1846, failed because of a shortage of small craft and the grounding of the flagship *Cumberland*. The second followed the arrival of the revenue steamer *McLane* (Captain W. A. Howard) in October. By then the defenses of Alvarado had been strengthened. Five batteries with about thirty-six guns guarded the river's mouth, and the three largest Mexican warships lay between them and the town. Conner led his squadron out of the Anton Lizardo roadstead, south of Veracruz, just after midnight on 15 October and arrived off the mouth of the river after daylight. A hoped-for breeze failed to come, and so he waited until afternoon to attack. Still without a breeze, he ordered his small vessels into two columns. The first he led himself in the *Vixen*, towing two schooner gunboats. The *McLane* led the second, towing the *Forward* and two more boats. The *Vixen* crossed the bar at 1:20 P.M. The slower *McLane* arrived off the bar at 2:15 P.M. She ran aground and her tows became hopelessly tangled and confused. This, and the fact that the three vessels that had crossed the bar, mounting just five guns, were no match for the Mexicans ashore and afloat, convinced Conner to call off the attack.[18]

To counteract the effects of the defeat and stop illicit trade from the Yucatan Peninsula, Commodore Matthew Calbraith Perry suggested to Conner an attack on the city of Tabasco and other towns along the like-named river. Perry hoped to take advantage of an accurate account of the town's defenses that he had received from Captain Howard, who had just returned from a reconnaissance mission up the Tabasco River in the revenue cutter *McLane*.[19]

After Conner gave his approval Perry, in his flagship the USS *Mississippi*, departed from Anton Lizardo for the mouth of the river on the morning of 16 October.[20] His squadron of three steamers and four schooners included the revenue cutters *McLane* (Captain Howard) and *Forward* (Captain H. B. Nones), plus a 253-man landing party. The navy steamer *Vixen* and the schooners *Nonata* and *Bonita* made up the remainder of the squadron.[21]

Perry anchored his flagship off the mouth of the Tabasco River on 23 October and transferred his flag to the *Vixen*, which towed the *Forward* and the *Bonita* across the bar. The *McLane*, towing the *Nonata* and a number of

Commodore M. C. Perry's Naval Expedition Crossing the Bar at the Mouth of the Tabasco River in the Mexican War, 14 June 1847. (*Courtesy* U.S. *Naval Historical Center.*)

boats, was once again stranded on the bar, but this time the squadron forged ahead. The *Nonata* sailed up river on her own, while the boats were rowed six miles to Frontera against a four-knot current. At Frontera Perry captured two steamers, three schooners, and the town without firing a shot, then converted the steamers *Petrita* and *Tabasquena* into U.S. gunboats. Putting most of his landing party aboard the *Petrita*, he steamed the seventy-five miles up river. The *Forward* and the *Nonata* were towed beyond Frontera by the *Vixen*. According to Samuel Eliot Morison, the riverbanks were "covered by a heavy hardwood jungle which harbored thousands of howling monkeys and birds which screamed at the invaders."[22]

The expedition proceeded unopposed past breastworks at Acachapan, where a landing party of marines spiked the guns, and on to the town of Tabasco. After a minor skirmish, Perry seized Tabasco and put a landing party ashore. At night the party returned to the ships, and by the following day Mexican troops had moved back into the town. There was a skirmish over a grounded vessel, but since a battle would have led to the destruction of Tabasco, Perry agreed to a truce and moved back down river to Frontera with his five captured ships.[23]

Returning to Anton Lizardo at the end of October, he left the *McLane* and the *Forward* behind to prevent shipping on the Tabasco River and to protect foreign residents at Frontera from reprisals by the Mexicans. His

The attack of the Mexicans *from the* Chapperal, *during the* Naval Expedition *to* Tabasco. (*Courtesy* U.S. *Naval* Historical *Center.*)

expedition had succeeded in capturing or destroying all the vessels in the river and in partially restoring fighting spirit to the squadron. The cutters blockaded the river, providing a safe anchorage for the small vessels of the United States. Perry subsequently praised all the commanders of his squadron except Captain Howard of the *McLane*:

> While I am gratified in bearing witness . . . to the valuable services of the Revenue Schooner "Forward" in command of Captain Nones, and to the skill and gallantry of her officers and men, it gives me infinite pause to be compelled, by a sense of imperative duty, to say that Captain Howard of the Revenue Cutter Steamer "McLane" managed his vessel with so little discretion that he placed her aground in a most dangerous position, by which serious obstacles were thrown in the way of the expedition; and had it not been for the persevering efforts of Captain Forrest, I doubt she would have been extricated from her perilous situation.[24]

It is possible that Perry was offended by Howard's sensitivity about having to serve under a navy lieutenant. When he originally received orders to that effect, Howard had protested vigorously, believing it was his duty to his service to do so.

The war took an enormous toll on the cutter fleet. The *McLane* was transferred along with the *Spencer* to lightship duty, the former serving off New Orleans and the latter off Hampton Roads. The *Morris* was lost when a hurricane drove her ashore three miles northwest of Key West in October 1846. Three steamers, the *Walker*, *Bibb*, and *Legare*, and the sailing cutters *Forward*, *Ewing*, *Wolcott*, and *Gallatin*, were transferred to the Coast Survey, where their work could be lightened. During the summer of 1847 the *Forward* required $2,500 of repairs. The *Van Buren* and the *Dallas* were auctioned off, the former selling for just $200 in New York. The *Taney* and the *Polk* were transferred to the navy, which used the latter as a marine hospital and later as a target for a new gun. The *Jefferson*, after being converted to sail power alone, ended her life in the Straits of Magellan. By January 1849, only eight cutters remained in service and another six were building.[25]

With only eight ready for sea duty, the service could not begin to protect the entire coast of the United States. A cutter was stationed at each of the following ports: Eastport, Boston, Newport, New York, Delaware, Norfolk, Mobile, and Lake Erie. Revenue boats were employed at Castine, Sackets Harbor, Frenchman Bay, Machias, Rochester, Wiscasset, South West Pass, Belize, Pointe à la Hache, Key West, and Oswego. Just two cutters patrolled the area between the Chesapeake Bay and Cape Florida. One cruised in the Gulf of Mexico off the Mississippi River. The gulf shore of Florida and the shores of Mississippi and Texas had no protection. Of the six new schooners being built, two were intended for service on the Atlantic coast and four were destined to serve off California and Oregon, but it would be some time before they were actually ready to guard the coast.[26]

Meanwhile, new demands were placed on the service, for a number of filibustering expeditions had left the United States for Cuba, and the cutters were called upon to protect U.S. neutrality. On 25 April 1851, the government ordered Captain T. C. Rudolph of the *Roger B. Taney* to proceed from New York to Savannah after information was received of a plan to launch an assault on Cuba from Burnt Ford on the St. Illa River. The *Taney* cruised between Savannah and Jacksonville keeping as close to shore as possible. After drawing opposite the St. Illa River, she proceeded up river to Burnt Ford, but no expedition was discovered. Continuing the cruise, she sailed on to St. Marys and from there to Jacksonville. On his return Captain Rudolph expressed the opinion that the filibustering expedition had been abandoned; he, at least, had not discovered one.[27]

Efforts to administer the newly acquired Mexican territory created sectionalism in the revenue service. Since only a vigorous nationalism could have sustained Fraser's reforms, they fell victim to the gathering storm.

Captain Richard Evans, Fraser's successor, was transferred out of Washington in 1849. Control of the Revenue Cutter Service thereafter fell into the hands of the commissioner of customs, who allowed collectors to reestablish their control over the service. Administrative control of the Lighthouse Service was returned to the fifth auditor of the treasury, while the Life-Saving Service remained independent. In 1852, a doomsday book was compiled on revenue cutter officers that included each man's political as well as service history. Once again, merit gave way to politics in the choice of personnel.[28]

The war did produce one favorable outcome for the nation and subsequently for the Revenue Cutter Service. The acquisition of vast territories in the West stimulated a golden age of American maritime development. Capital made available from shipping profits poured into economic development. The discovery of gold in California caused a rush to the West Coast, and Britain's repeal of her Corn Laws opened up the tea trade to American shippers. Thereafter, vessels laden with products rounded Cape Horn for California, continued to China to take on tea bound for Britain, and returned home to New York or Boston with products from the Old World. Immigrants often filled out the manifests on that last leg as well. All of this trade dramatically increased U.S. shipping tonnage and gave rise to the most beautiful moving art form created by man, the great clipper ships.

It also resulted in the establishment of a customs district on the West Coast. Following the acquisition of California, Congress sent Colonel James Collier to establish one at San Francisco. To assist him, Congress dispatched the revenue cutter *Cornelius W. Lawrence*. One of seven new vessels built to replace the cutters lost in the Mexican War, the *Lawrence* was constructed by William Easby at Foggy Bottom in Washington, D.C., on the present site of the Watergate Apartments and the John F. Kennedy Center for the Performing Arts. A native of Yorkshire, England, Easby had learned his trade at the Washington Navy Yard, where he became a master builder before opening his own yard. He had built at least one cutter, the very successful *Walter Forward*, prior to winning the contract for the *Lawrence*.[29]

The *Lawrence* was "staunchly built of white and live oak, yellow pine, cedar, locust, and mahogany and was copper fastened and sheathed." She bore the lines of a Baltimore clipper and was brig-rigged with raking masts for speed. Her overall length was 96½′. She measured 24′ in beam and displaced 144 tons. After laying her down in late 1847 or early 1848, Easby launched her on 20 August 1848. After her blocks were knocked away, she slid down the ways so quickly that Captain Alexander Fraser

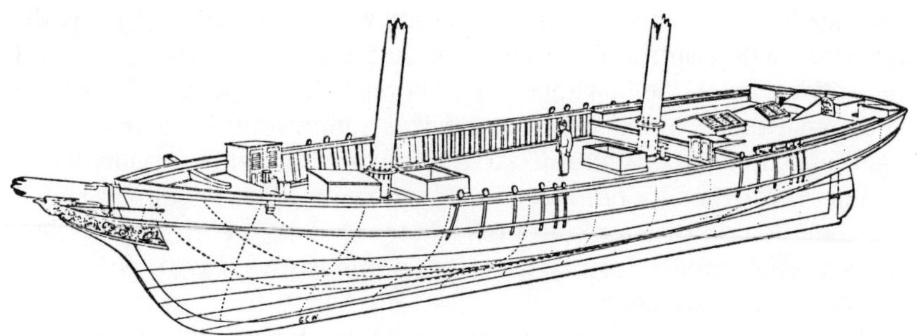

The USRC Joe Lane. (*Courtesy Smithsonian Institution.*)

just managed to leap aboard before she plunged into the Potomac with colors flying.[30] Her sails, awnings, tarpaulins, and hammocks were made by Kirby and Whittington of Baltimore. She carried "two 32-pounders, a long 18-pounder, . . . two 6-pounders, . . . carbines, percussion pistols, Colt revolvers, boarding pikes, and cutlasses."[31]

Having successfully sought command of the *Lawrence*—knowing he would be transferred out of Washington—Captain Fraser set sail from the capital on 1 November 1848. He carried orders to place himself under the control of the collector for the district of Oregon and to sail along the Oregon coast until California's commerce developed (no one yet anticipated the Gold Rush). Because she would be at sea for a long time, the *Lawrence* sailed from Washington with a large complement of officers. In addition to Fraser there was the executive officer, First Lieutenant J. Chaddock; two second lieutenants; two third lieutenants; and Dr. Overstreet, the surgeon. Thirty-five men constituted the *Lawrence*'s crew. After a brief stop at Norfolk for 1,825 pounds of black powder and other provisions, the cutter entered the Gulf Stream on 17 November.[32]

The passage to Rio de Janeiro was both exhausting and frustrating. Three of the *Lawrence*'s officers were political appointees who had never been aboard a square-rigger before. As a result, Fraser had to stand their watches. This was unpleasant enough; the task was made more onerous by persistently strong head winds, squalls, and electrical storms that took a heavy toll on the ship and her captain. According to Stephen H. Evans, "bands on bowsprits, bobstays, cranes, and chain slings on the lower yards gave way in the heavy weather." In the persistent dampness, vegetation grew from the ship itself. As the trip progressed the captain grew exhausted and issued the following order: "As a particular favor, it is requested that at least until the arrival of the vessel at Rio the duty shall

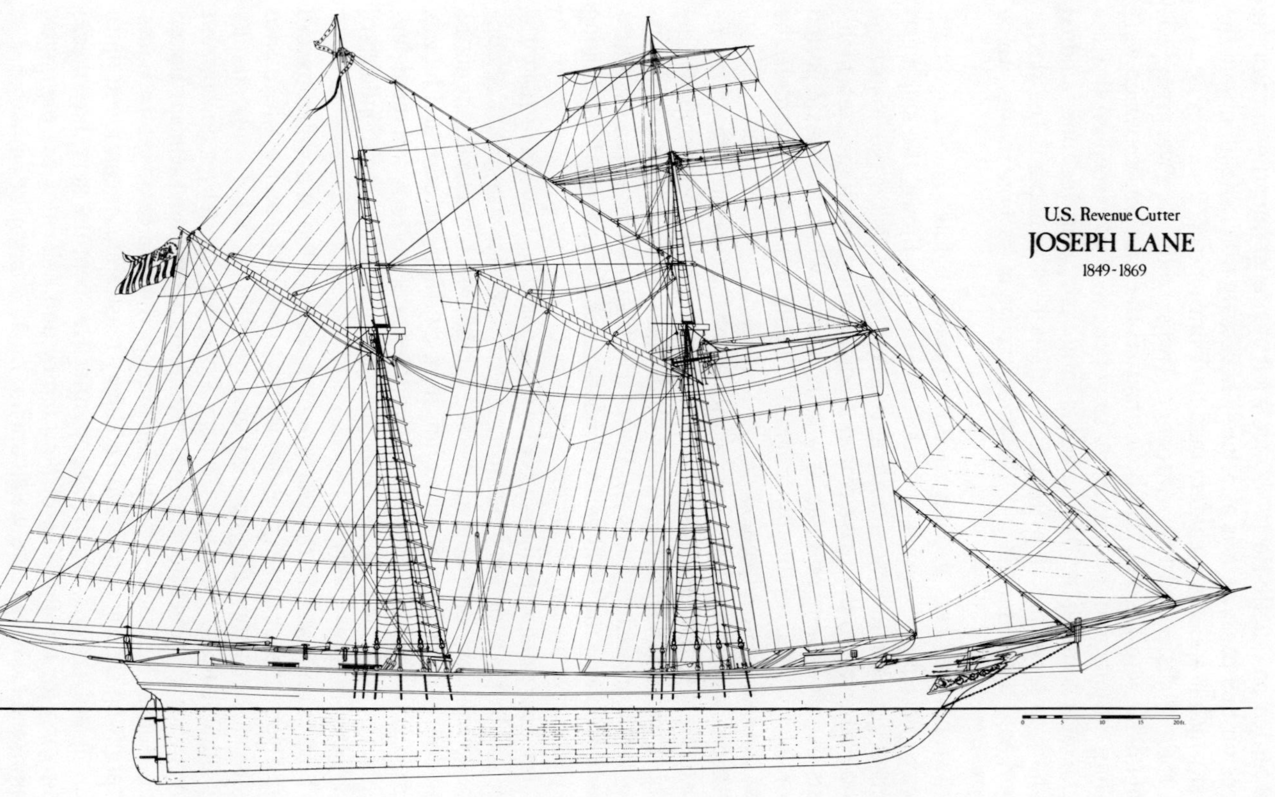

The USRC Joseph Lane, 1849–69. (*Drawing by* John A. Tilley, *courtesy* USCG Public Affairs Staff.)

be carried on quietly. Having scarcely felt any relief from the cares of the deck on this passage, it is absolutely necessary that I should obtain the rest which it appears predetermined to deprive me of."[33]

Fatigue sharpened Fraser's tongue. The surgeon, Dr. Overstreet, was unfamiliar with the sea, and believing that the *Lawrence*'s crewmen were taking advantage of his gullibility to get themselves placed on the sick list, Fraser commented that he would rather pay Overstreet one hundred dollars to leave the ship than fifty dollars to stay aboard. The doctor overheard the comment and "demanded to be put ashore in Rio," which he was.[34]

Two petty officers also departed the *Lawrence* before she reached California. Because of chronic seasickness Benjamin Brown, the ship's carpenter, got off in Rio. More troublesome was James Walker, the boatswain, who had come to the *Lawrence* from a whaler and treated the crew members as if they were on board a whaling vessel. When this was reported to Fraser Walker voluntarily resigned. "Finally, drunk and disorderly, he was put ashore in Valparaiso."[35]

There was a positive side to these unhappy events. Burdened by inexperienced officers, Fraser "ran the *Lawrence* like a school-ship." He established a small shipboard library and required officers to study surveying, law, seamanship, and navigation.[36] His idea influenced the establishment, following the Civil War, of a much-needed academy for the training of young revenue cutter officers.

The *Lawrence* had pulled into Rio, for repairs, on 17 January 1849. Expecting to be under way again in ten days, Fraser was most unhappy when he discovered that it would take two months to patch up the cutter. His dour personality prevented him from enjoying the port, and he was outraged by the cost of repairs, the indolence of workers, and the delays caused by Catholic holy days. His only consolation was the friendship of Commodore Storer, USN.[37]

Finally, on 7 March, the *Lawrence* took leave of Rio and sailed toward Cape Horn. It took three grueling months to reach Valparaiso, where once again she was cleaned, repaired, and provisioned. On 19 July she departed Valparaiso for Hawaii, where Fraser was to deliver government dispatches. En route he rendered assistance to the bark *LaGrange*, bound from Salem, Massachusetts, to San Francisco with a cargo of Argonauts. After giving six bags of coal to *LaGrange*'s master, Fraser continued on to Hawaii, arriving at Oahu on 3 September. He spent the next three weeks preparing for the final leg of his journey and delivering his messages. Before the *Lawrence* could weigh anchor on 28 September he had to ship seventeen islanders as crewmen, for several of his own crew had deserted at Honolulu. Desertions were a common problem for U.S. vessels visiting the paradise of Hawaii during that period. Finally, the *Lawrence* anchored off San Francisco on 31 October, nearly a year after leaving Washington.[38]

When Fraser arrived at San Francisco, the port was booming and the *Lawrence*'s services were desperately needed. The cutter, however, suffered the same fate as merchant ships there—her crewmen deserted for the gold fields. And unlike merchantmen, which could pay wages of one hundred dollars a month, Fraser could pay but a measly thirty-five. The first man deserted on 5 November; by the end of the month, nine and ten men were leaving each day. When three lieutenants resigned in March 1850, the captain was left alone with his duties.

Because of the expense of hiring a full complement of men to keep the *Lawrence* at sea, Colonel Collier had Fraser anchor her between Clark's and Rincon points, where she languished for more than a year. Then he hired two small schooners, the *Argus* and the *Catherine*, to patrol the bay as auxiliary cutters. The schooners, manned by just three or four men, were armed with some of the *Lawrence*'s weapons.[39]

The cutter's few remaining crew members performed a wide variety of tasks in the bay during that year at anchor. They boarded ships suspected of smuggling, which was widespread because there were just two collection offices in all of California. When ship's captains had trouble keeping their crewmen aboard they sometimes called on the *Lawrence* for help, and Fraser usually responded by putting the offenders in irons, either in their own ship or in the cutter. At one time in March 1850 there were a dozen men thus enchained in the *Lawrence*. The cutter also played a role in San Francisco's celebration of the state's admission to the Union. California became a state on 9 September 1850, but the news reached San Francisco belatedly and so it was not until 18 October that an officer from the *Lawrence* led ten men ashore with two brass guns and thirty-one blank cartridges to join in the festivities. More in line with the Revenue Cutter Service's traditional roles was the rescue of passengers flung into the bay when the boilers of the steamboat *Sagamore* burst. And the *Lawrence*'s crew helped to convert the *Thomas Bennett* from Charleston, South Carolina, into a pier and warehouse.[40]

While anchored in the busy harbor in 1850, the *Lawrence* was buffeted by three ships, one bark, and one schooner that between then carried away her flying jib boom, flying jib iron, and main gaff, destroyed carved work on her cat head, and fouled her jib boom.[41]

Changing circumstances finally allowed the *Lawrence* to escape from San Francisco Bay in the fall of 1850. The revenue cutter *Polk*, an iron bark, arrived for service on 27 September. This prompted a complaint from Fraser, who wanted to depart, that he had hardly been out of sight of his cutter since leaving Washington two years before. In October and November, the *Lawrence* was fitted out for a cruise to San Diego, for Collier agreed that her skipper had done more than his share of service at San Francisco. Few men, he noted in a letter to Fraser,

> had more difficult or responsible duties to perform and no man could have more faithfully and promptly discharged those duties. When it is remembered that you have been in a harbor where from five to six hundred vessels were riding at anchor—in the midst of a great excitement—with crews insubordinate & lawless—without the aid of civil authorities or civil process & when day & night you have been called upon to render assistance & to aid Masters of vessels in suppressing mutiny & violence, surely it becomes me to bear willing testimony to the necessity of your presence & your promptness in the discharge of your onerous duties.[42]

The *Lawrence* departed on 26 December 1850. In early January, Fraser charted the harbor at Catalina Island. On the nineteenth, he anchored off San Diego so that his crew could provision the ship and meanwhile did some exploring ashore. A few days later two crew members, William Graham and William Lobb, got into a fight. Graham bit off a piece of Lobb's nose and stabbed him in the face. Fortunately for Graham his adversary recovered; as punishment, he had his head shaved and was flogged and put ashore. That same morning the *Lawrence* set sail.[43]

From Point Loma the *Lawrence* crossed the Pacific to Hawaii, then returned to San Francisco on 4 May 1850. That day a great fire destroyed the town, and for the next month members of the *Lawrence*'s crew went ashore daily to guard the customhouse vault. Once back in the bay, they returned to the duties ceased months before. Night patrols of the bay were added to stop smuggling.

A significant change occurred on 7 June, when Fraser was granted a leave of absence and Captain Douglass Ottinger replaced him as the *Lawrence*'s commander. On leave from his revenue duties and in command of the Pacific mail steamship *Isthmus*, Ottinger did not accept permanent command until September. When Fraser departed the *Lawrence* he borrowed a Colt repeater and proceeded to Hawaii, then returned to the East Coast in 1852. Four years later, after Fraser supported a request for a new steam cutter for New York that an assistant secretary of the treasury opposed, the department arbitrarily suspended him.[44]

On 20 October 1851, Robert H. Waterman sailed the clipper ship *Challenge* into San Francisco after a 108-day passage from New York. Her owners, N. L. and G. G. ("No Loss and Great Gain") Griswald, had spared no expense in financing her construction. William H. Webb had built her for speed, and Waterman had been lured out of retirement because of his record-breaking China runs in the *Sea Witch*.

On the down side, the *Challenge* had shipped a crew between whom and the captain serious friction existed.[45] Waterman's account of what happened differed substantially from that of the *California Chronicle*. The captain claimed that

> when in the neighborhood of Rio, about fifty of the crew fell on the mate with the intention of killing him and afterwards me, by their own confession. I was on the poop taking observations while the mate stood forward at the gallery. They stabbed him and had beaten him shockingly before I could get to him. I struck down three of them, rescued the mate and quelled the mutiny. I flogged eight of them. Off Cape Horn, three men fell from the mizzentopsail yard and were killed and after a few weeks four more of the men died of dysentery.[46]

The *California Chronicle* depicted a "hell ship" that the sailors described as follows:

> The account given of captain Waterman by his crew, if true makes him one of the most inhuman masters of his age.
>
> If they are true, he should be burned alive—he should never leave the city a live man. Nine of his men are missing, and the sailors who are here declare that four were shaken down from the foretopsail yard into the sea where they were drowned, and five of them died from the effects of wounds and ill treatment.
>
> The scene at this time beggars all description. Five of them are mangled and bruised in the most shocking manner. One poor fellow died today and five others, it is expected, will soon be in the embrace of death. One of the men now lying on his deathbed had been severely injured in his genitals by a kick from this brute in human form. . . . The captain, the vile monster, has made his escape, and so has his brutal mate.[47]

With such lurid accounts of the voyage circulating in the city, Waterman was in danger. He requested Ottinger to remove seven men who were charged with mutiny from the *Challenge*. Later, on 31 October, a mob of over one thousand men went looking for Waterman, threatening both him and his ship. Ottinger, Lieutenant Richmond of the *Polk*, the U.S. marshal, local officials, and a vigilance committee defended the ship and her captain. The mob did minor damage before dispersing, while the *Lawrence*'s crew stayed aboard through the night to guard against further damage. Waterman was later tried for murder and convicted of a lesser charge of assault, perhaps in part because Ottinger appeared as a witness at the trial.[48]

The *Lawrence* had an encounter with a second clipper ship while in the Pacific. Having heard rumors of filibustering expeditions to Hawaii, Ottinger boarded four ships at the end of October. One was the *Gamecock*. No brigands were found aboard her.[49]

The *Lawrence* returned to San Francisco from a cruise on 25 November and anchored near Point Lobos. With the tide having ebbed and running south, and with the sea running in from the west, almost landward, disaster struck. Topping seas boarded the cutter and threatened to sweep her deck. At 8:30 P.M. her cable parted and she was driven into the breakers, striking bottom at three and a half fathoms with tons of water breaking over her deck. Lying with her bow toward the land, she went aground at about 9:00 P.M.[50] Because Ottinger had misjudged both his position and the tide, he lost the cutter. All hands, however, were saved.[51]

With the assistance of troops and teams from the Presidio in San Francisco, Ottinger and the *Lawrence*'s crew stripped the cutter over the next three days. Valuables, papers, navigational instruments, small arms, and various other items were stored at the Presidio. Sails, masts, spars, and rigging were also saved, along with the medicine chest. Ottinger believed that he could have salvaged the cutter, but also that he could purchase a new cutter more cheaply than he could repair the *Lawrence*. In any case he was dissatisfied with her sailing qualities. They were, he said, "very ordinary, most of the Coasting Schooners, and some of the Merchant Ships, could pass us to windward, aside from the new class of Clipper Ships some of which beat us at the rate of four or five knots an hour."[52]

Collector T. King purchased the schooner *Frolic* as a cutter for $4,000 and armed her with the *Lawrence*'s guns and ammunition, but when the treasury secretary disallowed the expense, King chartered the schooner as a cutter.[53] She sailed with $12,000 of equipment saved from the *Lawrence*, which, thus stripped down, sold for $2,360. With all other proceeds and expenses accounted for, the government received just $1,279 for the *Lawrence*.[54]

Because King defended Ottinger, he was not held accountable for the loss. In 1853 he returned to the East Coast. During the Civil War he commanded a number of cutters and, after the war, helped to design and build a number of new steam cutters for the service.[55]

CHAPTER ELEVEN

Origins of the Civil War

The Revenue Cutter Service played an active role in the historical developments that led to the Civil War. As one of the federal agencies responsible for checking smuggling, it was charged with stopping the slave trade. When the government tried to avert a domestic conflict by returning runaway slaves to their masters, revenue cutters were assigned that onerous task. And when South Carolina challenged federal authority during the administrations of both Jackson and Lincoln, the president called upon the Revenue Cutter Service to uphold national sovereignty. Finally, after all efforts at compromise between the Union and the Southern states failed, it was the revenue cutter *Harriet Lane* that fired the first shot at sea in the Civil War.

On 22 March 1794, Congress had declared it illegal for an American citizen to carry slaves from the United States to another nation or between foreign nations. Until 1808, one could still legally import slaves into the United States under the provisions of the Constitution. But penalties for violating the 1794 law were severe, including forfeiture of any ship involved, a $2,000 fine for each individual convicted of trading in slaves, and a fine of $200 for each slave illegally taken on board. Secretary of the Treasury Oliver Wolcott wrote American customs officers that the slave trade was an odious business, and he expected his department to enforce the law. The cutter *Governor Jay* sailing out of New York spoke two ships bound for Havana with a cargo of slaves in April 1799. When one of the two, the *Betsy*, subsequently sailed into Boston Harbor, Benjamin Lincoln fulfilled Wolcott's wishes by seizing her.[1]

Beginning on 1 January 1808, federal law closed all of the nation's ports to the foreign slave trade. Thereafter the Revenue Cutter Service made sporadic efforts to stop traffic, but there were many obstacles to success. Some local governments opposed enforcement, and international relations complicated matters. In the South, some revenue cutter skippers actually employed slaves on their own ships, which must have affected their attitude toward the law. Courts were often unsympathetic, and, of course, the memory of the fabulous profits that could be made in the slave trade lured many unscrupulous characters into the business.

Kenneth M. Stampp, the foremost historian of American black slavery, tells us that "in the absence of special enforcement machinery the law was violated with impunity; various estimates of slave importation between 1810 and 1820 run as high as sixty thousand." By the decade before the Civil War, this "illicit commerce reached such proportions as almost to constitute 'a reopening of the slave-trade.' " Many slavers were fitted out in New York City itself, where human cargo was offloaded with scarcely any concern for secrecy.[2]

The records of the Revenue Cutter Service certainly confirm Stampp's opinions. The slave trade flourished along the border between Florida and Georgia, where customs officials received little local support. The collector at Brunswick, Georgia, William McIntosh, reported that slaves were imported from the West Indies to Amelia Island, Florida, then smuggled from there to the mainland. On 12 April 1813 McIntosh apprehended Captain William Hale of St. Marys for engaging in the slave trade, but Hale escaped. Later, after seizing five African males whom Hale had tried to sell in Brunswick, McIntosh reported Hale to the marshal. Hale's vessel was subsequently seized, and McIntosh sent men out in a custom boat with orders to work along the shore. Still, McIntosh was pessimistic about the outcome in Hale's case. It was difficult to enforce the law, he wrote, because many Georgians opposed it as harmful to the interests of the state.[3]

We do not know the outcome of the Hale case, but A. T. Bullock, the collector at Savannah, was plagued by the same problem some four years later. African and West Indian slaves were being smuggled to Amelia Island and carried across the St. Marys River. To stop ships from landing, Bullock ordered Captain James Smith to cruise in his cutter as far south as St. Marys Bar. The collector noted, however, that it was beyond the power of the Revenue Cutter Service to guard the river. To stop slave traffic Bullock advised setting up a guard and paying informers. There was no alternative in a state that had not passed laws against the slave trade, and none of whose citizens, in his opinion, would cooperate except for money.[4]

From North Carolina, Thomas S. Singleton reported similar problems. Slavers smuggled their illicit cargo into Ocracoke and then proceeded the eighty or ninety miles up river to New Bern. According to Singleton, it was an easy matter to smuggle goods along the river because inhabitants were glad to participate in the lucrative business.[5]

The case of the *Antelope* illustrates how international complications further hampered enforcement efforts. At three o'clock in the afternoon of 29 June 1820, the revenue cutter *Dallas* (Captain John Jackson) captured the brig *Antelope* (Captain John Smith) with about 280 slaves aboard. The day before, after receiving word of a suspicious ship off the coast of St. Marys, Jackson had set sail for Amelia Island, where he took aboard twelve armed soldiers. Early on the twenty-ninth he spotted the *Antelope* sailing north between Amelia Island and the Florida coast. Having recently returned from Africa with her cargo, the *Antelope* tried to outrun the *Dallas* but was overhauled in midafternoon. Unwilling to concede defeat, Captain Smith ordered the brig's guns run out. His crew, however, refused to fire on the American flag and Smith had to surrender his vessel.[6]

Built in Freetown, Massachusetts (now Maine), the *Antelope* measured 69′ 2″ in overall length and 22′ 9″ in beam, and displaced a little over 112 tons. Her nationality was hard to determine. She had been seized at sea a number of times before the *Dallas* took her into custody, and when the latter landed the Africans at Savannah, consular officials from both Spain and Portugal registered their claims. Meanwhile, Richard Wylly Habersham, a U.S. district attorney in Georgia, developed a case under American law for the freedom of the blacks.[7]

While the case worked its way through the courts, John Morel, the U.S. marshal for the District of Georgia, took custody of the Africans. He kept them in an open area at the Savannah race grounds and charged the government for their maintenance, while at the same time leasing them out to work for private and public parties. During their first six months at Savannah, fifty of the Africans died, and more perished as the years passed.[8]

The case ultimately reached the Supreme Court, where Justice John

Marshall freed 131 of the Africans to go to Liberia. The 37 remaining survivors were bound for slavery in Cuba to satisfy Spanish claims, but Congressman Richard Henry Wilde of Georgia maintained that they preferred to remain with him and proposed to buy them. Although none of the slaves appeared to verify his claim, Wilde was allowed to keep the slaves.[9]

In a good book on the *Antelope*, James T. Noonan concluded that the whole affair was "characterized by fraud." "Worse than that," he wrote, "there was a sustained assault on individual human beings. For a period of eight years the process enslaved all of the Africans, and it permanently enslaved thirty-seven of them. During the litigation more of the free Africans perished than survived."[10] The result must have been discouraging to the officers and crew of the *Dallas*, though perhaps they were sustained by the imprisonment of Captain Smith and the sale of the *Antelope* for such affronts to decency.[11]

Some sense of the frustration of officials wanting to stop the illicit slave trade is felt in the letters of John Rodman, customs collector at St. Augustine, Florida. In June 1826 Rodman informed Treasury Secretary Richard Rush that according to a reliable source the little schooner *John Richard*, of over 70 tons, had been chartered to pick up forty slaves at Nassau in the Bahamas and carry them to two gentlemen at plantations along the coast. The plantation owners lived forty to fifty miles south of St. Augustine, and the only way to prevent their importing the slaves was to have the revenue cutter *Marion* (Captain Isaiah Doane), which had cleared for Charleston, returned immediately to that stretch of river below the port of St. Augustine. Three days later Rodman confirmed that his information was correct and that the *John Richard* had cleared Nassau for America. There is no record of a response. Five years later Rodman again wrote to the treasury secretary, this time Samuel Ingham, and this time about forty slaves imported into the same area of Florida to work on the plantation of one Mr. William H. Williams. Again there is no evidence of a response. Nor was a cutter assigned to patrol that stretch of coast.[12]

Piracy complicated efforts to suppress the slave trade in the Gulf of Mexico. The collector at New Orleans explained to the secretary of the treasury that slavery and piracy flourished in the western counties of Louisiana, where they were difficult to stop. He told the story of the French schooner *Confeinu*, which was carrying 189 male slaves when captured by the pirate schooner *Victory* of New Orleans. Subsequently, legal measures were taken by the owners of the *Confeinu* to regain possession of the slaves and to punish the owners of the *Victory*. Only six or seven of the slaves were ever found. The rest were sold, and the collector was pessimistic about his chances of gaining a conviction against the *Victory*'s owners, for they were represented by a former judge of the Supreme Court of Louisiana who had just been appointed to the office of secretary of state.[13]

The revenue cutter *Louisiana* (Captain John Jackson) enjoyed some minor successes in the gulf. In December 1821, a Venezuelan privateer seized the French brig *Pensée* with 220 Africans on board. Both the privateer and the *Pensée* were subsequently taken over by Captain Henley of the U.S. corvette *Hornet*. He brought the French brig into New Orleans, only to have the collector let the *Pensée* go free, probably owing to international considerations. Five months later Captain Jackson reported the same slaver cruising to the west of New Orleans, but he passed her up for the little 9-ton schooner *Pearl* of New Orleans. Jackson arrested her captain, lieutenant, and one boy for carrying slaves into Louisiana. The *Pensée*, meanwhile, proceeded on her way.[14]

U.S. naval ships patrolling the African coast frequently stopped ships for carrying slaves only to let them go because they were under French colors. France refused to join the international effort against the slave trade.[15]

International complications made possible all kinds of smuggling from U.S. ports. Between thirty and forty-five small fishing boats ranging from 35 to 60 tons fished on the Florida reef from the fall of 1828 through the summer of 1829. Without exception they carried two sets of papers, one American and the other Spanish. Their general rendezvous points were Key West and Havana or Matanzas, Cuba. They entered Key West under U.S. colors, Havana, under Spanish. The vessels actually did some fishing, but that was of secondary importance. Four masters admitted that it was a bad year when they did not smuggle between $80,000 and $200,000 of property. The collector of customs at St. Marks, Florida, wrote that he had seen boats in Havana with coffee and wine valued at $1,500 to $2,000 on which no U.S. customs dues had been paid. He had also been aboard a "smack" from New London, Connecticut, with a false cabin in which the captain could hide as much as $10,000 of property.[16]

Slavers went to even greater lengths to smuggle their cargo into the United States. A case reported by W. A. Whitehead, the collector at Key West, makes the point. A man from the Key West customs district bought slaves in the Bahamas and emancipated them. Then he entered into a contract with these ex-slaves, who bound themselves to him as indentured apprentices for ten years in return for "benefits" received. The secretary of the treasury declared this practice a ruse and a violation of the law.[17]

That ruling did not kill the idea. Advocates of reopening the slave trade in Louisiana tried to evade federal law through the subterfuge of an African apprentice bill. In 1858, the lower house of the Louisiana legislature passed a bill that "would have authorized the importation of Negro laborers under fifteen-year indentures." The upper house failed to pass it, but the idea lived on in efforts to organize an African labor-supply association in New Orleans and an African labor immigration company in Mississippi. In Florida, an editor simply invited smugglers to land their slaves illegally. "Commenting on the high slave prices, he reported that 'advocates for the re-opening of the trade in 'wool' are increasing. An investment in a ship load to be landed on the coast of Florida would be profitable. Who'll take stock?' "[18]

In a reversal of roles, Captain W. B. G. Taylor employed four of his own slaves aboard the cutter *Ingham* at Belize. For each of his slave's services, Taylor received thirty dollars a month. The collector at New Orleans, E. D. White, explained how this had happened. Wage receipts for the slaves were made out in the regular way. The slaves signed for their pay by affixing a cross, and the collector paid for their services thinking that they were free white men. When White learned the truth he pursued the matter with Captain Taylor, who reported that he had received permission to employ his slaves from the surveyor of the port of New Orleans. Believing that only the secretary of the treasury could authorize such a practice, White wrote to Secretary McLane asking him if it should continue and strongly recommending that it be stopped. In his opinion, it was a dangerous and improper precedent in light of the recent revolt led by Nat Turner in Virginia. It was absurd to teach slaves to use firearms, especially those who were put in a position to learn about the slave revolt in Santo Domingo. Furthermore, slaves could not appear as witnesses in the courts of Louisiana, so they made poor crew members indeed for a U.S. revenue cutter.[19] White's opposition to the employment of slaves on cutters was practical and reflected the interest of white Southerners. If the practice also repulsed him for humanitarian reasons, he did not say so.

McLane's answer to White's inquiry has not been found, but other correspondence on the issue indicates that he and at least one other treasury secretary opposed the employment of officers' slaves on cutters. On 23 October 1830, S. D. Ingham ruled that Captain William Polk's request for a ration allowance for his "colored servants" aboard the *Florida* at Wilmington, Delaware, was inadmissible.[20] Then in August 1832, five months after receiving the correspondence from White, McLane informed Captain Randolph of the *Crawford* at Norfolk, Virginia, that "the employment of his own slaves on board the Cutter as cook, Cabin and Wardroom stewards, being contrary to the regulations of the service," was "inadmissable."[21] Nevertheless, the practice apparently continued, for one of the abuses that Commandant Fraser terminated in 1843 was the employment of officer's slaves on cutters.[22] Such a practice has to have complicated the enforcement of laws against the slave trade.

There is little evidence that free black men were customarily employed as crewmen on cutters, but it was common practice to employ them as cooks and stewards on Boston cutters, at least before 1830. In March of that year the collector David Henshaw asked Secretary of the Treasury S. D. Ingham for permission "to continue this practice, if the commander of the Cutter should find it, as he has heretofore, more convenient than to have Whites in these stations."[23] No response by Ingham has been found, but there is no reason to believe that the practice was stopped.

Although he was too late to affect the decision of Congress, which built the *Harriet Lane* to save lives and property, the U.S. district attorney at New York, John McKeon, wrote Congressman Guy R. Pelton from New York arguing the case for a steam cutter to stop the slave trade. McKeon reported that he often had to hire steam tugs to stop suspected slavers from going through Long Island Sound and out to sea, and that a steam cutter would probably be more effective.[24]

The *Harriet Lane*, built by William H. Webb of New York and launched on 20 November 1857, did try and stop slavers in the years before the Civil War. From October 1859 to May 1860 the cutter cruised between New York and Cape Florida on an unsuccessful patrol. Back in New York Harbor, she seized several vessels suspected of having been fitted out as slavers. As in so many cases further south, charges were hard to prove. Captain John Faunce, acting on orders, intercepted the bark *Kate* off Sandy Hook on 3 July 1860 and took her back into the city under suspicion of trading in slaves. A tug in the vicinity was also stopped, and the Spanish captain of the *Kate* was found aboard. The tug and her crew were "subsequently delivered up to a United States Marshal for prosecution. Apparently *Kate* got off scot-free, for a month and a half later, she was again seized by *Harriet Lane*, bound for the coast of Africa."[25]

By 1850 the civil war that threatened to break out was postponed for a decade by a legislative compromise. A significant part of the Compromise of 1850 was the Fugitive Slave Act, which satisfied Southern demands for a federal statute to assure the return of runaway slaves. Southerners considered enforcement of the law essential to the continuation of the Union, while Northern abolitionists denounced it as inhumane. Northern revulsion was best expressed by Harriet Beecher Stowe in *Uncle Tom's Cabin*, an all-time best seller that had an enormous impact on public opinion, so great indeed that President Lincoln is reported to have said, when introduced to Mrs. Stowe a decade after the publication of her book, "So this is the little lady who made the big war."

The case of Anthony Burns intensified sectional hostility. A Virginia slave who had escaped to Boston in March 1854 by stowing away in a ship, Burns worked there as a free man until 24 May 1854, when he was seized and held for trial in a federal courthouse. Speeches in Faneuil Hall by the famous abolitionists Theodore Parker and Wendell Phillips stirred up a crowd of people who then, in an unsuccessful attempt to rescue Burns, assaulted the courthouse and killed a deputy. Burns was subsequently brought to trial. Although represented by Richard Henry Dana, author of *Two Years Before the Mast* and an outstanding attorney, he lost his bid for freedom. The court ordered him returned to his master. When some of Boston's leading citizens offered to purchase Burns's freedom for three times his market value, President Franklin Pierce refused the offer and chose instead to prove that the Fugitive Slave Act could be enforced, even in Boston.[26]

President Pierce sent four companies of marines and one artillery company to escort Burns to Boston Harbor, where the revenue cutter *Morris* (Captain John Whitcomb) was waiting to return him to Virginia. Launched at Baltimore, Maryland, on 26 April 1849, the *Morris* had sailed out of a number of northern ports before headquarters assigned her to Boston in the summer of 1851. Her services had been offered for the onerous task of returning Burns to his master by C. H. Peaslee, the collector at Boston. On 2 June 1854 armed guards escorted Burns to the steamer *John Taylor*, which would take him to the cutter, already towed down to Castle Island, whence she was to sail out of the harbor. Burns was marched aboard, but the steamer's departure was delayed for an hour so that a field piece could be loaded. Finally, at 3:20 P.M., the steamer escorted the *Morris* out of the harbor.[27]

Tens of thousands of angry Yankees watched the spectacle while "bells tolled the death of liberty in the cradle of the American Revolution." In his standard text book on the Civil War, James M. McPherson tells us that the impact of this event was so great as to turn moderates into Abolitionists. Personal liberty laws thereafter virtually nullified the fugitive slave law, and compromise gave way to violence.[28]

Six days after leaving Boston, the *Morris* arrived at Norfolk with Burns, a U.S. Marshal, and four assistants. Colonel Charles F. Suttle, Burns's owner, and a friend sailed out of Boston in the cutter, but they wanted to visit New York, so Captain Whitcomb put them on another vessel just off Sandy Hook.[29] As for Burns, his freedom was purchased by the citizens of Boston at a later date.

In the famous Nullification Controversy of 1832, when South Carolina challenged federal authority, the administration of Andrew Jackson used the *Morris* class of cutters to uphold national sovereignty. After Congress had passed the high protective tariffs of 1828 and 1832, John Calhoon developed a theory of rights that called upon the states, which he argued were sovereign, to interpose themselves between their citizens and the federal government. Acting on his theory of states' rights, South Carolina declared the tariff laws null and void and challenged the federal government by prohibiting the collection of duties within her boundaries. Under the ordinance of nullification, the use of federal force to collect duties was proclaimed a just cause for secession. President Andrew Jackson went ahead and asked Congress for the authority to enforce revenue laws, which was granted with the passage of the Force Bill. Jackson then wisely sent five fully armed revenue cutters to collect tariffs, reasoning that cutters, more than other ships, projected an image of power and diplomacy that was appropriate to such a dangerous situation.

The *Gallatin*, stationed at Wilmington, North Carolina, under the command of Captain William W. Polk, received orders to proceed to Charleston on 16 November 1832. Three cutters from New York followed: the *Alert* (First Lieutenant G. A. O'Brien), the *Jackson* (Captain William A Howard), and the *Dexter* (Captain Joseph Gold). The *McLane* from Alexandria, Virginia, made the count five. Before continuing on to Charleston, all the cutters stopped at Norfolk for provisions and arms.[30]

Even before South Carolina passed its nullification ordinance, Secretary McLane had taken action to protect the national interest. On 6 November 1832 he instructed Collector James R. Pringle at Charleston to anticipate a challenge to federal authority. Since McLane did not know the exact form such a challenge would take, he ordered Pringle, "a firm determined man," to enforce federal law as put forth in the 2 March 1799 import and tonnage bill. Under its provisions, all ships entering U.S. ports or approaching within four leagues of the coast from a foreign nation could be stopped and boarded. Customs officials could seal the hatches to cargo areas, place officers on board, and keep them there until satisfied that a ship was properly cleared and had paid the appropriate duties. The bill authorized the use of force in this process if necessary. On 6 November 1832, McLane told Collector Pringle that the *Alert* had been ordered to proceed to Charleston. Thus the collector was provided with two cutters, the *Alert* and the *Gallatin*.[31]

Later in the month, acting on information from loyal South Carolini-

The Morris-Class Cutters *Upholding Federal Authority in* Charleston Harbor *during the* Nullification Controversy, 1832–33.
(Oil *painting by* George Sottung, Claire White-Peterson *photo, courtesy* USCGA Library.)

ans, McLane authorized Pringle to replace any customs officers whose loyalty to the Union he questioned.[32] None of the cuttermen was recommended for removal, but Charles R. Holmes and William E. Hoyne, appraisers at the port of Charleston, and Major William Laval, measurer of salt and coal, were taken from office.[33]

McLane cautioned Pringle that force could probably not be used successfully and thus should be avoided if possible. To avoid a confrontation, which McLane thought a majority in the city wanted, he authorized the removal of the customs office to South Carolina's Fort Moultrie or Castle Pinckney, if and when that seemed advisable. President Jackson and Secretary McLane left the decision to the man on the spot, and Pringle proved worthy of the great trust placed in him. This dedicated public servant was fully prepared for confrontation when it came. He had permission to use the revenue cutters and force of arms if necessary, he knew that the bigger merchants of Charleston were reluctant to take on the nation for fear of losing their good credit rating, and he knew that the challenge was going to come from James Hamilton, an ex-governor of South Carolina.[34]

Thus prepared, Pringle stood firmly behind federal authority. He stationed the five cutters under the cover of Fort Moultrie's guns and beyond the reach of the city's guns. No ship from abroad could possibly reach Charleston without passing the cutters. Forewarned that Hamilton would try to import goods from abroad in defiance of the law, Pringle gave orders to enforce it. Soon thereafter, the brig *Catharine* (Captain David Maxwell) approached the city from Havana with a cargo of twenty-two boxes of sugar for the former governor. The crew from the *Alert* boarded and detained her, confiscated the sugar, and stored it in Fort Moultrie for safekeeping. Only after Hamilton complied with the law did the collector turn the cargo over to the ex-governor's agent, William Smith.[35]

This incident caused a minor international confrontation, but level heads fortunately prevailed and it passed into history without major consequence. The British ship *Roger Stewart* (Captain Robert Kerr) entered Charleston Harbor before 2 February 1833. Captain Polk of the *Alert* ordered Second Lieutenant Alexander Fraser, later commandant of the Revenue Cutter Service, to lead a boarding party onto the British vessel and inform Captain Kerr of the new procedures. Kerr was to anchor the *Roger Stewart* below Castle Pinckney. Apparently he refused to make a regular clearance of customs, for Pringle informed him that he was subject to a fine of $1,000 for failing to do so within twenty-four hours of entering U.S. territorial waters. Kerr then went to William Ogilby, the British consular officer for North and South Carolina, who protested to Pringle that Fraser had boarded the *Roger Stewart* "in a rude and insulting manner." Ogilby

Captain John Faunce. (Oil painting by George Sottung, Claire White-Peterson photo, courtesy USCGA *Library.)*

further inquired about the authority for such a boarding. President Jackson, Secretary McLane, and Pringle supported Fraser, and the *Roger Stewart* subsequently made a regular clearance. The $1,000 penalty was dropped, and Captain Kerr admitted that his charges against Fraser were false. There the matter ended. Thereafter British captains complied with cutter officers' orders and cleared customs in the regular manner.[36]

On 18 February 1833, Pringle advised Secretary McLane that the *Alert* should remain at Charleston for a while longer. All the other cutters left the city in April, but by then Henry Clay had maneuvered a compromise tariff bill through Congress and the Nullification Controversy was over, at least for the immediate future.

North and South continued to drift apart, however. Throughout the spring of 1861 support for secession raged in South Carolina and Major Robert Anderson, who with a small garrison had occupied Fort Moultrie, chose to move to the relative safety of Fort Sumter, in the middle of Charleston Harbor. After South Carolina seceded from the Union his

The USRC Harriet Lane. (*Courtesy* U.S. *Naval Historical Center.*)

presence there symbolized national sovereignty over the state. This enraged the Confederacy, which wanted the garrison removed. President Lincoln, who wanted to hold on to the fort as proof of federal authority, chose to resupply Anderson with foodstuffs but not military supplies. This placed the South on the horns of a dilemma. It would have to either accept the presence of Anderson's garrison or fire on a nonmilitary supply ship. The latter course was chosen, and it unified the North against the South more solidly than any other act had done.

Lincoln had first tried to send nonmilitary supplies to the garrison aboard the merchant ship *Star of the West*. She was driven off, so the president sent another transport, the *Baltic*, along with the navy gunboats *Pawnee* and *Pocahontas* and the revenue cutter *Harriet Lane* (Captain John Faunce). The cutter sailed for Charleston on 8 April and arrived on the eleventh, the night before the Civil War commenced. As she lay off the bar, the *Harriet Lane* stopped vessels from entering the harbor. When the mail steamer *Nashville*, en route from New York, refused to identify herself, the revenue cutter fired a shot across her bow with the desired effect. This was the first shot fired at sea in the Civil War. The *Nashville* was then given permission to proceed into Charleston Harbor, where she was seized by the Confederates for use as a commerce raider. During the bombardment of Fort Sumter the following day, the Union ships were forced to lay off because of a storm and thus played no role in the engagement.[37]

CHAPTER TWELVE

The Civil War

The Revenue Cutter Service was completely unprepared for the long and bloody Civil War. When it broke out, the service had just one 180′ sidewheel auxiliary cutter and twenty-three sailing cutters. Three of the latter were on the West Coast and six were on the Great Lakes. The Confederacy seized five of the cutters in Southern ports, and federal authorities destroyed one before it left Norfolk. This left just nine cutters in the Atlantic to perform the service's peacetime duties plus its many newly assigned wartime functions. New steamers were desperately needed. This was highlighted by the case of Captain H. B. Nones of the revenue cutter *Forward*, who, in trying to carry out orders to keep the sea lanes open between Perryville and Annapolis, asked any steamer he met to give his schooner a tow.[1]

The service acquired a fleet in a number of ways. Because priority was given to naval construction, privately owned vessels were purchased and leased and ships were even accepted as gifts. The service bought the steamer *Cuyahoga*, a Mexican War prize, along with the Clyde-built steam yacht *Lady le Merchant*, rechristened *Miami*, and the Chesapeake steamer tug *Reliance*. Several vessels were leased. James Gordon Bennett, Jr., son of the famous editor and publisher of the New York *Tribune*, was commissioned a first lieutenant in the Revenue Cutter Service and allowed to command his own 160-ton yacht *Henrietta*. After the war Bennett was elected commodore of the New York Yacht Club. Another club member, Thomas Boynton Ives, donated his schooner yacht *Hope* and received the same rank as Bennett. E. A. Stevens of Hoboken, New Jersey, gave the service his experimental iron-clad *Naugatuck*. A 100′-long semisubmersible, the *Naugatuck* could take on water in fore and aft compartments and sink 2′10½″ in fifteen minutes. She could blow out her tanks and resurface in eight minutes, and her twin screws could turn her end for end in seventy-five seconds.[2]

The *Bibb*, *Crawford*, *Varina*, *Corwin*, *Vixen*, *Howell Cobb*, *Agassiz*, *Arago*, and *Commodore Perry* were called back into the service from their more leisurely work with the Coast Survey.[3]

Serving on the Great Lakes were six small centerboard schooners built in 1856 at the Merry and Gay Shipyard at Miles, Ohio, measuring 63′ in length and 17′ in beam, and displacing an average of 60 tons. Secretary of the Treasury Salmon P. Chase ordered five of the six to proceed to the Atlantic coast via the St. Lawrence River. He left the *John D. Floyd* on Lake Superior, but her sisters, the *Aaron V. Brown* at Milwaukee, the *Isaac Toucey* at Michilimakinac, Michigan, the *Jacob Thompson* at Detroit, the *Jeremiah S. Black* at Erie, and the *Howell Cobb* at Oswego set out for Boston under the leadership of Captain Douglass Ottinger, who departed Milwaukee in the *Aaron Brown* on 31 October 1861 and gathered the others as he moved eastward. Some of the vessels were laid up for the season and had to be fitted out for the trip. Others needed major repairs, but all five got under way from Quebec on 1 December, just as ice was forming on the St. Lawrence. The *Aaron Brown* arrived at Boston on the eighteenth, followed by three of the cutters a few days later. As they neared Boston the *Howell Cobb* fell behind and was driven onto Cape Ann, where she was destroyed. Once the vessels reached Boston, they were ordered to replace more seaworthy cutters that had been assigned to naval duties.[4]

A modest building program added six new steamers in 1863: the *Ashuelot*, *Kankakee*, *Kewanee*, *Mahoning*, *Pawtuxet*, and *Wayanda*. The cutters, measuring about 135′ in length and displacing 350 tons, were driven at good speed by a single screw. They mounted six guns each and cost $100,000 to build. An additional steamer, the *Bronx*, was purchased late in the year.[5]

The U.S. Navy plied the seas during the Civil War as Britain had in her wars for centuries past, imposing blockades on enemy ports and taking

The USRC Henrietta, *Lieutenant* James G. Bennett, Jr., *Commanding.* (*Engraving from* Harper's Weekly, 10 *August* 1861, *courtesy* U.S. *Naval Historical Center.*)

command of the sea as a means to victory. It imposed a blockade on the Confederacy that, along with continued and increasing pressure from ground forces, defeated the South's bid for independence. Cutters served on blockade duty with the navy in the Atlantic Ocean and in the Chesapeake Bay. Many cutters served on the Potomac River, where they were effective in cutting off communications with the Lower South. The *Hope* stood guard with the South Atlantic Squadron. The *Agassiz* defended Fort Anderson at New Bern, North Carolina. The *Hercules* operated in the Chesapeake Bay. The *Philip Allen* lay off Fortress Monroe, Virginia, examining every merchantman that tried to proceed up the James River or into Norfolk, and the *Forward* cruised off Annapolis and Perryville, Maryland, as did the *Harriet Lane*.[6]

The effectiveness of the blockade was enhanced by the seizure of Confederate ports and the conquest of the Mississippi River. The former limited the access blockade runners had to the coast, and the latter cut off the Confederacy from its western states. During this phase of the war the *Harriet Lane* played a significant role, acquitting herself especially well in the raid on Hatteras Inlet and serving as Commodore David Dixon Porter's flagship during the seizure of New Orleans.

William H. Webb had built the *Harriet Lane* under the supervision of Samuel Pook and Captain John Faunce, USRCS, in 1857. Sought by New York underwriters, shipowners, and merchants following the loss of $10 million in property and a thousand lives at the port of New York in 1854–55, she was authorized by Congress two years later. Webb built her as an all-weather steamer to tow disabled ships and render assistance to their passengers and crew.[7]

The only revenue cutter ever named after a woman, the *Harriet Lane* bore the name of the niece of President James Buchanan. When launched on 20 November 1857, she "drew forth expressions of admiration for her light and graceful proportions."[8] She was built of wood with diagonal iron strapping that added support to her hull. She was 180′ long, 30′ in beam, and 12½′ in depth of hold, and she displaced over 639 tons. Her two inclined engines drove sidewheels that pushed her along at speeds of up to fourteen knots. Masts fore and aft provided auxiliary power. She had "three cabins, finished with great neatness, for the use of the captain and other officers, and room in steerage for a crew of sixty to eighty men." Her hull was pierced for ten guns.[9]

On 5 April 1857 the *Harriet Lane* was assigned to New York under the command of Captain Faunce. A native of Plymouth, Faunce had first gone to sea as a boy of twelve. He served in the merchant marine for twenty years and rose to command the ship *Isabella* out of Baltimore. In 1836 he joined the Revenue Cutter Service as an acting third lieutenant. He served aboard the *Campbell* in the Seminole War, was promoted to second lieutenant in 1841, and served in the revenue marine for over forty years, retiring as a captain in 1881.[10]

Four months after her assignment to New York, the *Harriet Lane* was transferred to the Navy Department to participate in a naval expedition against Paraguay. In February 1855 the dictator of that country, Carlos Antonio Lopez, fired at the navy survey vessel *Water Witch*. After considerable delay, Congress and President Buchanan ordered a naval expedition under Flag Officer William B. Shubrick to blockade Paraguay, destroy the fortifications at Humatia, and seize the capital city, Asuncion. The *Harriet Lane*, still commanded by Faunce, sailed for Paraguay on 7 October 1858.[11]

Both the cutter and Faunce acquitted themselves well on this expedition. Fifteen ships and one support vessel participated, and all of them went aground. This gave the *Harriet Lane* her opportunity, as Shubrick explained:

> All the vessels grounded more than once and it is proper, and it gives me pleasure to do so, that I should express my sense of the skill and zeal with which Captain Faunce has used the very efficient vessel under his command in extricating us from our difficulties. At one time I feared that the services of Fulton would be lost altogether to the expedition and they certainly would have been for a great length of time, if not entirely, but for the assistance afforded by the *Harriet Lane*.[12]

When the expedition arrived at Corrientes, Paraguay, it learned that an agreement had been reached. Copies of the treaties ending the conflict were placed aboard an English mail steamer and the *Harriet Lane* at Montevideo, and the two vessels left for New York. The *Harriet Lane* arrived first, on 20 April 1859, and was transferred back to the Revenue Cutter Service.[13]

From October 1859 to the outbreak of the Civil War, the *Harriet Lane* made efforts to stop the slave trade and carried out ceremonial functions for the United States government.[14] Then in April 1861, as mentioned, she fired the first shot at sea in the Civil War.

As soon as it became obvious that Major Anderson could not be relieved at Fort Sumter, a flag of truce was sent in and arrangements were made to evacuate his garrison. The major and his men went aboard the merchant ship *Baltic* and set sail for New York. The *Harriet Lane* accompanied them on their trip north, then put in at the Brooklyn Navy Yard for a quick refit and new arms, including four 32-pounders and an 8-inch rifle.

The cutter spent the next two weeks convoying vessels between the North and Maryland. On 22 April she convoyed five steamships and 4,700 soldiers from New York to Annapolis, en route to defend Washington, D.C. By the time the cutter reached Annapolis secession riots in the town had threatened the security of the U.S. Naval Academy, and Lieutenant George W. Rodgers had taken the USS *Constitution* into the Chesapeake Bay. The navy subsequently decided to move the academy to Newport for the duration of the war. The *Constitution*, with midshipmen aboard, was taken in tow by the USS *Cuyler* and convoyed there by the *Harriet Lane*. At the beginning of this journey, Captain Faunce had had to force a pilot with Southern sympathies to take them safely down the bay to Fortress Monroe. From Newport, the *Harriet Lane* returned to New York and convoyed the *Star of the South*, with 600 soldiers, to Maryland.[15]

For a short time the cutter patrolled the mouth of the Patapsco River to prevent supplies from reaching the enemy at Baltimore. While there, she seized two schooners with naval stores and a small sloop bound for Norfolk. After a spell of patrolling between Annapolis and Perryville, she was ordered to cruise with the South Atlantic Blockading Squadron. She spent much of May off Charleston before being ordered to the James River, where she fought a brief engagement with a Confederate battery in which five of her crewmen were wounded and she took out a Confederate 8-inch gun with a direct hit.[16]

Captain Faunce, having convinced higher authorities that the *Harriet Lane* needed her boilers and engine frames overhauled, returned her to the New York Navy Yard. On her trip north she transported prisoners taken from enemy privateers. She spent the end of July and August having the necessary work completed.[17]

When she arrived back in Hampton Roads, the *Harriet Lane* was sent to Savannah to take aboard witnesses in a "piracy" case. In a brief battle, the USS *St. Lawrence* had sunk the privateer *Petrel*, the former cutter *William Aiken* of Charleston. Since the United States did not recognize the sovereignty of the South, her privateers were tried as pirates. The *Harriet Lane*'s role in the affair was to transport crewmen from the *St. Lawrence* to serve as witnesses in the case.[18]

The *Harriet Lane* returned to Hampton Roads just in time to join the attack on Hatteras Inlet. When the Union navy expressed an interest in acquiring the inlet as a base for the blockading squadron, Lincoln's administration decided that it might be seized in a combined operation.

Departure of the Great Southern Expedition, under General Butler, from Fortress Monroe, 26 August 1861. The Harriet Lane *is on the left. (Copied from* Harper's Weekly, *1861, courtesy U.S. Naval Historical Center.)*

The mouth of the inlet depended for protection on Forts Hatteras and Clark, two poorly positioned sand and log fortifications with inadequate arms and too few defenders. Commodore Silas Stingham set out to attack the forts with the frigates *Minnesota* and *Wabash*, the gunboats *Pawnee* and *Monticello*, the sloop *Cumberland*, the sidewheel steamer *Susquehanna*, and the *Harriet Lane*. The transports *Adelaide* and *George Peabody* carried a thousand soldiers under the command of General Benjamin F. Butler.[19]

On the morning of 28 August the fleet concentrated its bombardment on Fort Clark, while Butler's troops landed three miles north of the fort under the protective bombardment of the *Harriet Lane* and the *Monticello*. Since the guns of the fort could not reach the fleet, Union naval forces drove its defenders away, suffering little damage themselves. General Butler was able to land only 315 of his men because heavy surf smashed two flatboats, swamped two iron boats, and grounded the *Pawnee*'s launch, but they did manage to occupy the abandoned Fort Clark.[20]

The following day Fort Hatteras fell, in part owing to effective shelling by the *Harriet Lane*. She opened fire at 10:15 A.M. and was joined in the attack by the *Cumberland*. Their bombardment was so heavy it forced the

The Harriet Lane, *Flagship of Commodore* David Dixon Porter's *Mortar* Flotilla *in the* Battle *of* New *Orleans, at the* Mouth *of the* Mississippi River. *The* Harriet Lane *is in the right front.* (*Claire* White-Peterson *photo, courtesy* USCGA *Library.*)

enemy into a bombproof in the center of the battery. The *Harriet Lane*'s 8-inch rifled gun sent several projectiles into the battery, one through the ramparts. At 11:05 A.M. an 11-inch shell exploded inside the bombproof near the magazine and the enemy "raised over the ramparts a white flag."[21]

Accepted as a great victory at the time, when the Union desperately needed one, the Hatteras operation is now viewed as having succeeded only because of an inadequate defense. Ultimately, Hatteras Inlet proved to be a poor site for a coaling station. Shoal waters, a shifting channel, and treacherous weather compelled the navy to seek another location for its blockading squadron. But none of this detracts from the job done by the *Harriet Lane*. She performed brilliantly, and made a strong impression on the people who lived at Hatteras.

Shortly after this operation, the Revenue Cutter Service sold the *Harriet Lane* to the navy. She subsequently served as the flagship of Commodore David Dixon Porter's mortar flotilla in the Battle of New Orleans. On 1 January 1863, she fell ignominiously to a Confederate boarding party in a bloody fray at Galveston, Texas. Her skipper, Commander Jonathan Wainwright, grandfather of the general with the same name who surrendered Bataan to the Japanese in World War II, was killed while trying to defend his ship. On 30 April 1864, after remaining at the Galveston dock for months, the *Harriet Lane* escaped through the Union blockade to Havana, where she lay idle throughout the war as the *Lavinia*. In 1867 she made her way to New York, was converted to a bark, and renamed *Elliot Richie*. She was abandoned off Pernambuco, Brazil, in 1884.[22]

Although the Union prevented the Confederacy from using the high seas, it failed to protect its thriving merchant marine. The South used ironclads, blockade runners, and commerce raiders in an attempt to break the Union blockade. While all of these efforts failed to affect the outcome of the war, Confederate commerce raiders, led by the *Alabama*, *Shenandoah*, and *Florida*, drove up insurance rates and thus caused Union merchant ships to flee the American flag for flags of convenience. This and other maritime problems resulted in a decline in the American merchant marine.

The revenue cutter *Caleb Cushing*, stationed at Portland, fell victim to one of the raiders in the summer of 1863, a time when the Confederacy reached its high tide with Robert E. Lee driving his army northward into Pennsylvania and Southern commerce raiders destroying large numbers of Northern merchantmen. A crew detached from the *Florida* that summer raided coastal shipping from Hatteras to Portland and destroyed the *Cushing*.

On 6 May, the *Florida* had captured the coffee-laden federal brig *Clarence* off the coast of Brazil. Lieutenant Charles W. Reed, a twenty-three year old graduate of the Naval Academy, set out in the *Clarence* with a twenty-man crew and one howitzer to raid the Union base at Hampton Roads. He captured and burned the brig *Mary Alvina* and the bark *Whistling Wind* off Hatteras, but Union vigilance kept him from pursuing his original intent. Transferring his flag to the bark *Tacony*, which he captured by posing as a mariner in distress, he sailed up the East Coast and destroyed shipping as he went. While none of his prizes was of particular value, their capture spread panic along the coast. Demands for protection inundated Secretary of the Navy Gideon Welles, who continued the blockade and ordered twenty ships from the New York, Philadelphia, and Boston navy yards to capture the privateer. Reed burned merchant ships, passenger liners, and six Gloucester fishing schooners. The merchants of Boston offered a $10,000 reward for him.[23]

Finding pursuers hot on his trail, Reed burned the *Tacony* and transferred to the *Archer*, a captured fishing schooner. In her, he quietly slipped into Portland Harbor disguised as a fisherman. His plans were to destroy two gunboats and a New York passenger steamer in the harbor.

Meanwhile, Captain George Clarke of the *Caleb Cushing* died of a heart attack. The cutter, a schooner armed with a 12- and a 32-pounder, waited at Portland for her new captain with about a third of her crew. On 27 June at 1:30 A.M., Reed and his raiders swarmed over the *Cushing*, put Lieutenant David Davenport and his men in irons, and set sail. The wind being light, Reed put two boats over the side, forgot his other plans for Portland, and towed the *Cushing* out of the harbor. The following morning Collector Jedediah Jewett of Portland rounded up the small steamer tug *Casco*, the 700-ton sidewheel steamer *Forest City*, and the screw-driven New York and Boston passenger steamer *Chesapeake*. He armed them with soldiers from Fort Preble and a number of citizen volunteers. Lieutenant James H. Merryman of the Revenue Cutter Service, who was just arriving in Portland to take command of the *Cushing*, jumped aboard the *Forest City* and joined in the chase. The *Forest City* overhauled the cutter about ten miles offshore but was driven off by the *Cushing*'s 32-pounder. Protected by fifty bales of cotton, the *Chesapeake* gave chase and closed with the cutter. The *Cushing* ran out of ammunition and could not defend herself, so Reed put Lieutenant Davenport and his crew of twenty into one of her boats, while his own crew left in her two remaining boats. Reed then torched the *Cushing*, which blew up and sank early that afternoon. Finally, he and his crew surrendered to Lieutenant Merryman of the *Forest City*. In two weeks of raiding Reed had burned and bonded twenty-two vessels, for which he was imprisoned in Portland's Fort Preble and later, for sixteen months, in Boston Harbor's Fort Warren.[24]

The Revenue Cutter Service undertook a number of unique operations during the Civil War. The cutter *Miami* transported President Lincoln behind enemy lines during the Peninsula Campaign in Virginia, and later the cutter *Naugatuck* led Commodore John Rodgers's squadron up Virginia's James River to Drewry's Bluff.

During the Peninsula Campaign of 1862, General George B. McClellan attempted to take Richmond by a combined operation on the peninsula between the James and York rivers. But McClellan was a procrastinator. He could not attack until he received more men, until the weather cleared, until Washington supported his efforts, and until he received siege guns. Meanwhile, the Confederacy continued to hold Norfolk, and the ironclad *Merrimac* (renamed *Virginia*) continued to threaten Union ships in Hampton Roads. With the Union army thus stalled before Norfolk, President Lincoln boarded the cutter *Miami* (Captain Douglass Ottinger) along with Treasury Secretary Salmon P. Chase, War Secretary Edwin M. Stanton, and Brigadier General Egbert L. Viele. On 6 May 1862 they set sail for Fortress Monroe to take a look at the situation for themselves. Hoping to seize Norfolk and put the *Virginia* out of commission, Lincoln

Destruction of the USRC Caleb Cushing *in Portland Harbor on 27 June 1863. (Copied from* Harper's Weekly, 1863, *Claire White-Peterson photo, courtesy Dennis* R. *Means.)*

and Chase searched for a location where the Union army could land. In the *Miami* they found the best spot. Two days later troops landed there and seized Norfolk. The Confederates blew up the *Merrimac* and then surrendered the city and six thousand men. Chase commented on the event as follows: "So has ended a brilliant week's campaign of the President, . . . for I think it quite certain that if we had not come down, Norfolk would still have been in possession of the enemy, and the *Merrimac* as grim and defiant and as much a terror as ever. The whole coast is now virtually ours."[25]

Shortly thereafter a Union flotilla under Commander John Rodgers tried to conquer Richmond from the James River. Rodgers's squadron, consisting of the *Monitor, Galena, Port Royal, Aroostook,* and revenue steamer E. A. *Stevens* (renamed *Naugatuck*), made its bid on 15 May. The *Naugatuck* (Lieutenant D. C. Constable) joined the flotilla because the James was full of shoal water above City Point and she could raise or lower her draft by making use of her ballast tanks, a unique ability. She led Rodgers's squadron up river as far as Drewry's Bluff, where sunken boats and spikes

The USRC Miami, 1862. (*Courtesy* USCG *Public Affairs Staff*.)

in the river stopped all progress and heavy bombardment from the shore forced a retreat. The *Galena*, which endured a rugged testing during the engagement, came out severely mauled. The *Naugatuck*'s 100-pounder rifled Parrott gun exploded, wounding one man and reducing her effectiveness, but she fought her broadside guns throughout the conflict. E. A. Stevens wrote Secretary Chase about the craft's performance:

> On her recent passage up the James River, and in the attack . . . her ability to submerge the whole hull under the water not only prevented her being struck by a single shot, but enabled her to pilot the other vessels of the fleet up the river, as she pumped out her water apartments and in that way got afloat whenever she got aground. The placing of the gun "en barbette" and the crew below the waterline prevented a large loss of life which otherwise might have followed the bursting of her gun.[26]

Many peacetime functions of the service not only continued during the war but took on additional significance because of it. Revenue cutters continued search and rescue operations, aiding an average of 115 vessels in distress each year between 1861 and 1865.[27] A dozen or more cutters continued to cruise for the protection of the revenue, a significant role not only because of the war but also because of the new, highly protective Morrill Tariff of 1861. Their success is evident in the fact that custom receipts rose from about $39.5 million in 1861 to $102 million in 1864.[28]

The USRC Naugatuck *during the* First Day's *Firing at Yorktown*, *April* 1862. *The* Naugatuck *is just to the right of the burning ship*. (*Copied from* Harper's Weekly, *January–June* 1862, *courtesy* U.S. *Naval Historical Center*.)

With increased threats of smuggling brought on by the war, the service added several new cutters in 1864. It purchased the steam cutters *Northerner* at Baltimore in April and *William* H. *Seward* at Wilmington, Delaware, in June; chartered the two steam tugs *Hector* and *Winslow* for service on the Great Lakes in September and October; and purchased the topsail schooner *Antietam* to suppress smuggling at Beaufort, North Carolina, in March. Although Beaufort was under Union control its citizens remained defiant, and the *Antietam* found more than enough work to do. She boarded as many as 86 vessels a day, and a total of 821 in August.[29]

During the Civil War, the Lighthouse Service relighted about 164 navigational lights and reestablished a number of lightships south of Chesapeake Bay because the Confederacy was destroying aids to navigation. As Union forces moved south, the Lighthouse Service placed special buoys, lights, and lightships in areas of naval activity. Lightships equipped with two white lights visible for a distance of twelve to fifteen miles were manned by twenty men, in addition to lightkeepers. Four rifled cannon were added for defense, and netting was positioned above the rail to prevent boarding. These aids were of great value to the Union

Bombardment of Fort Darling, *Drewry's Bluff*, Virginia, 15 *May* 1862. *The* USRC Naugatuck *is on the extreme right*. (*Contemporary pencil sketch, courtesy* Friends *of the* Navy Memorial *Museum*, 1974.)

navy, the Revenue Cutter Service, and U.S. merchant ships.[30] The U.S. Coast Guard would perform similar services during World War II and the Vietnam War.

The war forced many Southern officers to face the difficult question of where their loyalties lay. Every schoolboy and girl knows that Robert E. Lee agonized over the decision to join his native Virginia. Less well known is the fact that one-third of all U.S. naval officers joined the Southern cause, and that five of the seven revenue cutters based in the South were turned over to the Confederacy. At least five captains and fourteen lieutenants, besides the captains of the cutters turned over, resigned their commissions. A total of 219 revenue cutter officers served on fifty-seven cutters for the Union.

On 27 December 1860, just a week after South Carolina seceded, Captain Napoleon L. Coste surrendered the revenue cutter *William Aiken* to Charleston authorities. She was followed into Confederate service by the *Henry Dodge* (Captain William F. Rogers) at Galveston, the *Robert McClelland* (Captain John G. Breshwood) and the *Washington* (Captain Robert K.

The USRC Aiken. (*Copied from* Frank Leslie's Illustrated Newspaper, 1861, *courtesy* U.S. *Naval Historical Center.*)

Hudgins) at New Orleans, and the *Lewis Cass* (Captain James J. Morrison) at Mobile. The *Duane*, undergoing repairs at Norfolk, was destroyed when federal forces withdrew from the city.[31]

The only Southern-based cutter to escape to the north was the *James C. Dobbin* (Captain John A. Webster, Jr.), stationed at Savannah. When Captain Coste turned over the *William Aiken* to Charleston, Webster tried to escape to sea in the *Dobbin*, but foul weather and adverse winds kept him from sailing down river and the collector of the port refused to give him a tow. On 3 January a mob seized the cutter, put her crew in irons, and held her officers as prisoners on parole. At daylight a tug towed the *Dobbin* down river with the Palmetto flag at her peak. At high tide the mob ran her ashore under the guns of Fort Pulaski, took all of her boats, and went to the fort. At three o'clock that afternoon they returned, accompanied by an officer from the fort, who assumed command of the *Dobbin* in the name of Georgia. That same day, Collector John Boston learned what had happened and appealed to Governor Joseph E. Brown to allow the cutter to proceed to sea, in keeping with Secretary Chase's orders. With regrets for the illegal action, Governor Brown ordered the cutter and her officers released and the cutter towed to sea. Captain Webster lost no time getting under way and headed north, thus saving one Southern cutter for the Union.[32]

When Captain James Morrison surrendered the *Lewis Cass* to Alabama authorities, her junior officers and crew remained loyal to the Union. They were led back to Virginia and the protection of Union lines by Third Lieutenant Charles F. Shoemaker, who later became commandant of the Revenue Cutter Service. In July 1861 Shoemaker reported aboard the *Crawford*, just in time to join Commodore Silas Stingham's naval force at Hampton Roads. The junior officers of the *William Aiken*—Lieutenants John Underwood, Henry O. Porter, and Horace J. Gimball—also left for the North when their skipper, Napoleon Coste, turned the cutter over to the Confederacy; like Shoemaker, they served the Union aboard other cutters.[33]

The *Henry Dodge* was seized at Galveston on 2 March 1861. Her skipper, William F. Rogers, who had been promoted to captain on the first, was instrumental in her seizure. Other officers who joined the Confederacy with Rogers were Second Lieutenant William G. Roche and Third Lieutenant Robert M. Rogers.[34]

The *Dodge* joined the Confederate navy and, still under the command of Rogers, helped the army to protect the Texas coast until December 1862. She was then turned over to the army quartermaster at Houston. In 1864 she was purchased by private citizens who renamed her *Mary Sorley*. They operated her as a blockade runner until she was captured off Galveston on 4 April 1864.[35]

Secretary of the Treasury John A. Dix thrilled Northerners "with the hope that the time for delay was past, and that the growing rebellion would be put down with a firm hand" when, on 29 January 1861, he took action to avert the loss of the *McClelland*. Dix had sent a courier to Captain John G. Breshwood with orders to take the cutter from New Orleans to New York. Breshwood ignored the order, and Dix followed up with an order to Breshwood's second in command, Lieutenant S. B. Caldwell: "Tell Lieut. Caldwell to arrest Capt. Breshwood, assume command of the Cutter and obey the order I gave through you. If Capt. Breshwood after arrest undertakes to interfere with the command of the Cutter, tell Lieut. Caldwell to consider him as a mutineer & treat him accordingly. If anyone attempts to haul down the American flag shoot him on the spot." Unbeknownst to Dix, Caldwell had joined the Confederacy, as had Lieutenant Thomas D. Fister, third in command. His forceful words did not lead to the recovery of the cutter, though they reverberated throughout the North.[36]

At the request of Confederate Navy Secretary Stephen R. Mallory, Confederate Treasury Secretary Christopher G. Meminger turned over to the navy those cutters acquired by the South. Apparently President Jefferson Davis had intended to retain both the cutters and their personnel for revenue work with the idea that they would be useful once the war was over, but the needs of the Confederate navy won out.[37]

After being given to Alabama authorities, the revenue cutter *Lewis Cass* was renamed *Morgan* and turned over to the Confederate navy on 28 March. Captain Morrison retained command, but since Lieutenant Schoemaker had led her crew back to the Union, new officers and crew were needed. Lieutenants William T. Roche and Robert M. Rogers joined the *Morgan* from the revenue cutter *Henry Dodge* at Galveston, and two new third lieutenants, J. T. Ledyard and Robert G. Ward, joined her officer corps. Captain Morrison was ordered to report to Colonel William J. Hardee, the commander of Fort Morgan at the entrance to Mobile Bay. In May 1861 crewmen from the *Morgan* burned the buildings on Ship Island, halfway between Mobile and New Orleans. The *Morgan* returned to the navy on 14 August and was reported to be part of the naval defenses for the Mississippi River and Louisiana in April 1862. It is likely that she was lost in the fall of New Orleans on 25 April.[38]

The *Robert McClelland*, which Captain Breshwood turned over to Louisiana authorities at New Orleans, was given to the Confederate navy on 11 April 1861. Renamed *Pickens*, she served in the defense of the lower Mississippi River and the coast of Louisiana. On 30 May 1861 she overhauled the *Ariel* of Bath, Maine, and took her back to New Orleans, where the Union ship was condemned and sold at auction for $18,250. Prize money from the sale was divided among the *Pickens*'s officers and crew. She fought federal gunboats off the head of the Mississippi Passes as part of Commodore George N. Hollins's squadron in October 1862, still under the command of Captain Breshwood. To prevent her from being captured by the Union, Confederate authorities burned her at her dock in Algiers, across the river from New Orleans, on 25 April 1862.

The revenue cutter *Washington*, which Louisiana authorities seized at her Algiers dock on 31 January 1831, was also in New Orleans when David Glasgow Farragut's fleet arrived. She sank at her dock at the foot of Canal Street, as George W. Cable, author of short stories and novels of Creole life, watched from a nearby store.[39]

The cutter *William Aiken*, an 82-ton schooner and the former Charleston pilot boat *Eclipse*, was the first boat in the South Carolina navy. Purchased through a letter of marque by Charleston citizens, she was renamed *Petrel* and sent after Northern merchantmen under the command of Captain

William Perry, who mistakenly engaged the frigate *St. Lawrence* of fifty-two guns. In the ensuing and uneven fight, the *Petrel* took a fatal blast from the frigate's entire fo'c's'le battery, which sent her to the bottom and killed four of her forty-man crew. The thirty-six survivors were transferred to the U.S. gunboat *Flag* in Savannah and taken to Philadelphia, where they were imprisoned and tried as pirates. Fortunately for the prisoners, Judge Greer of the Circuit Court of Philadelphia refused to hear the case, arguing that captives taken at sea should be treated the same as those taken on land. A subsequent similar judgment by Judge Daly of New York put the question to rest.[40]

The revenue cutter officers who joined the Confederacy served in a number of capacities. For some time their status was in doubt. Neither the Confederate Treasury Department, the Navy Department, nor the War Department knew just what to do with them. Finally, on 24 December 1861, the Confederate Congress authorized the president to employ them "in such naval or military service as the public interest may require, and at such salary as he may determine: Provided, it shall not exceed the pay to which the officer so employed was entitled to receive from the United States." Some served as commissioned officers in the army and navy, while others apparently continued to serve as revenue cutter officers, and even those who accepted army and navy commissions apparently retained their revenue cutter commissions.[41]

Former revenue cutter officers who chose to continue under their revenue commissions were Captains Breshwood (the *Robert McClelland*), Morrison (the *Lewis Cass*), and Rogers (the *Henry Dodge*). Thomas D. Fister, who attended but did not graduate from the Naval Academy, not only retained his revenue cutter commission but was also promoted from second to first lieutenant in December 1864. So the revenue cutter commission remained viable throughout the war. The jobs performed by these officers included recruiting naval personnel, "the handling of public auction and sale of destroyed navy ships, commanding a receiving ship, conducting prisoners to Richmond, and assisting at ship construction yards."[42]

Captain Richard Evans, who had served as a revenue cutter officer for over thirty years, was taken into the Confederate navy as a master on 6 December 1861, but he continued to be called captain and was paid his old captain's salary. Evans served as skipper of the Confederate receiving ship *United States* at Norfolk, and worked at the Richmond Naval Works in 1862–63 and at the Richmond Navy Yard, Rocketts, in 1863–64.[43]

Captain Osmond Peters, who had twenty-eight years of experience in the Revenue Cutter Service, served the State of Virginia as head of trans-

Destruction of the Privateer Petrel, *Former* USRC Aiken, *by the* St. Lawrence, 28 July 1861. (*Courtesy* U.S. Naval Historical Center.)

portation in the ordnance department at the Gosport Navy Yard. After 29 October 1861 he served in the same capacity with an army commission, and when Norfolk was evacuated, he moved to the Naval Ordnance Works at Charlotte, North Carolina, where he supervised the transportation of public stores for the navy.[44]

The Peace at Appomattox brought to an end the tragic American Civil War and left the Revenue Cutter Service, like the nation, crying for reconstruction. It also saw the end of the age of sail, for by 1865 two-thirds of the cutters were steam-powered. Sail power would never again rule the seas, though it had shaped both the service and its sailors.

Notes

Chapter 1

1. For the history of this period see Merrill Jensen, *The New Nation*; John Fiske, *The Critical Period of American History*; and Gordon S. Wood, *The Creation of the American Republic*, 1776–1787.

2. John C. Fitzpatrick, ed., *The Writings of George Washington* 30: 291–92.

3. Leonard D. White, *The Federalists*, 116–23, 304.

4. James Truslow Adams, "Benjamin Lincoln," in *Dictionary of American Biography* [hereafter cited as DAB], ed. by Allen Johnson, 11: 259–61; Douglas Southall Freeman, *George Washington* 4: 394, 5: 385B; Francis Vinton Greene, *The Revolutionary War*, 207–11; Frank Edward Ross, "John Lamb," DAB 555–56; Harold C. Syrett, ed., *The Papers of Alexander Hamilton* [hereafter cited as A. H. *Papers*], 21: 54–55 note 1; Edward E. Curtis, "Otho H. Williams," DAB 20: 284–85; Frank Monaghan, "Jedediah Huntington," DAB 9: 416–17; John Habersham to Alexander Hamilton, 7 Dec. 1795, A. H. *Papers* 19: 472, 472 note 1.

5. White, *The Federalists*, 435–40.

6. Hyman R. Kaplan, "Hamilton's Revenue Fleet," U.S. Naval Institute *Proceedings*, 160–63; Edmund Berkeley, "The Naval Office in Virginia, 1776–1789," *The American Neptune*, 20–33, especially 24–26.

7. White, *The Federalists*, 261, 461, 462.

8. Alexander Hamilton, Treasury Department circulars to the collectors of customs, 2 Oct. 1789 and 23 Sep. 1790.

9. White, *The Federalists*, 461; Sharp Delany, Letter book, 10–11.

10. Sharp Delany to Alexander Hamilton, 4 May 1790. See also Sharp Delany to Alexander Hamilton, 31 Oct. 1789 and 23 Mar. 1790; Alexander Hamilton to

William Webb, 27 May 1790; and Alexander Hamilton to Sharp Delany, 30 Apr. 1790, A.H. *Papers* 6: 399.

11. Hamilton, "Report on Defects in the Existing Laws of Revenue," 22 Apr. 1790, A. H. *Papers* 6: 380–83.

12. Ibid., 380–81.

13. Statute 1, 175 (4 Aug. 1790).

14. Hamilton, "Report on Defects in the Existing Laws of Revenue," A. H. *Papers* 6: 380–81.

15. George Washington to Hamilton, Mount Vernon, 20 Sep. 1790, in Fitzpatrick, *The Writings of George Washington*, 31: 118–19.

16. Hamilton to Washington, 10 Sep. 1790, A. H. *Papers* 7: 31–32. The Boston collector was Benjamin Lincoln, and Joseph Whipple was collector at Portsmouth (see also Joseph Whipple to Hamilton, Portsmouth, 7 Oct. 1791, A. H. *Papers* 9: 297–99; Hamilton to Washington, 29 Sep. 1790, A. H. *Papers* 7: 77–79.

17. Hamilton to Washington, New York, 29 Sep. 1790, and Joseph Whipple to Hamilton, Portsmouth, 9 Oct. 1790, A. H. *Papers*, 7: 77–79, 104–5; Hamilton to Jedediah Huntington, 19 Nov. 1790, and Jeremiah Olney to Hamilton, Providence, 14 Feb. 1791, 17 Feb. 1791, 11 Jun. 1791, and 31 Aug. 1791, A. H. *Papers* 7: 158, 8: 30, 51, 466–67, 9: 96; Hamilton to Washington, 8 Oct. 1790, A. H. *Papers* 7: 101–2; Hamilton to Washington, 26 Jul. 1791, Washington to Hamilton, 5 Aug. 1792, John Daves to Hamilton, New Bern, 17 Jul. 1792, A. H. *Papers* 12: 116–17, 117 notes, 117–18, 166–68, 42, 7: 65.

18. Washington to Hamilton, Mount Vernon, 27 Sep. 1790, A. H. *Papers* 7: 75–76, 76 notes 4, 5, and 6.

19. Thomas Randall *et al.* to Hamilton, 15 Jul. 1793, Comfort Sands to Hamilton, 15 Jul. 1793, Benjamin Walker to Hamilton, 15 Jul. 1793, and Hamilton to Washington, 20 Jul. 1793, all in A. H *Papers* 15: 98–99, 118; Washington to Hamilton, 20, 27, and 29 Sep. 1790, A. H. *Papers* 7: 61–62, 75–76, 77–79; Fitzpatrick, *The Writings of George Washington* 31: 125.

20. James Gunn to Alexander Hamilton, Augusta, Georgia, 11 Nov. 1790, A. H. *Papers* 7: 147.

21. Washington to Hamilton, Mount Vernon, 27 Sep. 1790, A. H. *Papers* 7: 75–76, 76 notes 4, 5, and 6.

22. Hamilton to Washington, 29 Sep. 1790, and Washington to Hamilton, Mount Vernon, 6 Oct. 1790, A. H. *Papers* 7: 77–79, 97.

23. T. Williams to Secretary Timothy Pickering, Boston, 31 May 1798, in Dudley W. Knox, *Naval Documents Related to the Quasi-War between the United States and France* 1: 96–97.

24. Oliver Wolcott to Benjamin Lincoln, 2 Jul. 1798, in Knox, *Naval Documents* 1: 158–59.

25. Hopley Yeaton to the president, Portsmouth, 11 Dec. 1789, in James G. Heydenreich, "Hopley Yeaton in the Continental Navy, 1776–1781," *The Bulletin* of the USCGA Alumni Association, 11 (see also Gerald D. Foss, "First Captain of the U.S. Coast Guard," *The Northern Light*, 13; William Bell Clark and William James Morgan, eds., *Naval Documents of the American Revolution* 6: 27, 27 note, 1031, 1031

note [Clark edited vol. 1–4, and Morgan has edited all subsequent vol.; hereafter cited as Morgan, *Naval Documents*]; Robert B. Burnet, "Tobias Lear," DAB 11: 76–77; Morgan, *Naval Documents* 6: 27, 27 note, 1031, 1031 note; Robert B. Burnet, "Tobias Lear," DAB 11: 76–77; Washington to Hamilton, Mount Vernon, 6 Oct. 1790, in Fitzpatrick, *The Writings of George Washington* 31: 130–31; Washington to Hamilton, 20 Sep. 1790, A. H. *Papers* 7: 61–62.

26. Washington to Hamilton, Mount Vernon, 20 Sep. 1790, A. H. *Papers* 7: 61–62; William Jackson to Alexander Hamilton, Wilmington, North Carolina, 25 Apr. 1791, Hamilton to Tobias Lear, 25 May 1791, Washington to Hamilton, Charleston, 8 May 1791, Augusta, 20 May 1791, and 6 Oct. 1790, and Hamilton to Washington, 29 Sep. 1790, A. H. *Papers* 8: 311, 358–59, 331, 349–50; A. H. *Papers* 7: 79, 79 note 13, note 14, 97–98.

27. Washington to Hamilton, Augusta, 20 May 1791, A. H. *Papers* 8: 349–50.

28. Hamilton to Washington, 29 Sep. 1790, and Washington to Hamilton, 6 Oct. 1790, A. H. *Papers* 7: 77–79, 97–98 (see also Washington to Hamilton, Mount Vernon, 20 Sep. 1790, in Fitzpatrick, *The Writings of George Washington* 31: 118–19; Edward Brick, "Joshua Barney," DAB 1: 632–35).

29. Hamilton to Otho H. Williams, 17 Nov. 1791 and 20 Apr. 1791, and Hamilton to Simon Gross, 20 Apr. 1791, A. H. *Papers* 8: 301–2; A. H. *Papers* 9: 508–9, 509 note 1 and note 2.

30. Washington to Hamilton, 5 Aug. 1792, and Hamilton to Otho H. Williams, 13 Aug. 1792, A. H. *Papers* 12: 166–68, 199.

31. Hamilton to Washington, New York, 29 Sep. 1790, A. H. *Papers* 7: 77–79; Washington to Hamilton, Mount Vernon, 6 Oct. 1790, in *The Writings of George Washington* 31: 130–31.

32. Irving H. King, *George Washington's Coast Guard*, 18–32; Florence Kern, "Robert Cochran's U.S. Revenue Cutter *South Carolina*, 1793/1798."

33. Ibid., chap. 3.

34. Ibid., 33–36.

35. Ibid., chap. 3, 172–73.

36. Ibid; Howard I. Chapelle, *The History of American Sailing Ships*, 180.

37. King, *George Washington's Coast Guard*, chap. 3, 172–73; Chapelle, *American Sailing Ships*, 180.

38. King, *George Washington's Coast Guard*, 39, 57, 58; Sharp Delany to Alexander Hamilton, Philadelphia, 23 Feb. 1790, A. H. *Papers* 6: 275–76 (see also Sharp Delany to Alexander Hamilton, 31 Oct. 1789, and appendix A, in Sharp Delany letter book; Washington to Hamilton, Mount Vernon, 8 Nov. 1790, A. H. *Papers* 7: 143–44; Hamilton to Otho H. Williams, 22 Jan. 1791, A. H. *Papers* 7: 447–48; Hamilton to George Wray, 23 Jan. 1791, A. H. *Papers* 7: 449–50).

39. Washington to the Marquis de LaFayette, Mount Vernon, Virginia, 15 Nov. 1781, in Jared Sparks, ed., *The Writings of George Washington* 8: 203–7; Treasury Department circular to the collectors of customs, 1 Oct. 1790, in A. H. *Papers* 7: 87–88.

40. Harold and Margaret Sprout, *The Rise of American Naval Power*, 1776–1918, 22; Sherman F. Mittell, ed., *The Federalists*, 67–68.

41. Sharp Delany to Alexander Hamilton, Philadelphia, 7 Oct. 1790, A. H. *Papers* 7: 98; Treasury Department circular to the collectors of the customs, 1 Oct. 1790, in A. H. *Papers* 7: 87–88; Florence Kern, *James Montgomery's* U.S. *Revenue Cutter* General Greene, 1791–1797, 25–28.

42. King, *George Washington's Coast Guard*, 42–47, 172–173.

43. Ibid.

44. Ibid., 43, 61; Hamilton to Delany, 14 Dec. 1792, in Correspondence of the Secretary of the Treasury with Collectors of Customs, 1789–1833, roll 20 [hereafter cited as Treasury secretary correspondence].

45. King, *George Washington's Coast Guard*.

46. Ibid.

47. Hamilton to Benjamin Lincoln, Treasury Department, 25 Jan. 1790, A. H. *Papers* 6: 207–9.

48. Hamilton, Treasury Department circular to the collectors of customs, 1 Oct. 1790, A. H. *Papers* 7: 87–88, 88 note 3; U.S. Coast Guard, Office of Assistant Commandant, *Record of Movements: Vessels of the United States Coast Guard* 1: 96a; Hamilton to Simon Gross, 20 Apr. 1791, and Joseph Whipple to Hamilton, Portsmouth, 9 May 1791, A. H. *Papers*, 301–2, 337; Benjamin Lincoln to Hamilton, Boston, 29 Apr. and 3 May 1791, A. H. *Papers* 8: 317, 317 note 1; Otho H. Williams to Hamilton, 3 Jan. 1792, and Hamilton to Williams, 12 Jan. 1792, A. H. *Papers* 10: 503, 512; Tench Coxe to Benjamin Lincoln, 20 Apr. 1791, Treasury secretary correspondence, roll 6, no. 43; Hamilton to Sharp Delany, 14 Dec 1792, A. H. *Papers* 13: 323.

49. Sprout, *The Rise of American Naval Power*, 7–34; Robert Greenhalgh Albion and Jennie Barnes Pope, *Sea Lanes in Wartime*, 75.

50. Sprout, *The Rise of American Naval Power*, 36.

51. Treasury secretary correspondence, roll 6, p. 186. The author altered Hamilton's punctuation.

52. Benjamin Lincoln to Hamilton, Boston, 5 Jul. 1794, A. H. *Papers* 16: 368–69.

53. Benjamin Lincoln to Hamilton, Boston, 20 Aug. 1794, A. H. *Papers* 17: 117 (see also 117–18, 118 notes 1 and 2).

54. Walter Lowrie and Walter S. Franklin, eds., *American State Papers, vol.* 1, *Naval Affairs*, 9–10.

55. Sprout, *The Rise of American Naval Power*, 35; *American State Papers*, 6; Department of the Navy, *United States Frigate* Constitution 1: 7.

56. Chapelle, *The History of the American Sailing Navy*, 117–18.

57. *American State Papers*, 6; Hamilton to Otho H. Williams, 13 Jun. 1791, A. H. *Papers* 8: 472; Hamilton to Washington, Treasury Department, 10 Sep. 1790, A. H. *Papers* 7: 31–32; Washington to Hamilton, Mount Vernon, 20 Sep. 1790, A. H. *Papers* 7: 61–62, appendix A.

58. *American State Papers*, 6; Washington to Hamilton, Mount Vernon, 20 Sep. 1790, A. H. *Papers* 7: 61–62; Hamilton to Washington, Treasury Department, New York, 29 Sep. 1790, A. H. *Papers* 7: 77–79; Treasury Department circular to the collectors of customs, 1 Oct. 1790, A. H. *Papers* 7: 87–88.

59. *American State Papers*, 8; Joseph Whipple to Hamilton, Portsmouth, 15 Feb. 1791, A. H. *Papers* 8: 40.

60. George Gibbs, ed., *Memoirs of the Administrations of Washington and John Adams, Edited from the Papers of Oliver Wolcott, Secretary of the Treasury* 1: 40; Tench Coxe to Hamilton, 30 Jun. 1794, A. H. *Papers* 16: 538; Tench Coxe to Daniel Stevens, 3 Jul. 1794, A. H. *Papers* 16: 562; Coxe to Hamilton, 5 Jul. 1794, A. H. *Papers* 16: 566–67; Edmund Randolph to William Bradford, Hamilton, and Henry Knox, 11 Jul. 1794, A. H. *Papers* 16: 588–90 (see also A. H. *Papers* 17: 339, 454, 455, 457, 467–69, 471–75, and 18: 10–11, 170–71).

61. *American State Papers*, 8–10; Coxe to Hamilton, 25 Dec. 1794, A. H. *Papers* 17: 466–67; A. H. *Papers* 17: 454, 469.

62. Hamilton to Thomas Pinckney, Treasury Department, 30 Dec. 1794, USCGA Library.

63. Oliver Wolcott to the secretary of the navy, Treasury Department, 6 Dec. 1794 and 25 Sep. 1799, Oliver Wolcott manuscripts, 35: 86, and 37: 76; Wolcott manuscripts 30: 17; Knox, *Naval Documents*, 2: 58, 3: 37, 5: 463.

64. Benjamin Stoddert to Wolcott, Philadelphia, Navy Department, 22 Jun. 1798, in Knox, *Naval Documents* 1: 130.

65. Knox, *Naval Documents* 2: 129–34.

66. Sprout, *The Rise of American Naval Power*, 50–51; *American State Papers*, 74–75, 86–87; C. O. Paulin, "Early Naval Administration under the Constitution," United States Naval Institute *Proceedings* 30: 1001, 1023–28.

Chapter 2

1. King, *George Washington's Coast Guard*, chapter 8.

2. Alexander Hamilton to George Washington, Feb. 28, 1794, A. H. *Papers* 16: 102–3 note 2; Hamilton to Benjamin Lincoln, Treasury Department, 7 Mar. 1794, enclosure to Thomas MacDonough, and Hamilton to Lincoln, 16 Jun. 1794, all in Wolcott manuscripts 27: 103–5; Hamilton to Sharp Delany, 24 Jan. 1795, A. H. *Papers* 18: 180–81.

3. King, *George Washington's Coast Guard*, chap. 7; Melvin H. Jackson, *Privateers in Charleston*, 1793–1796, 11, 48–52, 102–3 note 2, 73.

4. King, *George Washington's Coast Guard*, chapter 7.

5. Ibid.; Jackson, *Privateers in Charleston*, 106.

6. Albion, *Sea Lanes in Wartime*, 80–81.

7. Oliver Wolcott to Benjamin Lincoln, 28 Mar. 1799, and 12 Feb. 1800, Letters sent by the treasury secretary to collectors of customs, 1789–1847, 307, 358.

8. Treasury Department circular to the collectors of customs, Treasury Department, 21 Mar. 1798, Wolcott manuscripts 39: 32; Gardiner W. Allen, *Our Naval War With France*, 41, and Oliver Wolcott to the masters of the revenue cutters on the South Carolina station, T.D.: 25 May 1798, Wolcott manuscripts 34: 83; Knox, *Naval Documents* 1: 7–9.

9. Oliver Wolcott to Samuel Sewall, Treasury Department, 7 Dec. 1797, Wolcott manuscripts 33: 70.

10. King, *George Washington's Coast Guard*, 145–48.

11. Ibid.; Samuel Eliot Morison, *The Maritime History of Massachusetts*, 1783–1860, 102.

12. King, *George Washington's Coast Guard*, 148–49; Chapelle, *The History of American Sailing Ships*, 182–83; Howard I. Chapelle, *The History of the American Sailing Navy*, 146–48; Oliver Wolcott to the secretary of the navy, T.D., T. 13 Sep. 1798, Wolcott manuscripts 35: 18, 18a; Knox, *Naval Documents* 7: 366, 367, 369, 370, 371; Commander R. R. Waesche, "Armaments and Gunnery in the Coast Guard," U.S. Naval Institute *Proceedings* (May 1929), 381; *Philadelphia Daily Advertiser*, 6 and 10 Aug. 1798; *American Daily Advertiser*, 10 Aug. 1798; *Humphreys Mast Yard Book for the Revenue Cutters* Scammel II, Eagle II, Pickering, General Greene II, Diligence II, and *Humphreys Letter Book* (the last four citations were copied in a set of notes on early cutters that the late M. V. Brewington prepared in the 1930s; Brewington's notes are now in my possession, thanks to the generosity of his widow, Mrs. M. V. Brewington, and will be referred to hereafter as Brewington notes).

13. King, *George Washington's Coast Guard*, 149.

14. Ibid., 147–51.

15. Ibid., 151–52.

16. Ibid., 152–53.

17. Hamilton, "Report on Defects in the Existing Laws of Revenue," 22 Apr. 1790, A. H. *Papers* 6: 380–81.

18. *Laws of the United States of America* (Boston) 1: 190–91.

19. King, *George Washington's Coast Guard*, 77–78 and 153.

20. Ibid., 153.

21. Ibid., 144–45 and 154–55; Albion, *Sea Lanes in Wartime*, 80–81; Allen, *Our Naval War with France*, 41, 61–62, and appendix 4; Knox, *Naval Documents* 1: 166–67, 210, 244, 518; secretary of the navy to Lt. Edd Prebble, Philadelphia, 4 Jan. 1799, secretary of the navy to Benjamin Lincoln, 4 Jan. 1799, secretary of the navy to Steven Higginson, Philadelphia, 31 Jan. 1799, and secretary of the navy to Uriah Tracy of the Senate, 18 April 1800, all in Knox, *Naval Documents* 2: 208, 210, 297, and 5: 425.; Oliver Wolcott to Benjamin Lincoln, 2 Jul. 1798; secretary of the navy to Steven Higginson and to Oliver Wolcott, 5 Jul. 1798, and secretary of the navy to Benjamin Lincoln, Navy Department, 4 Jan. 1799, in Knox, *Naval Documents* 1: 158–59, 166–67, and 2: 210 (see also 2: 114, 115, 116, 120, 121).

22. King, *George Washington's Coast Guard*, 156–58.

23. Ibid., 155–58.

24. Timothy Pickering to Capt. John Adams, 22 Oct. 1798, in Knox, *Naval Documents* 1: 533–54.

25. King, *George Washington's Coast Guard*, 158–61.

26. Ibid., 161–62; Albion and Pope, *Sea Lanes in Wartime*, 83, 70, and 81.

27. King, *George Washington's Coast Guard*, 162–64.

28. Knox, *Naval Documents* 7: 311–12 and 372–73 (see also King, *George Washington's Coast Guard*, 165, appendix B, and 209 note 77).

29. King, *George Washington's Coast Guard*, 153–54, 162–64.

30. Ibid., 108–9.

31. Ibid., 106–7 and 104–5.

32. Ibid., 107–8 (see also Merrill Jensen, ed., *Tracts of the American Revolution, 1763–1776*, xvi–xvii and John C. Miller, *Origins of the American Revolution* 83–84.

33. King, *George Washington's Coast Guard*, 98–99.

34. Ibid., 99–100.

35. Treasury Department circular to the captains of revenue cutters, 4 June 1791, A. H. *Papers* 8: 432–33.

36. King, *George Washington's Coast Guard*, 101–2.

37. Log of the *Massachusetts*; Journal of the revenue cutter *Argus* (see also White, *The Federalists*, 462–63).

38. Log of the *Massachusetts*, 54, 56, 83, and 87; Journal of the Revenue Cutter *Argus*, winter of 1800; White, *The Federalists*, 262–63.

39. King, *George Washington's Coast Guard*, 109–10.

40. King, *George Washington's Coast Guard*, 111–14; chapter 5, especially 84–89.

41. Ibid., 115–16.

42. Ibid., 118.

43. Ibid., 118–20.

44. Ibid., 166–68.

45. Ibid., 168–69.

46. Ibid., 169–70.

Chapter 3

1. Robert G. Albion, et al., *New England and the Sea*, 45 and 54.

2. Ibid., 60–61.

3. Albion and Pope, *Sea Lanes in Wartime*, 93–94.

4. Quoted in ibid., 96 (see also Thomas A. Bailey, *A Diplomatic History of the American People*, 10th ed., 117–45).

5. Albert Gallatin to the collector of customs, Norfolk, 18 July 1807, Treasury secretary correspondence, roll 18, no. 44.

6. Paul Leicester Ford, ed., *The Writings of Thomas Jefferson*, 10 vols. 8: 91.

7. Ibid., 9: 202.

8. White, *The Jeffersonians*, 34–35, 423–24.

9. Statute 451.

10. Albert Gallatin to Gabriel Christie, collector at Baltimore, 30 Dec. 1807 and 4 Jan. 1808, Treasury secretary correspondence, roll 2, nos. 145 and 146.

11. John Bach McMaster, *A History of the People of the United States, from the Revolution to the Civil War* 8 vols., 3: 279.

12. Albion and Pope, *Sea Lanes in Wartime*, 98–99.

13. Embargo circulars, p. 217 (see also Albert Gallatin to Gabriel Christie, 9 Jan. 1808, Treasury secretary correspondence, roll 2, no. 148).

14. Letters on Revenue Cutter Service, 1 Oct. 1790–2 Apr. 1833, Treasury Department, National Archives, 58–59.

15. Treasury secretary correspondence, roll 3, no. 14.

16. Elijah Cobb, *A Cape Cod Skipper*, 59–64, 64–69.

17. Ibid.

18. John Brice to Albert Gallatin, Baltimore, 14 Jan. 1808, Treasury secretary correspondence, roll 3, no. 15.

19. John Shee, collector, to Albert Gallatin, Philadelphia, 26 Dec. 1807, Treasury secretary correspondence, roll 22, no. 34.

20. Benjamin Lincoln to Albert Gallatin, Boston and Charlestown, 4 Jan. 1808, Treasury secretary correspondence, roll 11, no. 193.

21. Morison, *The Maritime History of Massachusetts*, 187–88.

22. Jeremiah Olney, collector, custom house district of Providence, 22 Aug. 1808 and 23 Sep. 1808, Treasury secretary correspondence, roll 28, nos. 177 and 180.

23. John Brice to Albert Gallatin, Baltimore, 14 Jan. 1808, Treasury secretary correspondence, roll 3, no. 15.

24. Albert Gallatin to James H. McCulloch, collector, Baltimore, 14 Dec. 1809, Treasury secretary correspondence, roll 2, no. 218.

25. S. Christiel, collector, Baltimore, 11 Feb. 1808, Treasury secretary correspondence, roll 3, no. 17.

26. Ibid.

27. Albion, *Sea Lanes in Wartime*, 100–101; Leonard D. White, *The Jeffersonians: A Study in Administrative History, 1801–1829*, 447–49; Henry Adams, ed., *The Writings of Albert Gallatin* 1: 388 (16 May 1808), 390 (23 May 1808), 417 (14 Sep. 1808), 448 (28 Dec. 1808); Letters on Revenue Cutter Service, 64 (27 Dec. 1808); Thomas Lehre to Jefferson, 31 Jan. 1809, quoted in Louis Martin Sears, *Jefferson and the Embargo*, 133; Benjamin Lincoln to Albert Gallatin, Boston, 22 Mar. 1808, Treasury secretary correspondence, roll 11, no. 195; H. Dearborn to A. Gallatin, customhouse, Boston, 21 Aug. 1812, Treasury secretary correspondence, roll 11, no. 294; roll 32, no. 349; Massachusetts Historical Society *Proceedings*, 2d series, 20 (1806–7), 310–11 (9 Aug. 1808).

28. Albert Gallatin to A. B., collector, Saint Marys, Georgia, 27 Dec. 1808, Treasury secretary correspondence, roll 38, vol. 2, no. 91; A. T. Bullock to A. Gallatin, customhouse, Savannah, 12 Sep. 1811, Treasury secretary correspondence, roll 38, vol. 2, no. 2; Wm. H. Crawford to collector of customs, Brunswick, Georgia, 26 Apr. 1822, Treasury secretary correspondence, roll 38, vol. 2, no. 141.

29. White, *The Jeffersonians*, 443–46; Albert Gallatin to James H. McCulloch, Baltimore collector, 25 Apr. 1808, and 25 Dec. 1808, Treasury secretary corespondence, roll 2, nos. 178 and 205.

30. Treasury secretary correspondence, roll 2, no. 141.

31. Jere Olney to Albert Gallatin, collector's office, Providence, 13 Jul. 1808, Treasury secretary correspondence, roll 28, no. 175.

32. Jere Olney, collector, to Albert Gallatin, customhouse, district of Providence, 10 Oct. 1808, Treasury secretary correspondence, roll 28, no. 181.

33. Letters from the collector, Portsmouth, 14 Feb. 1809 and 11 Sep. 1809, Treasury secretary correspondence, roll 26 (see also ibid., 31 Dec. 1808).

34. 22 Feb. 1809, Treasury secretary correspondence, roll 26.

35. Collector's office, Portsmouth, New Hampshire, 11 Sep. 1809, to Albert Gallatin, ibid.

36. Collector's office, Boston, 26 Aug. 1808, Treasury secretary correspondence, roll 11, no. 215.

37. B. W. to Albert Gallatin, Boston, 15 Nov. 1808, Treasury secretary correspondence, roll 11, no. 222.

38. B. W. to A. Gallatin, Boston, 30 Nov. 1808, Treasury secretary correspondence, roll 11, no. 228.

39. Treasury secretary correspondence, roll 11, no. 224.

40. Robert G. Albion with Jennie B. Pope, *The Rise of New York Port, 1815–1860*, 197.

41. White, *The Jeffersonians*, 428–30.

42. Albert Gallatin to George Hoffman, 28 Jul. 1808, Treasury secretary correspondence, roll 37; Albert Gallatin to Hart Massey, collector, Sackets-Harbor, New York, 3 Aug. 1809, 12 Oct. 1809, 8 Nov. 1809, 5 Jul. 1810, 3 Aug. 1810, 20 Nov. 1810, and 17 Dec. 1810, Treasury secretary correspondence, roll 31, nos. 2, 2½, 4, 6, 7, 9, and 11.

43. Treasury secretary correspondence, roll 31, no. 10; McMaster, *A History of the People of the United States* 3: 305.

44. White, *The Jeffersonians*, 450–51; Sears, *Jefferson and the Embargo*, 170.

45. McMaster, *A History of the People of the United States* 3: 305.

46. Ibid., 306.

47. Treasury secretary correspondence, roll 2, nos. 72–78, 84, 85, and 91; Albert Gallatin to H. B. Trish, collector, New Orleans, 4 Jun. (?) 1804, roll 16, no. 14; Albert Gallatin to W. Brown, collector, New Orleans, 10 Oct. 1804, and 14 Dec. 1804, roll 16, nos. 16 and 17; roll 16, nos. 235–38.

48. Treasury secretary correspondence, roll 16, nos. 235–38, 256.

49. U.S. Coast Guard, *Record of Movements* 1: 313.

50. Albert Gallatin to Wm. Brown, collector, New Orleans, 16 May 1806, Treasury secretary correspondence, roll 16, no. 29.

51. Albert Gallatin to Wm. Brown, collector, New Orleans, 10 Dec. 1804, Treasury secretary correspondence, roll 16, nos. 18 and 19.

52. Treasury secretary correspondence, roll 16, nos. 32, 33, 260, 275, and 276.

53. Treasury secretary correspondence, roll 16, nos. 433–35.

54. Joseph Whipple to Albert Gallatin, collector's office, Portsmouth, New Hampshire, 10 Nov. 1800, 28 Nov. 1801, 4 Aug. 1802, and 27 Sep. 1802, Treasury secretary correspondence, roll 26; roll 20, no. 73; *Record of Movements* 1: 310.

55. Joseph Whipple to Albert Gallatin, 10 Nov. 1800, 28 Nov. 1801, 4 Aug. 1802, 27 Sep. 1802, 31 Dec. 1802, 18 Mar. 1803, 31 Dec. 1803, 15 Apr. 1803, 16 Oct. 1804, 24 Feb. 1805, and 10 Feb., 9 Apr., 11 Oct., 25 Nov. and 23 Dec. 1808, Treasury secretary correspondence, roll 26.

56. H. A. S. Dearborn to A. Gallatin, customhouse, Boston, 10 Jul. 1812, Treasury secretary correspondence, roll 11, no. 286, and roll 32, nos. 300, 302, 306, 315, 316, 327, 354, and 358.

57. Treasury secretary correspondence, roll 2, nos. 14, 15, 22, 134, and 135; roll 18, nos. 8, 16, 17, 18, 20, 21, 24, 25, 30, 36, 37, and 39; *Record of Movements* 1: 310.

58. Treasury secretary correspondence, roll 2, nos. 14, 15, 22, 134, and 135; roll 18, nos. 8, 16, 17, 18, 20, 21, 24, 25, 30, 36, 37, and 39; *Record of Movements* 1: 310.

59. Treasury secretary correspondence, roll 2, nos. 14, 15, 22, 134, and 135; roll 18, Nos. 8, 16, 17, 18, 20, 21, 24, 25, 30, 36, 37, and 39; *Record of Movements* 1: 310.

60. G. Christie to Albert Gallatin, Baltimore, 22 May, 10 Jun., and 26 Sep. 1807, Treasury secretary correspondence, roll 3, nos. 3, 6, and 9; J. H. McCullock to Albert Gallatin, Baltimore, 3 and 18 Jan. 1809, and Gallatin, Baltimore, 3 and 18 Jan., 20 Feb. and 10 Mar. 1809, Treasury secretary correspondence, roll 3, Nos. 45, 46, 51, 53, and 57; Albert Gallatin to the collector, Norfolk, 3 Jul. 1807, Treasury secretary correspondence, roll 18, no. 42; roll 2, no. 136 and 138; roll 3, no. 147.

61. G. Christie to Albert Gallatin, Baltimore, 22 May, 10 Jun., and 26 Sep. 1807, Treasury secretary correspondence, roll 3, nos. 3, 6, and 9, and J. H. McCullock to Albert Gallatin, Baltimore, 13 and 18 Jan., 20 Feb., and 10 Mar. 1809, Treasury secretary correspondence, roll 3, Nos. 45, 46, 51, 53, and 57; Albert Gallatin to the collector, Norfolk, 3 Jul. 1807, Treasury secretary correspondence, roll 18, no. 42; roll 2, Nos. 136 and 138; roll 3, no. 147.

62. G. Christie to Albert Gallatin, Baltimore, 22 May, 10 Jun., and 26 Sep. 1807, Treasury secretary correspondence, roll 3, nos. 3, 6, and 9, and J. H. McCullock to Albert Gallatin, Baltimore, 3 and 18 Jan., 20 Feb., and 10 Mar. 1809, Treasury secretary correspondence, roll 3, Nos. 45, 46, 51, 53, and 57; Albert Gallatin to the collector, Norfolk, 3 Jul. 1807, Treasury secretary correspondence, roll 18, no. 42; roll 2, Nos. 136 and 138; roll 3, no. 147.

63. Albert Gallatin to the collector, Norfolk, 5 Dec. 1807, and D. Sheldon, for the secretary of the treasury to the collector, Norfolk, 31 May 1808, Treasury secretary correspondence, roll 18, nos. 48 and 56; *Record of Movements* 1: 78–79.

64. Albert Gallatin to Thomas Newton, Esq., chairman of Committee of Commerce and Manufactures, Treasury Department, 29 Nov. 1808, reprinted in Horatio Davis Smith, *Early History of the United States Revenue Marine Service*, 1789–1849, 22–23; Kensil Bell, *Always Ready*, 42–43; Stephen H. Evans, *The United States Coast Guard*, 1790–1915, 42–43 (see also Gallatin, *Writings* 1: 397; *The Writings of Thomas Jefferson* 12: 93).

65. Treasury secretary correspondence, roll 2, no. 207, roll 20, no. 305, roll 32, no. 326.

66. Jn. Steele, collector, to Albert Gallatin, collector's office, Philadelphia, 2 Feb. 1809, Treasury secretary correspondence, roll 2, no. 155.

67. Albert Gallatin to Abraham Bishop, collector of New Haven, 16 Jan., 10 Mar., 24 Apr., and 29 Apr. 1809, all copied by Wm. H. Ellis, collector, 1834, Treasury secretary correspondence, roll 32, Nos. 139, 140, 141, and 143.

68. Treasury secretary correspondence, roll 32, nos. 326, 358, 360, 364, 366, 367, and 368.

69. Treasury secretary correspondence, roll 32, no. 372.

70. Evans, *The United States Coast Guard*, 18; Treasury secretary correspondence, roll 32, no. 402.

71. White, *The Jeffersonians*, 453–54, and W. Freeman Galpin, "The American Grain

Trade under the Embargo of 1808," *Journal of Economic and Business History* 2: 85 (see also Treasury secretary correspondence, roll 3, no. 15).

72. Treasury secretary correspondence, roll 20, nos. 95, 97, 100, 101, 106, 107, and 109, and roll 22, nos. 3, 4, 5, and 10.

73. White, *The Jeffersonians*, 454–58.

74. Letters from the collector, Boston, to Albert Gallatin, 22 Aug. 1808 and 13 Sep. 1808, Treasury secretary correspondence, roll 11, nos. 2 (?) and 217.

75. Adams, *Writings of Gallatin* 1: 427 (8 Nov. 1808).

76. Statute 2, 499, sec. 7 (25 Apr. 1808).

77. Adams, *Writings of Gallatin*, 1: 397 (29 Jul. 1808); *The Writings of Thomas Jefferson* 12: 93.

78. Adams, *Writings of Gallatin*, 1: 403–4 (9 Aug. 1808).

79. White, *The Jeffersonians*, 460; Adams, *Writings of Gallatin*, 1: 406 (17 Aug. 1808) and 488 (28 Dec. 1808).

80. Adams, *Writings of Gallatin*, 1: 447 (28 Dec. 1808).

81. McMaster, *A History of the United States* 3: 307.

82. Jere Olney, collector, customhouse district of Providence, to Albert Gallatin, 23 and 25 Jan. 1809, Treasury secretary correspondence, roll 28, nos. 191, 193, and 194.

83. Jere Olney, collector, customhouse district of Providence, to Albert Gallatin, 23 and 25 Jan. 1809, Treasury secretary correspondence, roll 28, nos. 191, 193, and 194.

84. White, *The Jeffersonians*, 462–71.

Chapter 4

1. Sprout, *The Rise of American Naval Power*, 76–85.

2. Evans, *The United States Coast Guard*, 20; Bell, *Always Ready*, 45; *Record of Movements* 1: 119; Chapelle, *The History of American Sailing Ships*, 188–89, 192.

3. Smith, *Early History*, 30; Evans, *The United States Coast Guard*, 20.

4. Evans, *The United States Coast Guard*, 20; Bell, *Always Ready*, 45; Chapelle, *The History of American Sailing Ships*, 188–89, 192; *Record of Movements* 1: 78, 113, 117, 119; Smith, *Early History*, 30.

5. *Record of Movements* 1: 120 (see also Chapelle, *The History of American Sailing Ships*, 190; Evans, *The United States Coast Guard*, 21; Bell, *Always Ready*, 45–46; Theodore Roosevelt, *The Naval War of 1812* 1: 265).

6. *Record of Movements* 1: 118; F. H. to Albert Gallatin, customhouse, New Bern, 20 Aug. 1810, Treasury secretary correspondence, roll 15, no. 129.

7. The Charleston *Courier*, 20 Apr. 1813, quoted in Smith, *Early History*, 29–30 (see also *Record of Movements* 1: 78).

8. Ibid.

9. Chapelle, *The History of American Sailing Ships*, 189–92; *Record of Movements* 1: 132.

10. Chapelle, *The History of American Sailing Ships*, 188–89; Evans, *The United States*

Coast Guard, 20–21; Bell, *Always Ready*, 46–68; S. H. McCulloch to G. W. Campbell, customhouse, Baltimore, 17 May 1814, Treasury secretary correspondence, roll 3, no. 105.

11. Quoted in *Record of Movements* 1: 117–18 (see also William L. Travis to S. H. McCulloch, Williamsburg, Virginia, 14 Jun. 1812, reprinted in Smith, *Early History*, 26–27; Evans, *The United States Coast Guard*, 20–21; Bell, *Always Ready*, 46–48; Theodore Roosevelt, *The Naval War of* 1812, 1: 243–44, including notes).

12. *Record of Movements* 1: 118.

13. McCulloch to G. W. Campbell, customhouse, Baltimore, 17 May 1814, Treasury secretary correspondence, roll 3, no. 105.

14. Ibid.

15. McCulloch to G. W. Campbell, customhouse, Baltimore, 27 May and 14 Jul. 1814, Treasury secretary correspondence, roll 3, nos. 106 and 110; R. Jones to McCulloch, Baltimore, 21 Jun. 1813, Treasury secretary correspondence, roll 2, no. 272; G. W. Campbell to McCulloch, Baltimore, 21 May 1814, Treasury secretary correspondence, roll 2, no. 274.

16. Evans, *The United States Coast Guard*, 22; Bell, *Always Ready*, 49–50; Smith, *Early History*, 30.

17. Albert Gallatin to Larkin Smith, collector, Norfolk, 4 Jul. 1812, Treasury secretary correspondence, roll 18, no. 103.

18. Collector's office, district of Portsmouth, 10 Feb. 1813, Treasury secretary correspondence, roll 26.

19. *Record of Movements*, 1: 114.

20. Ibid., 115–16; Bell, *Always Ready*, 48–49.

21. *Record of Movements* 1: 115–16; Bell, *Always Ready*, 48–49.

22. Albion and Pope, *Sea Lanes in Wartime*, 125.

Chapter 5

1. Albion and Pope, *Sea Lanes in Wartime*, 139–42; Charles Carroll Griffin, *The United States and the Disruption of the Spanish Empire*, 1810–1822, 97–105.

2. Albion and Pope, *Sea Lanes in Wartime*, 142; Griffin, *The United States and the Destruction of the Spanish Empire*, 101, 103, 104.

3. Albion and Pope, *Sea Lanes in Wartime*, 144–45.

4. Sprout, *The Rise of American Naval Power*, 95; Albion and Pope, *Sea Lanes in Wartime*, 145–46.

5. *Record of Movements* 1: 313–14.

6. Treasury secretary correspondence, roll 16, nos. 312, 313, 316–18, 50, and 57.

7. Ibid., roll 2, no. 299, and roll 18, no. 153.

8. Ibid., roll 3, nos. 136, 168, 172, and 180–82.

9. Ibid.

10. Evans, *The United States Coast Guard*, 22; Chapelle, *The History of the American Sailing Navy*, 125, 127; Treasury secretary correspondence, roll 16, no. 327; Chapelle, *The History of American Sailing Ships*, 192–94.

11. Treasury secretary correspondence, roll 16, no. 325.

12. Treasury secretary correspondence, roll 20, no. 399.

13. Chapelle, *The History of American Sailing Ships*, 192–94 and 198; *Record of Movements* 1: 346, and 2: 390 and 415; Treasury secretary correspondence, roll 18, no. 178; roll 24, nos. 63, 68, 69, and 127.

14. Chapelle, *The History of American Sailing Ships*, 192–94 and 198; *Record of Movements* 1: 141, 339, and 2: 384, 394; Treasury secretary correspondence, roll 18, nos. 131, 144, 147, and 148. Another cutter on the Savannah station was lost in December 1830. The *Sam Patch*, which had just arrived from New York on 23 May 1830, was lost off St. Augustine.

15. *Record of Movements* 1: 123; Treasury secretary correspondence, roll 3, no. 130.

16. Evans, *The United States Coast Guard*, 22–23; Bell, *Always Ready*, 54–55; Treasury secretary correspondence, roll 16, nos. 327 and 351; *New York Evening Post*, 20 Oct. 1819; Stanley Faye, "Privateersmen of the Gulf and Their Prizes," *The Louisiana Historical Quarterly* 22, no. 4: 1083; John Smith Kendall, "The Successor of Lafitte," *The Louisiana Historical Quarterly* 24, no. 2: 363–64.

17. Evans, *The United States Coast Guard*, 22–23; Bell, *Always Ready*, 54–55; Treasury secretary correspondence, roll 16, nos. 327 and 351; *New York Evening Post*, 20 Oct. 1819; Frye, "Privateersmen of the Gulf" 1083; Kendall, "The Successor of Laffite," 363–64.

18. Treasury secretary correspondence, roll 16, no. 333.

19. Kendall, "The Successor of Lafitte," 363–645; Faye, "Privateersmen of the Gulf," 1083.

20. Treasury secretary correspondence, roll 16, nos. 84 and 327.

21. Ibid., nos. 342, 348, 349, and 122.

22. Ibid., nos. 122, 342, and 348.

23. See ibid., nos. 342, 348, 351, 352, and 90, and *The Savannah Republican*, 23 May 1820.

24. *The Savannah Republican*, 23 May 1820; *Record of Movements* 1: 76.

25. *The Savannah Republican*, 29 Aug. 1820.

26. *New York Evening Post*, 18 Nov. 1822; Treasury secretary correspondence, roll 16, nos. 365, 374.

27. *The Savannah Republican*, 13 Nov. 1822.

28. Treasury secretary correspondence, roll 16, nos. 360, 370, and 374.

29. Treasury secretary correspondence, roll 16, nos. 402, 403, and 404; *Niles Weekly Register*, 2 Jun. 1827; Kendall, "The Successor of Lafitte," 368–69.

30. Kendall, "The Successor of Lafitte," 369–70.

31. Treasury secretary correspondence, roll 16, nos. 402–4; *Niles Weekly Register*, 2 Jun. 1827; and Kendall, "The Successor of Lafitte," 370–71.

32. *The Louisiana Portrait Gallery*, vol. 1, 78–79; Kendall, "The Successor of Lafitte," 372.

33. *Record of Movements* 1: 123–24; Treasury secretary correspondence, roll 2, nos. 286, 292, 311, and 312; roll 3, nos. 130, 133, 136, 142, 153, 184, 185, 199, and 200.

34. *Record of Movements* 1: 123–24; Treasury secretary correspondence, roll 2, nos. 286, 292, 311, and 312; roll 3, nos. 130, 133, 136, 142, 184, 185,199, and 200.

35. *Record of Movements* 1: 123–24; Treasury secretary correspondence, roll 2, nos. 286, 292, 311, and 312; roll 3, nos. 130, 133, 136, 142, 153, 184, 185, 199, and 200.

36. *Record of Movements* 1: 123–24; Treasury secretary correspondence, roll 2, nos. 286, 292, 311, and 312; roll 3, nos. 130, 133, 136, 142, 153, 184, 185, 199, and 200.

37. *Record of Movements* 1: 124–25; Treasury secretary correspondence, roll 3, nos. 136, 168, 172, and 180–82.

38. *Record of Movements* 1: 124–25; Treasury secretary correspondence, roll 3, nos. 136, 168, 172, and 180–82.

39. *Record of Movements* 1: 125.

40. Treasury secretary correspondence, roll 3, nos. 294 and 328.

41. Ibid., roll 2, nos. 319, 332, 348, and 352; roll 3, nos. 219, 220, 288, and 302; roll 5, no. 5; roll 16, no. 108; roll 18, no. 195.

42. Ibid., roll 3, nos. 302, 306, 309, 311, 312, 318, 320–23, 325, and 330; *Record of Movements* 2: 416.

43. Treasury secretary correspondence, roll 3, nos. 302, 306, 309, 311, 312, 318, 320–23, 325, and 330; *Record of Movements* 2: 416. The *Pulaski* was launched on 31 Aug. 1825 and the *Marion* a little over a week later. The *Marion* (Captain Doane) was ready to sail for Florida on 17 Oct. but the *Pulaski* (Captain William W. Polk) was held up until 14 Nov., when her 6-pounders finally arrived.

44. Treasury secretary correspondence, roll 3, no. 328.

45. Ibid., roll 21, nos. 150, 157, 161, 206, and 209; roll 23, nos. 21 and 86; roll 39, no. 169; roll 38, no. 102.

46. Ibid., roll 23, no. 86.

47. Ibid., roll 38, nos. 81 and 116.

48. *Record of Movements* 1: 309.

49. Ibid., 141–42.

50. Ibid., 91–92.

51. Ibid., 79.

52. Ibid., 120–21.

53. Ibid., 120–21; Treasury secretary correspondence, roll 32, no. 151.

54. *Record of Movements* 1: 80, 83, and 306; 2: 421.

55. Morison, *The Maritime History of Massachusetts*, 270.

Chapter 6

1. Robert G. Albion with Jennie Pope, *The Rise of New York Port*, 1815–1860.

2. Ibid., 2–3 and 10–13.

3. Treasury secretary correspondence, roll 5, no. 28 (see also roll 32, no. 511; roll 18, no. 266; roll 24, no. 177; roll 25, nos. 24 and 186½; roll 26, nos. 76 and 104; roll 32, no. 176).

4. Ibid., roll 5, no. 28.

5. Ibid.

6. Ibid., roll 15, no. 325.

7. Albion, *The Rise of New York Port*, 214.

8. Treasury secretary correspondence, roll 18, no. 326.

9. Ibid., roll 25, nos. 186, 186½, and 194.

10. Ibid., roll 38, no. 44.

11. John Chandler, collector and superintendent of the revenue cutter *Detector*, to Capt. William A. Howard, commanding the revenue cutter *Detector*, Portland, 17 Feb. 1830, Treasury secretary correspondence, roll 25, no. 57.

12. Treasury secretary correspondence, roll 14, nos. 115, 216, 231, 232, 235, 269, 279, 315, 349, and 350.

13. Letters from Wm. Pickering to Louis McLane, 28 Dec. 1831, 12 Mar. 1832, and 19 May 1832, Treasury secretary correspondence, roll 26 (see also roll 17, nos. 387 and 392, and roll 26, no. 113).

14. Treasury secretary correspondence, roll 17, nos. 387, 389, 392, 427, and 451.

15. Albion, *The Rise of New York Port*, 214; Treasury secretary correspondence, roll 17, nos. 387, 389, 391, 427, and 451.

16. Treasury secretary correspondence, roll 5, nos. 80 and 81.

17. Ibid., roll 14, no. 216.

18. Ibid., roll 14, nos. 231 and 232.

19. Ibid., no. 235.

20. Ibid., nos. 269 and 350.

21. Ibid., no. 350.

22. Ibid., nos. 279, 315, 349, and 350.

23. Ibid., roll 32, nos. 178, 208, 210, and 214.

24. Chapelle, *The History of the American Sailing Navy*, 513.

25. Contract for revenue cutter *Roger B. Taney*, between Isaac Webb and John Allen with Samuel Swartwout, collector for port of New York, 1 Sep. 1830.

26. Treasury secretary correspondence, roll 5, no. 79.

27. Bell, *Always Ready*, 69–70.

28. Smith, *Early History*, 74; ibid., 96–97.

29. Fraser quoted in Smith, *Early History*, 74.

30. Fraser quoted in Bell, *Always Ready*, 99 (see also ibid., 95–96).

31. Bell, *Always Ready*, 99.

32. Statute 1, 605 and 729; Wolcott manuscripts 37: 107 and 112; Treasury secretary correspondence, roll 7, no. 51; Correspondence regarding marine hospital, 1802–69, New London, Connecticut; Treasury secretary correspondence, roll 1, nos. 329 and 340–41; White, *The Federalists*, 121; Lawrence F. Schmeckebier, *The Public Health Service*, 3.

33. Treasury secretary correspondence, roll 2, nos. 338 and 337; roll 14, no. 40; roll 32, no. 468.

34. Ibid., roll 3, no. 354; roll 2, nos. 376, 376½, and 380.

35. Ibid., roll 2, no. 361.

36. Ibid., roll 38, II, nos. 217 and 219.

37. Ibid., nos. 220, 221, 274, 275, and 233.
38. Ibid., no. 233.
39. Ibid.
40. Ibid.
41. Ibid.
42. Ibid., no. 235.
43. Ibid., no. 295.
44. Ibid.
45. Ibid., roll 18, no. 229; roll 18, no. 231.
46. Ibid., roll 21, nos. 54, 55, and 57.
47. Albert Gallatin to Wm. Brown, collector, New Orleans, 20 Feb. 1805, Treasury secretary correspondence, roll 16, no. 21.
48. Albert Gallatin to Peter Muhlenburg, collector, Philadelphia, 7 Oct. 1802, Treasury secretary correspondence, roll 20, no. 45.
49. Albert Gallatin to Thos. H. Williams, collector, New Orleans, 1 Jun. 1812, Treasury secretary correspondence, roll 16, no. 48.
50. Treasury secretary correspondence, roll 16, no. 411.
51. Ibid., roll 3, no. 481.
52. Ibid., nos. 472 and 473.
53. Ibid., roll 23, no. 231.
54. Bell, *Always Ready*, 96–97.
55. Ibid., 97.
56. Ibid., 97–98.
57. Ibid., 98.
58. Ibid.
59. Harold Burstyn, "Seafaring and the Emergence of American Science," in *The Atlantic World of Robert G. Albion*, ed. by Benjamin W. Labaree, 76–109, especially 77, 79–80, 82–85, 85–86, and 98–99.
60. Treasury secretary correspondence, roll 38, II, nos. 209 and 257.
61. Smith, *Early History*, 35–36.
62. Ibid., 35; Treasury secretary correspondence, roll 17, no. 266.
63. Treasury secretary correspondence, roll 25, nos. 73, 96.
64. Smith, *Early History*, 36–37.
65. Treasury secretary correspondence, roll 3, no. 488.
66. Ibid., roll 32, no. 211.
67. Smith, *Early History*, 37.

Chapter 7

1. Treasury secretary correspondence, roll 12, nos. 111, 154, 225, 256, and 264, and roll 13, nos. 317 and 352; Andrew Jackson to the secretary of the treasury, 16 Sep. 1829.
2. Treasury secretary correspondence, roll 17, no. 148, 208, 263, 271, 276, 278, 301, 303, 310, 381, 389, and 392; Albion, *The Rise of New York Port*, 214.

3. Chapelle, *The History of American Sailing Ships*, 202–3.

4. Ibid., 203; Treasury secretary correspondence, roll 14, nos. 14 and 36.

5. Contract for revenue cutter *Roger B. Taney*.

6. Chapelle, *The History of American Sailing Ships*, 203; Alexander Hamilton to the secretary of the treasury, 16 Sep. 1829.

7. Treasury secretary correspondence, roll 14, no. 65.

8. *Record of Movements* 2: 389.

9. Chapelle, *The History of American Sailing Ships*, 203–4; *Record of Movements* 2: 389.

10. Treasury secretary correspondence, roll 24, nos. 188 and 193.

11. Ibid., roll 25, no. 264.

12. Ibid., roll 32, no. 175.

13. Chapelle, *The History of American Sailing Ships*, 205 (see also Evans, *The United States Coast Guard*, 24–25, and Treasury secretary correspondence, roll 14, no. 115).

14. Contract for revenue cutter *Roger B. Taney*.

15. Chapelle, *The History of American Sailing Ships*, 204–5; contract for revenue cutter *Roger B. Taney*.

16. Treasury secretary correspondence, roll 17, no. 435; Chapelle, *The History of American Sailing Ships*, 204; Treasury secretary correspondence, roll 17, nos. 106, 208, 221, 260, 268, 270, 286, 340, and 414 (see also Treasury secretary correspondence, roll 16, nos. 370 and 417; roll 18, no. 185).

17. Treasury secretary correspondence, roll 39, no. 129 (see also roll 16, nos. 370 and 417; roll 17, nos. 106, 208, 221, 260, 268, 270, 286, 340, and 414; roll 18, no. 185).

18. Ibid., roll 39, no. 129.

19. Smith, *Early History*, 36.

20. Chapelle, *The History of American Sailing Ships*, 206.

21. Treasury secretary correspondence, roll 17, no. 435.

22. Ibid.

23. Chapelle, *The History of American Sailing Ships*, 204–5; Treasury secretary correspondence, roll 3, nos. 329, 530, and 532; roll 18, nos. 227 and 228.

24. *Record of Movements* 2: 391–93.

25. Smith, *Early History*, 36.

26. *Record of Movements* 1: 105.

27. Chapelle, *The History of American Sailing Ships*, 204–5.

28. *Record of Movements* 2: 412.

29. Ibid., 412–14.

30. Ibid.

31. Ibid.

32. Ibid.

33. Ibid.

34. Ibid.

35. Truman R. Strobridge, "Captain Daniel Dobbins: One Man History Has Forgotten," *The Coast Guard Engineer's Digest* 4–7.

36. Strobridge, "Captain Daniel Dobbins," 7–8.

Chapter 8

1. George E. Buker, *Swamp Sailors: Riverine Warfare in the Everglades, 1835–1842*, 16–31.

2. *Record of Movements* 1: 83, 307–8; Evans, *The United States Coast Guard*, 25–26.

3. *Record of Movements* 1: 143–44.

4. Buker, *Swamp Sailors*, 17–20; *Record of Movements* 1: 81.

5. Buker, *Swamp Sailors*, 17–20, 136; *Record of Movements* 1: 81, 131.

6. *Record of Movements* 1: 132.

7. Buker, *Swamp Sailors*, 23–24; *Record of Movements* 1: 131, 132, 144.

8. Buker, *Swamp Sailors*, 25–26.

9. Ibid., 26–29; *Record of Movements* 1: 81.

10. Buker, *Swamp Sailors*, 35–37; *Record of Movements* 1: 81, 132, 133; 2: 393.

11. Buker, *Swamp Sailors*, 35.

12. Ibid., 36–37; *Record of Movements* 1: 81, 132, 133.

13. Buker, *Swamp Sailors*, 36–37; *Record of Movements* 1: 81, 132, 133.

14. Winslow Foster, commanding the *Jefferson*, to secretary of the treasury, in *Record of Movements* 2: 392.

15. *Record of Movements* 2: 36–37; 1: 81, 132, 133.

16. Ibid., 1: 131–33.

17. Buker, *Swamp Sailors*, 80–81.

18. *Record of Movements* 1: 82.

19. Ibid., 135.

20. Ibid., 49–68.

21. Buker, *Swamp Sailors*, 69.

22. Ibid., 71; *Record of Movements* 1: 303, 307.

23. Buker, *Swamp Sailors*, 71–73; *Record of Movements* 1: 307. The *Madison* cruised as far north as Brunswick, Georgia, until August, when she returned to her revenue duties at Portsmouth.

24. Buker, *Swamp Sailors*, 73–77; *Record of Movements* 1: 304, 305. The sources differ about the number of scalps; one says there were eleven, the other says seven.

25. Buker, *Swamp Sailors*, 78–79.

26. Ibid., 97–114.

27. Ibid., 95–96.

28. Ibid., 115–18; *Record of Movements* 1: 83, 300, 307, 308, and 310.

29. Buker, *Swamp Sailors*, 118–19.

30. Ibid., 124.

31. Ibid., 125.

32. Ibid., 127–29.

33. Ibid., 129–35.

34. Ibid., 129–35.

35. *Record of Movements* 1: 300, 308, 310.

36. Buker, *Swamp Sailors*, 136–40.

Chapter 9

1. Leonard D. White, *The Jacksonians*, 138; Bell, *Always Ready*, 71–72.

2. White, *The Jacksonians*, 138 (see also Bell, *Always Ready*, 71–72).

3. Bell, *Always Ready*, 72.

4. Ibid., 75–76; Evans, *The United States Coast Guard*, 34–35.

5. Philip McFarland, *Sea Dangers*, 52–56, 60, 77.

6. J. C. Spencer to Hon. J. W. Jones, speaker of the House of Representatives, 10 Jan. 1844, quoted in Smith, *Early History of the U.S. Revenue Marine*, 57–58; White, *The Jacksonians*, 37–38; Evans, *The United States Coast Guard*, 34–35, 37; Bell, *Always Ready*, 76–77.

7. Evans, *The United States Coast Guard*, 31–34.

8. Bell, *Always Ready*, 79–80.

9. Alexander V. Fraser's annual report on the Revenue Marine Service, 9 Jan. 1844, reprinted in Smith, *Early History of the U.S. Revenue Marine*, 58–62.

10. Bell, *Always Ready*, 77–78, 89–90; Evans, *The United States Coast Guard*, 54–55; Smith, *Early History*, 57, 67–68.

11. Smith, *Early History*, 68–69.

12. *A Brief Sketch of the Character and Services of Captain Josiah Sturgis*, 34; Bell, *Always Ready*, 78–79; Evans, *The United States Coast Guard*, 55.

13. J. C. Spencer to Hon. J. W. Jones, speaker of the House of Representatives, 10 Jan. 1844, quoted in Smith, *Early History*, 57.

14. Treasury secretary correspondence, roll 17, no. 240.

15. Correspondence of Levi Woodbury, quoted in Smith, *Early History*, 62–63 (see also 70–71; *Record of Movements* 1: 108–9).

16. Fraser's annual report of the Revenue Marine Service, 19 Jan. 1844, in Smith, *Early History*, 59.

17. Ibid., 9 Jan. 1844, 59–60, 62.

18. Robert G. Albion, *Five Centuries of Famous Ships*, 142.

19. R. H. Thornton, *British Shipping*, 67.

20. Jeanne Figueira, "The Story of Hunter's Wheel," *Commandant's Bulletin*, 18–19.

21. Smith, *Early History*, 64.

22. Ibid., 69–71; Bell, *Always Ready*, 90–94.

23. Figueira, "The Story of Hunter's Wheel," 20.

24. Smith, *Early History*, 70–71; Figueira, "The Story of Hunter's Wheel," 19–20.

25. Evans, *The United States Coast Guard*, 45–48.

26. Ibid., 51; Smith, *Early History*, 70–71.

27. Smith, *Early History*, 70–71.

28. Evans, *The United States Coast Guard*, 38–40, 44–51; Bell, *Always Ready*, 87–88, 91–93.

29. House Report 125, 18th Cong., 1st sess., p. 2 (22 May 1824).

30. House Doc. 69, 18th Cong., 2d sess., p. 3 (31 Jan. 1825), for Crawford quote; White, *The Jeffersonians*, 22–24.

31. Evans, *The United States Coast Guard*, 29; Carl Cutler, *Queens of the Western Ocean*, 226; David Stick, *Graveyard of the Atlantic*, 245.

32. Stick, *Graveyard of the Atlantic*, 27–42, 245.

33. Evans, *The United States Coast Guard*, 29; Cutler, *Queens of the Western Ocean*, 226.

34. Benjamin Lincoln to Albert Gallatin, Boston, 25 Sep. 1805, Treasury secretary correspondence, roll 11, no. 164.

35. Treasury secretary correspondence, roll 25, nos. 83, 84, and 89.

36. John Chandler, collector, to Lieutenant Green Walden, collector's office, district of Portland and Falmouth, 4 Mar. 1831, Treasury secretary correspondence, roll 25, no. 145.

37. J. H. McCulloch, collector, to Richard Rush, customhouse, Baltimore, 21 Jul. 1826, Treasury secretary correspondence, roll 3, no. 332; roll 18, no. 193.

38. Joshua Taylor to S. D. Ingham, and S. D. Ingham to Joshua Taylor, Treasury secretary correspondence, roll 38, nos. 227 and 287.

39. Treasury secretary correspondence, roll 38, nos. 99 and 109.

40. Ibid., roll 25, no. 207; John Chandler, collector, and superintendent of lighthouses in Maine, to Capt. Henry D. Hunter, commanding revenue cutter *Morris*, collector's office, district of Portland and Falmouth, 5 Sep. 1832, Treasury secretary correspondence, roll 25.

41. Benjamin Lincoln to Albert Gallatin, Hingham, 24 Sep. 1808, Treasury secretary correspondence, roll 11, no. 218.

42. Evans, *The United States Coast Guard*, 55–56; order of George M. Bibb, secretary of the treasury, 19 Feb. 1845, in Smith, *Early History*, 73; *Record of Movements* 1: 46 and 83; 2: 421; Treasury secretary correspondence, roll 4, no. 22; roll 14, no. 170; roll 17, no. 240; David Stick, *North Carolina Lighthouses*, 42–43.

43. Evans, *The United States Coast Guard*, 55–56; order of George M. Bibb, secretary of the treasury, 19 Feb. 1845, published in Smith, *Early History*, 73; *Record of Movements* 1: 46, 83; 2: 421; Treasury secretary correspondence, roll 4, no. 22; roll 14, no. 170; roll 17, no. 240.

44. Robert G. Albion, *Square Riggers on Schedule*, 226–27.

45. Albion, *Square Riggers on Schedule*, 227.

46. Wick York: "The Architecture of the U.S. Life-Saving Stations," *The Log of Mystic Seaport*, 3; Albion, *Square Riggers on Schedule*, 227.

47. Evans, *The United States Coast Guard*, 36–37; White, *The Jacksonians*, 38–39.

48. White, *The Jacksonians*, 438–39.

49. Evans, *The United States Coast Guard*, 57.

50. Ibid.

51. Ibid.; White, *The Jacksonians*, 438–39; York, "The Architecture of the U.S. Life-Saving Stations," 3.

52. Dennis R. Means, "A Heavy Sea Running: The Formation of the U.S. Life-Saving Service, 1846–1878," *Prologue*, 226–27, 239 note 24.

53. White, *The Jacksonians*, 538; House Doc. 45, 28th Cong., 1st sess., p. 1 (10 Jan. 1844).

54. White, *The Jacksonians*, 538; House Doc. 45, 28th Cong., 1st sess., p. 1 (10 Jan. 1844).

Chapter 10

1. R. J. Walker, secretary of the treasury, to Capt. John A. Webster, Newport, 19 May 1846, in Smith, *Early History*, 74–76, 77 (see also *Record of Movements* 1: 49, 98, 103).

2. Walker to Webster, Newport, 19 May 1846, in Smith, *Early History*, 74–76; *Record of Movements* 1: 146; Robert L. Scheina, "A Modelbuilder's Dilemma," *The Mariners' Museum Journal*, 16.

3. Walker to Webster, Newport, in Smith, *Early History*, 74–76; *Record of Movements* 1: 105, 108, 112, 146.

4. Smith, *Early History*, 77.

5. *Record of Movements* 1: 46.

6. *Record of Movements* 1: 47–49.

7. Smith, *Early History*, 74, 76; Evans, *The United States Coast Guard*, 61; and *Record of Movements* 1: 108, 109–10, 301; 2: 422.

8. Smith, *Early History*, 74, 76; Evans, *The United States Coast Guard*, 61; and *Record of Movements* 1: 108, 109–10, 301; 2: 422. It was not uncommon for cutters to be hit by lightning. The *Roger B. Taney* was also hit near Tybel Island on 30 Aug. 1857.

9. Bell, *Always Ready*, 104; Smith, *Early History*, 76; *Record of Movements* 1: 98.

10. Bell, *Always Ready*, 104–5.

11. *Record of Movements* 1: 112.

12. Smith, *Early History*, 78; Bell, *Always Ready*, 105; *Record of Movements* 1: 70–71.

13. Bell, *Always Ready*, 106; Smith, *Early History*, 77; *Record of Movements* for cutters in the Mexican War.

14. Evans, *The United States Coast Guard*, 61; Smith, *Early History*, 77.

15. *Record of Movements* 1: 50; Bell, *Always Ready*, 106–7; Evans, *The United States Coast Guard*, 61.

16. K. Jack Bauer, *The Mexican War, 1846–1848*, 106–9; Raphael Semmes, *Service Afloat and Ashore during the Mexican War*, 75–79, 80–82; Justin Smith, *The War with Mexico*, 2: 191–93, 195–96.

17. Bauer, *The Mexican War*, 106–9, 111–12; Semmes, *Service Afloat and Ashore*, 75–79.

18. Bauer, *The Mexican War*, 112–13, 116–17; Samuel Eliot Morison, *Old Bruin: Commodore Matthew C. Perry, 1794–1858*, 191–92; Semmes, *Service Afloat and Ashore*, 88–89; *Record of Movements* 1: 99.

19. Bauer, *The Mexican War*, 337–40.

20. Ibid., 117–18; Commodore M. C. Perry to Commodore Conner, *Record of Movements* 1: 100–101.

21. Perry to Conner, *Record of Movements* 1: 100–101.

22. Morison, *Old Bruin*, 194–95; Bauer, *The Mexican War*, 117–18; Perry to Conner, *Record of Movements* 1: 100.

23. Perry to Conner, U.S. steamer *Mississippi*, Anton Lizardo, 11 Nov. 1846, Commodore David Conner papers, lot 73, box 1; Perry to Conner, *Record of Movements* 1: 100–101; Bauer, *The Mexican War*, 117–18; Evans, *The United States Coast Guard*, 62–63; Semmes, *Service Afloat and Ashore*, 89–90; Smith, *The War with Mexico* 2: 200.

24. Perry to Conner, U.S. steamer *Mississippi*, 3 Nov. 1846, Commodore David Conner papers, lot 73, box 1; W. A. Howard to Commodore Perry, McLane, 24 Dec. 1846, Conner papers, lot 73, box 1; Conner papers, lot 188, box 10; Perry to Conner, journal of *Forward*, Conner to secretary of the navy, secretary of the treasury to Captain Nones, all in *Record of Movements* 1: 101–102; Morison, *Old Bruin*, 194–98, 200–201; Bauer, *The Mexican War*, 119; Evans, *The United States Coast Guard*, 62–63; Smith, *The War with Mexico* 2: 200.

25. *Record of Movements* 1: 70–71, 80, 104, 110, 112, 147, 301; Bell, *Always Ready*, 108–109.

26. Smith, *Early History*, 78–79.

27. *Record of Movements* 2: 421–22.

28. Evans, *The United States Coast Guard*, 64–65.

29. James P. Delgado, "In the Midst of a Great Excitement: The Argosy of the Revenue Cutter C. W. *Lawrence*," *The American Neptune*, 119–20.

30. Delgado, "C. W. *Lawrence*," 120.

31. Ibid.

32. Evans, *The United States Coast Guard*, 68; Delgado, "C. W. *Lawrence*," 120–21.

33. Delgado, "C. W. *Lawrence*," 121; Evans, *The United States Coast Guard*, 69.

34. Evans, *The United States Coast Guard*, 68.

35. Ibid., 68–69.

36. Ibid., 70.

37. Ibid., 69; Delgado, "C. W. *Lawrence*," 121.

38. Delgado, "C. W. *Lawrence*," 151; Morison, *The Maritime History of Massachusetts*, 78.

39. Delgado, "C. W. *Lawrence*," 122–23.

40. Ibid., 123–25.

41. Ibid., 125.

42. Ibid.

43. Ibid., 126.

44. Ibid., 126–27.

45. Albion, *Five Centuries of Famous Ships*, 199–201.

46. Ibid., 200.

47. Ibid.

48. Delgado, "C. W. *Lawrence*," 127–28.

49. Ibid., 128.

50. Ibid., 128–29.

51. Ibid., 129; *Record of Movements* 1: 110.

52. Delgado, "C. W. *Lawrence*," 129.

53. Ibid.

54. Ibid., 129–30.

55. Ibid.

Chapter 11

1. "An act to prohibit the carrying on the slave trade, from the United States to any foreign place or country," *Laws of the United States of America from the 4th of March, 1789, to the 4th of March* 1815 2: 383–84; Oliver Wolcott to Jeremiah Olney, Treasury Department, 21 Aug. 1799, Letters sent by the treasury secretary, roll 1, 333–34; Wolcott to Benjamin Lincoln, Treasury Department, 30 Apr. 1799, Letters sent by the treasury secretary, roll 1, 308 (see also Wolcott to Lincoln, Treasury Department, 6 May 1799, 10 Jun. 1799, 29 May 1800, and Wolcott to Olney, Treasury Department, 28 Jun. 1799, roll 1, 309, 319–20, 331, 365).

2. Kenneth M. Stampp, *The Peculiar Institution*, 271–72.

3. Correspondence of the treasury secretary, roll 38, no. 143.

4. Ibid., no. 4.

5. Ibid., no. 241.

6. John T. Noonan, *The Antelope*, 11, 13, 31–33; *Record of Movements* 1: 142.

7. *The Catholic Transcript*, 28 Oct. 1977, 5; Noonan, *The Antelope*, 31–38.

8. Noonan, *The Antelope*, 33, 45–46, 48, 49, 66, 77–80, 120–21, 123–26, 130, 134, 139, 143–44, 156.

9. *The Catholic Transcript*, 28 Oct. 1977, 5.

10. Noonan, *The Antelope*, 156.

11. *Record of Movements* 1: 142.

12. Correspondence of the treasury secretary, roll 39, nos. 148, 149, 186, and 187.

13. Ibid., roll 16, nos. 352 and 353. For the difficulty of gaining a conviction in Louisiana, see also roll 16, nos. 302–6.

14. Ibid., roll 16, nos. 357 and 362.

15. Morison, *Old Bruin*, 61–76. For further cases of international complication see Treasury secretary correspondence, roll 16, nos. 302–6.

16. Treasury secretary correspondence, roll 38, no. 2.

17. Ibid., nos. 67 and 105.

18. Stampp, *The Peculiar Institution*, 276, 277.

19. Treasury secretary correspondence, roll 16, nos. 389, 516, 492, 496, and 499.

20. Ibid., roll 32, no. 475.

21. Ibid., roll 18, no. 295.

22. Evans, *The United States Coast Guard*, 55.

23. Treasury secretary correspondence, roll 14, no. 21.

24. Philip E. Yanaway, "The United States Revenue Cutter *Harriet Lane*, 1857–1884," *The American Neptune*, 175–77.

25. Yanaway, "The United States Revenue Cutter *Harriet Lane*," 182–83.

26. *Boston Slave Riot, and Trial of Anthony Burns*, 79, 85–86.

27. Ibid.; *Record of Movements* 1: 43.

28. James M. McPherson, *Ordeal By Fire*, 79–80; J. G. Randall, *The Civil War and Reconstruction*, 166–67; Marie A. Kasten, "Anthony Burns," Johnson, DAB 3: 308; *Boston Slave Riot*, 79, 85–86.

29. *Record of Movements* 1: 43.

30. Ibid., 79.

31. Treasury secretary correspondence, roll 32, no. 20; John Spencer Bassett, ed., *Correspondence of Andrew Jackson* 4: 481.

32. Treasury secretary correspondence, roll 32, no. 21; Bassett, *Correspondence of Andrew Jackson* 4: 474, 481, 485–88.

33. Treasury secretary correspondence, roll 32, no. 47.

34. Ibid., nos. 23, 24, 46, 48, 49, 50, and 64.

35. Ibid., nos. 64, 24, 25, 49, and 50.

36. Ibid., nos. 25, 51, 53, 54, 55, 56, 57 and 60.

37. Richard N. Current, *Lincoln and the First Shot*; Yanaway, "The Revenue Cutter *Harriet Lane*," 186–87; Frank H. Pulsifer, "Reminiscences of the *Harriet Lane*," *Journal of the* U.S. *Coast Guard Association* 1: 31.

Chapter 12

1. Evans, *The United States Coast Guard*, 78–79; Kern, *The United States Revenue Cutters in the* Civil War, 2–1 to 2–14.

2. Bell, *Always Ready*, 115–16; Evans, *The United States Coast Guard*, 79; Kern, *The United States Revenue Cutters*, 8–4 to 8–9, 4–1 to 4–2, 11–2 to 11–3.

3. Bell, *Always Ready*, 114; Kern, *The United States Revenue Cutters*, 6–7.

4. Kern, *The United States Revenue Cutters*, 9–1 to 9–7.

5. Evans, *The United States Coast Guard*, 79–80; Kern, *The United States Revenue Cutters*, 14–2 to 14–8.

6. Bell, *Always Ready*, 115–17, 121–22; Evans, *The United States Coast Guard*, 77.

7. Yanaway, "The United States Revenue Cutter *Harriet Lane*," 175–77.

8. *The New York Times*, 20 Nov. 1857, 1.

9. Yanaway, "The United States Revenue Cutter *Harriet Lane*," 177–79; *The New York Times*, 12 Mar. 1858, 1.

10. Yanaway, "The United States Revenue Cutter *Harriet Lane*," 177 note 9, 179–80.

11. Ibid., 180–81; *Record of Movements* 1: 35–36.

12. *Record of Movements* 1: 36.

13. Yanaway, "The United States Revenue Cutter *Harriet Lane*," 180–82; *Record of Movements* 1: 37.

14. Yanaway "The United States Revenue Cutter *Harriet Lane*," 182–86.

15. Ibid., 187–88.

16. Ibid., 188–90; Bell, *Always Ready*, 116–17.

17. Yanaway, "The United States Revenue Cutter *Harriet Lane*," 190.

18. Ibid., 190; W. E. Ehrman, "Rebel Cutter Takes on U.S. Navy," *The Bulletin* of the U.S. Coast Guard Academy Alumni Association, 20–22.

19. Rowena Reed, *Combined Operations in the* Civil War, 11–14.

20. Reed, *Combined Operations*, 12–14.

21. *Harper's Weekly*, 14 Sep. 1861, 578.

22. *Civil War Naval Chronology, 1861–1865* 2: 26, 3: 3, 150; 4: 50–51, 6: 249; Yanaway, "The United States Revenue Cutter *Harriet Lane*," 192–205.

23. Albion, *Sea Lanes in Wartime*, 164–65; Barbara C. Long, "When the Civil War Came to Maine," *Yankee*, 198–205; U.S. Office of Naval War Records, *Official Records of the Union and Confederate Navies in the War of the Rebellion*, series 1, 2: 654–57.

24. Albion, *Sea Lanes in Wartime*, 165; Long, "When the Civil War Came to Maine," 205–11; *Official Records of the Union and Confederate Navies*, series 1, 2: 322–29, 654–57; Bell, *Always Ready*, 122–26; *Civil War Naval Chronology* 3: 101, 104, 4: 207; Kern, *The United States Revenue Cutters*, 12–7.

25. Benjamin P. Thomas, *Abraham Lincoln*, 319–20; *Civil War Naval Chronology* 2: 61, 62.

26. Evans, *The United States Coast Guard*, 80–81; Reed, *Combined Operations in the Civil War*, 166–67.

27. Evans, *The United States Coast Guard*, 78.

28. Ibid.; Bell, *Always Ready*, 120.

29. Kern, *The United States Revenue Cutters*, 16–2 to 16–6.

30. Evans, *The United States Coast Guard*, 84–85; *Harper's Weekly*, 14 Sep. 1861.

31. Ehrman, "Rebel Cutter Takes on U.S. Navy," 20; *Record of Movements* 1: 85, 97, 149, 2: 390, 415, 419; Ralph W. Donnelly, "Officers of the Revenue Marine Service in the Confederacy," *The American Neptune*, 298, 302, 303; *Civil War Naval Chronology* 1: 2, 4, 5; Kern, *The United States Revenue Cutters*, 3–3 to 3–4.

32. Kern, *The United States Revenue Cutters*, 5–3 to 5–4.

33. Evans, *The United States Coast Guard*, 76; Kern, *The United States Revenue Cutters*, 3–2, 4–6.

34. Donnelly, "Officers of the Revenue Marine Service," 302–3; Kern, *The United States Revenue Cutters*, 3–7 to 3–8.

35. *Civil War Naval Chronology* 6: 222.

36. Willis J. Abbot, *Blue-Jackets of '61*, 5; *Harper's Weekly*, 16 Feb. 1861, 103, and 9 Mar. 1861, 151; John A. Dix to Wm. Hemphill Jones, New Orleans, Treasury Department, 29 Jan. 1861.

37. Donnelly, "Officers of the Revenue Marine Service," 298, 299, 304.

38. Ibid., 298–300; Ralph W. Donnelly, "Revenue Marine Service: The Nucleus of the Confederate Navy," *The American Neptune*, 90–92.

39. Donnelly, "Officers of the Revenue Marine Service," 298, 300, 303; *Civil War Naval Chronology* 6: 282; Donnelly, "The Nucleus of the Confederate Navy," 87–90.

40. Ehrman, "Rebel Cutter Takes On U.S. Navy," 20–22; *Civil War Naval Chronology* 6: 282, 329.

41. Donnelly, "Officers of the Revenue Marine Service," 299, 301–4; James M. Matthews, ed., *The Statutes at Large of the Provisional Government of the Confederate States of America*, 229.

42. Donnelly, "Officers of the Revenue Marine Service," 303–4.

43. Ibid., 301–2.

44. Ibid., 302.

Bibliography

Published

Abbot, Willis J. *Blue Jackets of '61*. New York: Dodd, Mead, 1891.

Adams, Henry, ed. *The Writings of Albert Gallatin*. Vol. 1. New York: Antiquarian Press, 1960.

Albion, Robert G. *Five Centuries of Famous Ships*. New York: McGraw-Hill, 1978.

Albion, Robert, et. al. *New England and the Sea*. Middletown, Connecticut: Wesleyan University Press, 1972.

Albion, Robert Greenhalgh. *Square-Riggers on Schedule*. Princeton: Princeton University Press, 1938.

Albion, Robert Greenhalgh, and Jennie Barnes Pope. *Sea Lanes in Wartime*. 2d ed. New York: Anchor Books, 1968.

Albion, Robert Greenhalgh, with the collaboration of Jennie Barnes Pope. *The Rise of New York Port, 1815–1860*. New York: Charles Scribner's, 1939.

Allen, Gardiner W. *A Naval History of the American Revolution*. 2 vols. Boston: Houghton Mifflin, 1913.

———. *Massachusetts Privateers of the Revolution*. Cambridge: The Harvard University Press, 1927.

———. *Our Naval War with France*. Boston: Houghton Mifflin, 1909.

Bailey, Thomas A. *A Diplomatic History of the American People*. 10th ed. New York: Appleton-Century-Crofts, 1980.

Bailyn, Bernard. *The Ideological Origins of the American Revolution*. Cambridge, Massachusetts: The Belknap Press, 1967.

———. *The New England Merchants in the Seventeenth Century*. New York: Harper & Row, 1964.

Barrow, Thomas C. *Trade and Empire: The British Customs Service in Colonial America, 1660–1775*. Cambridge, Massachusetts: Harvard University Press, 1967.

Bassett, John Spencer, ed. *Correspondence of Andrew Jackson*. 6 vols. New York: Kraus Reprint, 1969.

Bauer, K. Jack. *The Mexican War 1846–1848*. New York: Macmillan, 1974.

Baughman, James P. *The Mallorys of Mystic: Six Generations in American Maritime Enterprise*. Middletown, Connecticut: Wesleyan University Press, 1972.

Bell, Kensil. *Always Ready*. New York: Dodd, Mead, 1943.

Bemis, Samuel Flagg. *Jay's Treaty: A Study in Commerce and Diplomacy*. New Haven: Yale University Press, 1962.

Berry, Erick. *You Have to Go Out*. New York: David McKay, 1964.

Boston Slave Riot, and Trial of Anthony Burns. Boston: Fetridge, 1854.

A *Brief Sketch of the Character and Services of Captain Josiah Sturgis*. Boston: William White and H. P. Lewis, 1844.

Brief Sketch of the Naval History of the United States Coast Guard. Washington, D. C.: Byron S. Adams.

Brewington, Marion V. *Chesapeake Bay: A Pictorial Maritime History*. New York: Bonanza Books, 1953.

Buker, George E. *Swamp Sailors: Riverine Warfare in the Everglades, 1835–1842*. Gainesville: The University Presses of Florida, 1975.

Chapelle, Howard I. *The History of the American Sailing Navy*. New York: Bonanza Books, 1949.

———. *The History of the American Sailing Ships*. New York: Bonanza Books, 1935.

———. *The Search for Speed under Sail*. New York: Norton, 1967.

Civil War Naval Chronology, 1861–1865. Washington: Department of the Navy, 1971.

Clark, Arthur H. *The Clipper Ship Era, 1843–1869*. New York: G. P. Putnam's, 1930.

Clark, William Bell, and William James Morgan, eds. *Naval Documents of the American Revolution*. 7 vols. Washington, 1964–72.

Cobb, Elijah. *A Cape Cod Skipper*. New Haven: Yale University Press, 1925.

———. *Elijah Cobb, 1768–1848: A Cape Cod Skipper*. New York: American Maritime History, 1970.

Current, Richard N. *Lincoln and the First Shot*. Philadelphia, 1963.

Cutler, Carl C. *Greyhounds of the Sea*. New York: Halcyon House, 1930.

———. *Queens of the Western Ocean*. Annapolis, Maryland: U. S. Naval Institute, 1961.

Dana, Richard Henry. *Two Years before the Mast*. New York: The Limited Editions Club, 1947.

Department of the Navy. *United States Frigate* Constitution. Washington: Government Printing Office, 1932.

Evans, Stephen H. *The United States Coast Guard, 1790–1915*. Annapolis, Maryland: The U. S. Naval Institute, 1949.

Fiske, John. *The Critical Period of American History*. Boston: Houghton Mifflin, 1888.

Fitzpatrick, John C., ed. *The Writings of George Washington*. 39 vols. Washington: Government Printing Office, 1931–44.

Ford, Paul Leicester, ed. *The Writings of Thomas Jefferson*. 10 vols. New York: G. P. Putnam's, 1892–99.

Foss, Gerald D. *Three Centuries of Freemasonry in New Hampshire*. Concord, New Hampshire, 1972.

Freeman, Douglas Southall. *George Washington: A Biography*. 7 vols. New York: Charles Scribner's, 1948–58.

Gibbs, George, ed. *Memoirs of the Administrations of Washington and John Adams, Edited from the Papers of Oliver Wolcott, Secretary of the Treasury*. 2 vols. New York, 1946.

Gipson, Lawrence Henry. *The Coming of the Revolution, 1763–1775*. New York: Harper & Row, 1962.

Greene, Francis Vinton. *The Revolutionary War and the Military Policy of the United States*. Port Washington, New York: Kennikat Press, 1967.

Griffin, Charles Carroll. *The United States and the Disruption of the Spanish Empire, 1810–1822*. New York: Octagon Books, 1974.

Hammond, Otis G., ed. *Collections of the New Hampshire Historical Society*. Vol. 15, *Letters and Papers of Major-General John Sullivan*. Concord: New Hampshire Historical Society, 1939.

Hutchins, John G. B. *The American Maritime Industries and Public Policy, 1789–1914*. Cambridge: Harvard University Press, 1941.

Jackson, Melvin H. *Privateers in Charleston, 1793–1796*. Washington: Smithsonian Institution Press, 1969.

Jensen, Merrill. *The New Nation*. New York: Alfred A. Knopf, 1950.

Jensen, Merrill, ed. *Tracts of the American Revolution*. New York: Bobbs-Merrill, 1967.

Johnson, Allen, ed. *Dictionary of American Biography*. 22 vols. New York: Charles Scribner's, 1928–58

Kern, Florence. *The United States Revenue Cutters in the Civil War*. Bethesda, Maryland: Alised Enterprises, 1988.

Kilby, William H. *Eastport and Passamaquoddy*. Ann Arbor, Michigan: University Microfilms, 1970.

King, Irving H. *George Washington's Coast Guard*. Annapolis, Maryland: Naval Institute Press, 1978.

Knox, Dudley W., ed. *Naval Documents Related to the Quasi-War between the United States and France*. 7 vols. Washington: Government Printing Office, 1935–38.

Labaree, Benjamin W., ed. *The Atlantic World of Robert G. Albion*. Middletown, Connecticut: Wesleyan University Press, 1975.

Laws of the United States of America. Vol. 1. Boston: Printed at the State Press by Adams and Larkin, 1755.

Laws of the United States of America from the 4th of March, 1789, to the 4th of March, 1815. 5 vols. Philadelphia: John Bioren and W. John Duane, 1815.

Lists of Light-Houses . . . of the United States. Washington: George W. Bowman, 1861.

The Louisiana Portrait Gallery. Vol. 1. New Orleans: The Louisiana State Museum, 1979.

Lowrie, Walter, and Walter S. Franklin, eds. *American State Papers*. Vol. 1, *Naval Affairs*. Washington: Gales and Seaton, 1834.

McFarland, Philip. *Sea Dangers*. New York: Schocken Books, 1985.

McMaster, John Bach. A *History of the People of the United States, from the Revolution to the Civil War*. 8 vols. New York: D. Appleton-Century, 1885–1938.

McPherson, James M. *Ordeal by Fire*. New York: Alfred A. Knopf, 1982.

Matthews, James M., ed. *The Statutes at Large of the Provisional Government of the Confederate States of America*. Richmond: R. M. Smith, 1864.

Middlebrook, Louis K. *Maritime Connecticut during the American Revolution*. Salem, Massachusetts: The Essex Institute, 1925.

Miller, John C. *The Federalist Era, 1789–1801*. New York: Harper & Row, 1960.

———. *Origins of the American Revolution*. Boston: Little, Brown, 1943.

Mittell, Sherman F., ed. *The Federalists*. No. 11, 62–69. Washington, D. C.: National Home Library Foundation, n.d.

Morgan, Edmund S. and Helen M. *The Stamp Act Crisis*. New York: Collier, 1965.

Morison, Samuel Eliot. *The Maritime History of Massachusetts, 1783–1860*. Boston: Houghton Mifflin, 1930.

———. *Old Bruin: Commodore Matthew C. Perry, 1794–1858*. Boston: Little, Brown, 1967.

Morison, Samuel Eliot, and Henry Steele Commager. *The Growth of the American Republic*. Vol. 1. New York: Oxford University Press, 1962.

Noonan, John T. *The Antelope*. Berkeley: University of California Press, 1977.

Randall, J. G. *The Civil War and Reconstruction*. Boston: D. C. Heath, 1953.

Reed, Rowena. *Combined Operations in the Civil War*. Annapolis, Maryland: Naval Institute Press, 1978.

Rider, Sidney S. *An Historical Inquiry Concerning the Attempt to Raise a Regiment of Slaves by Rhode Island during the War of the Revolution*. Providence: Sidney S. Rider, 1880.

Roosevelt, Theodore. *The Naval War of 1812*. 2 parts. New York: G. P. Putnam's, 1904.

Schmeckebier, Lawrence F. *The Public Health Service*. Baltimore: Johns Hopkins Press, 1923.

Sears, Louis Martin. *Jefferson and the Embargo*. Durham, North Carolina: Duke University Press, 1927.

Semmes, Raphael. *Service Afloat and Ashore during the Mexican War*. Cincinnati: William H. Moore, 1851.

Smelser, Marshall. *The Congress Founds the Navy, 1787–1798*. Notre Dame, Indiana: University of Notre Dame Press, 1959.

Smith, Darrell Hevenor, and Fred Wilbur Powell. *The Coast Guard*. Washington: The Brookings Institute, 1929.

Smith, Horatio Davis. *Early History of the United States Revenue Marine Service, 1789–1849*. Bryn Mawr, Pennsylvania: Polk Printing, 1932.

Smith, Justin. *The War with Mexico*. 2 vols. Gloucester, Massachusetts: Peter Smith, 1963.

Snow, Elliot, and H. Allen Gosnell. *On the Deck of "Old Ironsides."* New York: MacMillan, 1932.

Sparks, Jared, ed. *The Writings of George Washington*. 12 vols. Boston: Ferdinand Andrews, 1839.

Sprout, Harold and Margaret. *The Rise of American Naval Power, 1776–1918*. Princeton: Princeton University Press, 1967.

Stackpole, Edouard Alexander. *The Sea-Hunters*. Philadelphia: Lippincott, 1953.

Stampp, Kenneth M. *The Peculiar Institution*. New York: Vintage Books, 1956.

Stick, David. *Graveyard of the Atlantic*. Chapel Hill: The University of North Carolina Press, 1952.

———. *North Carolina Lighthouses*. Raleigh: North Carolina Department of Cultural Resources, 1986.

Syrett, Harold C., ed. *The Papers of Alexander Hamilton*. 26 vols. New York: Columbia University Press, 1961–79.

Thomas, Benjamin P. *Abraham Lincoln*. New York: The Modern Library, 1968.

Thornton, R. H. *British Shipping*. Cambridge: At the University Press, 1939.

Turnbull, Archibald Douglas. *Commodore David Porter, 1780–1843*. New York: Century, 1929.

U. S. Coast Guard, Office of Assistant Commandant. *Record of Movements: Vessels of the United States Coast Guard*. 2 vols. Washington: U. S. Coast Guard, 1933.

U. S. Office of Naval War Records. *Official Records of the Union and Confederate Navies in the War of the Rebellion*. 30 vols. Washington: Government Printing Office, 1894–1922.

White, Leonard D. *The Federalists*. New York: The Free Press, 1965.

———. *The Jacksonians*. New York: The Free Press, 1965.

———. *The Jeffersonians: A Study in Administrative History, 1801–1829*. New York: The Free Press, 1965.

Whitehill, Walter Muir, ed. *New England Blockaded in 1814: The Journal of Henry Edward Napier, Lieutenant in* H. M. S. *Nymphe*. Salem: Peabody Museum, 1939.

Wood, Gordon S. *The Creation of the American Republic, 1776–1787*. Chapel Hill: The University of North Carolina Press, 1969.

The Writings of Thomas Jefferson. 20 vols. Washington, D. C.: Thomas Jefferson Memorial Association, 1903.

Articles and Pamphlets

Bennett, Robert F. "The Life Savers: For Those in Peril on the Sea." Part 1. U. S. Naval Institute *Proceedings* 102 (Mar. 1976): 54–63.

Berkeley, Edmund. "The Naval Office in Virginia, 1776–1789." *The American Neptune* 33, no. 1 (Jan 1973): 20–33.

Delgado, James P. "In the Midst of a Great Excitement: The Argosy of the Revenue Cutter C. W. *Lawrence*." *The American Neptune* 45, no.2 (Spring 1985): 119–31.

Donnelly, Ralph W. "Officers of the Revenue Marine Service in the Confederacy." *The American Neptune* 40 (Oct., 1980): 298–304.

———. "Revenue Marine Service: The Nucleus of the Confederate Navy." *The American Neptune* 48 (Spring 1988): 87–95.

Ehrman, W. E. "Rebel Cutter Takes on U. S. Navy." *The Bulletin* of the U. S. Coast Guard Academy Alumni Association (Nov.-Dec. 1979): 20–22.

Faye, Stanley. "Privateersmen of the Gulf and Their Prizes." *The Louisiana Historical Quarterly* 22, no. 4 (Oct. 1939): 1012–94.

Figueira, Jeanne. "The Story of Hunter's Wheel." *Commandant's Bulletin* (16 Mar. 1984): 18–21.

Foss, Gerald D. "First Captain of the U. S. Coast Guard." *The Northern Light* (Jun. 1973): 12–14

Galpin, W. Freeman. "The American Grain Trade under the Embargo of 1808." *Journal of Economic and Business History* 2 (1929–30): 71–100.

Heydenreich, James G. "Captain Hopley Yeaton, 1740–1812." *The Bulletin of the USCGA Alumni Association* (Sep.-Oct. 1967): 275–83.

———. "Hopley Yeaton and the Revenue Marine Service." *The Bulletin* of the USCGA Alumni Association (May-Jun. 1968): 33–42.

———. "Hopley Yeaton in the Continental Navy, 1776–1781." *The Bulletin* of the USCGA Alumni Association (Jan.-Feb. 1968): 2–10, and (Mar.-Apr. 1968): 3–10.

———. "Hopley Yeaton: Twilight and Sunset." *The Bulletin* of the USCGA Alumni Association (Nov.-Dec. 1968): 25–35.

———. "The Life and Times of Hopley Yeaton, 1740–1812." *The Bulletin* of the USCGA Alumni Association (Nov.-Dec. 1967): 360–67.

Jackson, Melvin H. "The Consular Privateers: An Account of French Privateering in American Waters, April to August, 1793." *The American Neptune* 22, no. 2 (Apr. 1962): 81–98.

Kaplan, Hymen R. "Hamilton's Revenue Fleet." U. S. Naval Institute *Proceedings* 88, no. 10 (Oct. 1962): 160–63.

Kendall, John Smith. "The Successor of Lafitte." *The Louisiana Historical Quarterly* 24, no. 2 (Apr., 1941): 360–77.

Kern, Florence. *Hopley Yeaton's* U. S. *Revenue Cutter* Scammel. Washington, D. C.: Alised Enterprises, 1976.

———. *James Montgomery's* U. S. *Revenue Cutter* General Green, 1791–1797. Washington, D. C.: Alised Enterprises, 1977.

———. *John Foster Williams'* U. S. *Revenue Cutter* Massachusetts, 1791–1792. Washington, D. C.: Alised Enterprises, 1976.

———. *John Howell's* U. S. *Revenue Cutter* Eagle. Washington, D. C.: Alised Enterprises, 1978.

———. *Jonathan Malthie's* U. S. *Revenue Cutter* Argus. Washington, D. C.: Alised Enterprises, 1976.

———. *Robert Cochran's* U. S. *Revenue Cutter* South Carolina, 1793–1798. Washington, D. C.: Alised Enterprises, 1978.

———. *The United States Revenue Cutter* Vigilant. Washington, D. C.: Alised Enterprises, 1976.

———. *William Cooke's* U. S. *Revenue Cutter* Diligence, 1792–1798. Washington, D. C.: Alised Enterprises, 1979.

Long, Barbara C. "When the Civil War Came to Maine." *Yankee* (Oct. 1979): 198–211.

Massachusetts Historical Society *Proceedings*. 2d ser., 20 (1906–9).

Maxam, Oliver M. "The Life-Saving Stations of the United States Coast Guard." U. S. Naval Institute *Proceedings* 55 (May 1929): 374–80.

Means, Dennis R. "A Heavy Sea Running: The Formation of the U. S. Life-Saving Service, 1848–1878." *Prologue* 19, no. 4 (Winter 1987): 223–43.

Merryman, J. H., and Sumner Increase Kimball. "The United States Revenue Marine." Photostat of *Extracts from Hamersly's Naval Encyclopedia* (Philadelphia, 1881): 687–91.

Paulin, C. O. "Early Naval Administration under the Constitution." U. S. Naval Institute *Proceedings* 32, no. 3 (Sept. 1906): 1001–30.

Pulsifer, Frank H. "Reminiscences of the *Harriet Lane*." *Journal of the* U. S. *Coast Guard Association* 1 (1917): 29–34.

Scheina, Robert L. "A Modelbuilder's Dilemma." *The Mariners' Museum Journal* 14, no. 1 (Spring 1987): 16.

Smelser, Marshall, and William I. Davidson. "The Longevity of Colonial Ships." *The American Neptune* 33, no. 1 (Jan. 1973): 16–19.

Snow, Elliot. "Making Fresh Water by Distilling Sea Water in 1791: Experiments of Captain John Foster Williams, U. S. R. C. S." *Journal of the American Society of Naval Engineers* 40, no. 4 (Nov. 1928): 541–45.

Strobridge, Truman R. "Captain Daniel Dobbins: One Man History Has Forgotten." *The Coast Guard Engineer's Digest* 133, no. 178 (Jan., Feb., Mar. 1973): 52–57.

Vance, Roger P. "The First Federal Customs." Part 1. U. S. Naval Institute *Proceedings* 102 (Mar. 1976): 46–53.

Waesche, R. R. "Armaments and Gunnery in the Coast Guard." U. S. Naval Institute *Proceedings* 55 (May 1929): 381–84.

Yanaway, Philip E. "The United States Revenue Cutter *Harriet Lane*, 1857–1884." *The American Neptune* 36 (Jul. 1976): 174–205.

York, Wick. "The Architecture of the U. S. Life-Saving Stations." The *Log* of Mystic Seaport 34, no. 1 (Spring 1982): 3–20.

Unpublished

Brewington, Marion V. Folder of notes on the early revenue cutters. Author's collection.

Conner, Commodore David. Papers. New York Public Library.

Contract for revenue cutter *Roger* B. *Taney*, between Isaac Webb and John Allen with Samuel Swartwout, collector for port of New York, 1 Sep. 1830. Webb Institute.

Correspondence of the Secretary of the Treasury with Collectors of Customs, 1789–1833. 39 rolls. Microcopy no. 178. National Archives Microfilm Publications.

Correspondence regarding marine hospital, 1802–1925. Carton on New London, Connecticut. Federal Archives and Records Center, Waltham, Massachusetts.

Correspondence regarding the Revenue Marine, 1792–1932. Records on New London, Connecticut. Federal Archives and Records Center, Waltham, Massachusetts.

Delany, Sharp. Letter book. USCGA Library.

Dix, John A. Letter to William Hemphill Jones, New Orleans, Treasury Department, 29 Jan. 1861. USCGA Library.

Embargo circulars. National Archives.

Evans, S. H., and A. A. Lawrence. "The History and Organization of the United States Coast Guard." Unpublished manuscript, Oct. 1938. USCGA Library.

Evans, Stephen Hadley. "Forerunners of the Cutter Fleet." An unpublished manuscript, 15 Mar. 1962. USCGA Library.

Fitzgerald, John. Letter to Alexander Hamilton, n.d. USCGA Library.

Hamilton, Alexander. Letter to Jedediah Huntington, Treasury Department, 20 Dec. 1792. Federal Archives and Records Center, Waltham, Massachusetts.

———. Letter to John Fitzgerald, New York, 10 Oct. 1789. USCGA Library.

———. Letter to Thomas Pinckney, Treasury Department, 30 Dec. 1794. USCGA Library.

———. Letter to William Webb, Bath, Maine, 27 May 1790. USCGA Library.

———. Treasury Department circulars to the collectors of customs, 2 Oct. 1789 and 23 Sep. 1790. USCGA Library.

Hawes, Lilla M., director of the Georgia Historical Society. Letter to Paul H. Johnson, librarian, USCGA, Savannah, Georgia, 24 Mar. 1976. USCGA Library.

Jackson, Andrew. Letter to the secretary of the treasury, 16 Sep. 1829. USCGA Library.

Journal of the revenue cutter *Argus*, Jul. 1799–1809, Captain Elisha Hinman. Federal Archives and Records Center, Waltham, Massachusetts.

Keyes, R. L. Report on the *Argus*. New London County file. Mystic Seaport, Mystic, Connecticut.

Letters on Revenue Cutter Service., 1 Oct. 1790–2 Apr. 1833. Treasury Department. National Archives.

Letters sent by the Secretary of the treasury to collectors of customs at all ports, 1789–1847, and at Small Ports, 1847–1879. 43 rolls. Microcopy no. 175. National Archives Microfilm Publications.

Lighthouse Letters, May 22, 1792–Sep. 30, 1802. 2 rolls. Microcopy no. 63. National Archives Microfilm Publications.

Log of the revenue cutter *Massachusetts*, 1791–95. USCGA Library.

Remick, Oliver P. Correspondence. USCGA Library.

Return of provisions received and issued and of rations due on board the revenue cutter *Argus*, 1 Nov.-30 Nov. 1800. Inclusive. Federal Archives and Records Center, Waltham, Massachusetts.

Revenue cutter journals, 1791, 1800–1809, 1842–66. Federal Archives and Records Center, Waltham, Massachusetts.

"Revenue Cutter Vessels, 1790–1880." Record Group 26. The National Archives.

Revenue marine vouchers, 1791–1800. Federal Archives and Records Center, Waltham, Massachusetts.

Wolcott, Oliver, Jr. Manuscripts. 51 vols. and 18 boxes. Connecticut Historical Society.

Wolcott, Treasury Secretary Oliver. Letter accompanying his report on the petitions of inhabitants of Newport, Rhode Island, to Treasury Department, 6 Feb. 1798. John Carter Brown Library, Brown University.

Yeaton, Mary. Diary, 7 Jun.–5 Oct. 1801. Typed copy. USCGA Library archives.

Newspapers and Magazines

The Catholic Transcript

Harper's Weekly

New York Evening Post

The New York Times

Niles Weekly Register

The Savannah Republican

Index

Fortress Monroe, 161, 163, 164

About the Author

Irving King, author of *George Washington's Coast Guard*, is professor of history and head of the department of humanities at the U.S. Coast Guard Academy in New London, Connecticut.

The Naval Institute Press is the book-publishing arm of the U. S. Naval Institute, a private, nonprofit professional society for members of the sea services and civilians who share an interest in naval and maritime affairs. Established in 1873 at the U. S. Naval Academy in Annapolis, Maryland, where its offices remain today, the Naval Institute has more than 100,000 members worldwide.

Members of the Naval Institute receive the influential monthly naval magazine *Proceedings* and substantial discounts on fine nautical prints, ship and aircraft photos, and subscriptions to the Institute's recently inaugurated quarterly, *Naval History*. They also have access to the transcripts of the Institute's Oral History Program and may attend any of the Institute-sponsored seminars regularly offered around the country.

The book-publishing program, begun in 1898 with basic guides to naval practices, has broadened its scope in recent years to include books of more general interest. Now the Naval Institute Press publishes more than forty new titles each year, ranging from how-to books on boating and navigation to battle histories, biographies, ship guides, and novels. Institute members receive discounts on the Press's more than 300 books.

For a free catalog describing books currently available and for further information about U. S. Naval Institute membership, please write to:

Membership Department
U. S. Naval Institute
Annapolis, Maryland 21402

or call, toll-free, 800-233-USNI.